100 THINGS
COLTS FANS
SHOULD KNOW & DO
BEFORE THEY DIE

100 THINGS COLTS FANS SHOULD KNOW & DO BEFORE THEY DIE

Phillip B. Wilson

TRIUMPH
BOOKS

Library of Congress Cataloging-in-Publication Data

Wilson, Phillip B., 1965-
   100 things Colts fans should know & do before they die / Phillip B. Wilson.
      pages cm. — (100 things...fans should know)
   Includes bibliographical references.
   ISBN 978-1-60078-840-6 (pbk.)
   1. Indianapolis Colts (Football team)—Miscellanea. I. Title. II. Title: One hundred things Colts fans should know & do before they die.
   GV956.I53W45 2013
   796.332'640977252—dc23
                                                    2013027109

This book is available in quantity at special discounts for your group or organization. For further information, contact:
   Triumph Books LLC
   814 North Franklin Street
   Chicago, Illinois 60610
   (312) 337-0747
   www.triumphbooks.com

Printed in U.S.A.
ISBN: 978-1-60078-840-6
Design by Patricia Frey
Photos courtesy of AP Images unless otherwise indicated

To Dee and David B., who sustain me.

To Morgan and Brandon,
who are always close to my heart.

Contents

Foreword

What the Colts Horseshoe Means

It's kind of like growing up in the circus, with the sawdust in your veins.

I've been blessed to be around the franchise and the National Football League for 41 years. George Halas was at my wedding, and I got to meet and know him. He was obviously one of the men who started the league. In those early years, I was able to touch the end of some eras like Halas and John Unitas, Weeb Ewbank. As a kid, I met Carroll Rosenbloom.

The horseshoe sets a universal symbol, which is tremendous, and you're blessed when it shows up. An interesting omen: when we moved into our house in 1966, from Lincoln to Winnetka, Illinois, I found out that, on one of the doors going into the house, there was a horseshoe put there in the '50s by the previous owner. It was kind of a strange omen that the horseshoe was just there, years before we ended up buying the team.

For me, I really focused on learning to be a historian about a good many years of the franchise. And the years I missed in the '50s and '60s, I got caught up with that by talking to some of the other players who were around the Baltimore era when I was a kid, whether it was Mike Curtis or Tom Matte or Rick Volk. My first year with the team, in 1972, I lived with Joe Thomas, our general manager, in Golden, Colorado. The questions I had for him were non-stop. I watched film with Teddy Marchibroda at night when I was 15. Years later, I sat around and heard the stories from Art Donovan and Bill Pellington when we were at a bar in Baltimore. I had a chance to witness a lot, then all of a sudden at age 37 when I became owner, I really had a huge notebook of just history. I grew up with those players, who told me again and again, "When your day comes…"

I know what the assistant equipment manager goes through because I did it. I know exactly the hours that they work. I know what it's like to do every single job in this organization. I've worked in the ticket office. I've advanced games in public relations where I've gone out on the road and done the pregame advance like we used to do. I can feel the sweat on the jockstraps that I picked up and threw in the bin when I was a 13-year-old kid. The horseshoe, there's obviously tremendous pride in it, and at the same time as owner, I knew that I had the ability to set up what I thought was the best structure and the best way to get to greatness. Being able to have contact with guys like Art Rooney Jr. and John Mara, having known their fathers obviously for as long as we've been in the league, has been so important as I think of the Colts and what we're about.

When I think of the Colts, it's hard to separate the family from them. Obviously to my three daughters, that's all they've ever known since they were born. I think of it as something that is just literally connected to the family name and the legacy. I'm really excited that when I had my chance to put it together in '97 and become owner, I was ready to use all the things that I had learned to try to create greatness, to try to create an understanding.

I wasn't part of the '60s era, I wasn't there in the summer of love in '67…well I was but as a kid playing football and basketball. My hair wasn't long, and I was seven years old. I wasn't part of that revolution. Being from the '70s and influenced by musical artists like John Lennon, Bob Dylan, and Marvin Gaye and others, I really feel it was about how not only do you want to win and have greatness, but how you want to affect the world and how you want to affect your community, how important it is to use the incredible love and popularity of the game to help make the world a better place.

When I think about the Colts, I think it's a third arm or third leg or a second hat; it's just so tightly connected into my heart and my bloodstream. It's been an adventure that I look at as very exciting because at 53 years old and already having gone through a full generation of ownership, which is young for an owner still, it's on to the next generation and the next chapter.

As exciting and incredible as the last 15 years have been, I'm really looking forward to what the future holds. It's tough making the generational switch, so to speak, but it's exciting and time goes by so quickly. Here we are reshaping this new era. I've had a lot of good fortune in terms of being successful on and off the field, business-wise and football-wise, having a chance to get Peyton Manning and then to get Andrew Luck. Those are times where the football Gods look after you and you're thankful for that.

But it takes a lot more. Winning two AFC Championship Games, winning a Super Bowl, hosting a Super Bowl all within five years—these are things that, as an owner, you dream of and aspire to, but you know how difficult that is.

There's nothing like winning AFC Championship Games in your own stadium. It's so special. And of course winning the Super Bowl instead of just getting there, it's so special. Then hosting the Super Bowl is so special. All of that going down between 2006 and 2012, it's just incredible. The goal has always been three Super Bowls in a row. That's the standard. That's the thing that hasn't been done that always remains the goal because it hasn't been done.

Off we go with the new era and different times, but when I think of that horseshoe, I think of life itself. It's such a part of my soul and my heart that it's hard to explain. It's like part of your meaning, like part of your DNA from being around it. I was born at the right time to be able to touch virtually all of the eras of the Colts. Even if I wasn't there when they were shaping the NFL, I had the chance to know those people who were there and could learn from them. At the same time, there's so much more to come, so much more to learn. That's what excites me.

I hope that some day I can sit there like Buffalo Bills owner Ralph Wilson, still be alive at 93 and look back on a life and still have more and more chances to add to the legacy of the horseshoe, only God knows. I love what we've done. No one has won more games in the last decade. There are some records, like the seven consecutive 12-win seasons in a row, which may never be broken.

But onward we move…and I'm as excited about the future as I am about the past.

—Jim Irsay
Owner and CEO, Indianapolis Colts

Acknowledgments

The Colts were exceedingly helpful, especially chief operating officer Pete Ward and director of media content Craig Kelley. You never gave me an ounce of grief, although I couldn't have been more of a pest. Thank you, gentlemen. Owner Jim Irsay delivered the perfect jump-start to this book. Gut instinct said you would nail this, Jimmy. There are no words to describe the heart of head coach Chuck Pagano, who agreed to relive 2012 one final, emotional time. Never again, Chuck, I promise.

This venture wouldn't have been the same without vice president of equipment operations Jon Scott, my Colts complex tour guide and hook-up for a hilarious chapter on Peyton Manning. Other staffers who deserve thanks are vice president of ticket operations/guest services Larry Hall, radio voice Bob Lamey, senior director of marketing Stephanie Pemberton, owner executive assistant Cathy Catellier, COO executive assistant Traci Morgan (just leave a message!), receptionist Sue Kelly, marketing coordinator Ashley Powell, director of broadcast services Jeffrey Gorman, and the media relations staff of Avis Roper, Matt Conti, and Pamela Humphrey.

Where would a scribe be without my friends at *The Indianapolis Star*, Terry Hutchens, Mike Chappell, Phil Richards, and Bob Kravitz, as well as former colleagues Robin Miller, Tom Rietmann, and Conrad Brunner. Impeccable insight, as always, fellas.

It boggles the mind to think about how much former players and coaches shared. Raymond Berry and Gino Marchetti were off-the-charts incredible. So, too, were Tony Dungy, Edgerrin James, Lenny Moore, and George Taliaferro. The list goes on. It meant a lot to catch up with Jim Mora, Ted Marchibroda, Marv Levy, Tarik Glenn, Joe Staysniak, Will Wolford, Ken Dilger, and Barry Krauss.

Appreciate Bill Brooks taking the time, as did Hunter Smith, and apologies to Darrin Gray for not getting back to you again.

Lucas Oil Stadium director Mike Fox is a fountain of behind-the-scenes knowledge. So, too, is Myra Borshoff. My *Bob & Tom* buddies, Tom Griswold and Bob Kevoian, have been a non-stop blast since you let me into your studio three years ago. The hook-up with Duke Tumatoe provided one of the more laugh-out-loud chats. Well, Mr. Tumatoe and Dean Biasucci, I'm still laughing, Dean. You're better than Matt Dillon in my book. Thoughtful others who took the time were Bill Tobin, John Unitas Jr., Rohn Stark, Jim "Lassie" O'Brien, Stan White, Mike Prior, David Frick, Michael Chernoff, Michael Smith, and Bill Hudnut.

Thanks to the San Francisco 49ers for arranging a chat with head coach Jim "Captain Comeback" Harbaugh. I appreciate the contributions of Tom Zupancic, Jon Torine, Mel Kiper, Tim Bragg, Don Fischer, and Ray Compton. Another shout-out goes to John Ziemann and Baltimore's Sports Legends Museum.

Appreciate the tour. Great exhibit. The hospitality and food were excellent at Randy Collins' Blue Crew Sports Grill as well as at the Indianapolis Colts Grille with Michael Duganier. The Blue Crew Fan Club came up clutch. Thanks to Collins, Dan Cole, Eric Van Wagner, Tim Millikan, Nathan and Angie Tilse, as well as Colts season ticketholder SuEllyn Stevens.

Books For Youth's Stacy Lozer was pure joy. Any reason to call Anderson University's director of communications/community relations Chris Williams means it's a good day. Nancy Hulse was so kind to share the memory of her son Danny. Lisa Hartman did the same for her now-healthy son Jackson. Thanks to Teresa Black, Linda White, April Nading, and Jay Williamson.

Yes, the Dee Johnson quoted once is my wife. She provided a memory from her Colts season ticketholder days that preceded our meeting. I have the Colts to thank for bringing us together. She has been so supportive while my mind, body, soul, and heart were on an extended vacation. You can have the basement back now, baby.

I would be remiss to not say one more thank you to Heritage House's Myranda Hartwell and Maggie Conner, who reached out to me to provide one of the most heartwarming stories of 2012.

Finally, rest in peace, Danny Hulse and Danny Webber.

Introduction

When Terry Hutchens kindly suggested me for this venture, it sounded like a lot of fun—a lot of work, but an opportunity to take a creative journey. The Colts' Craig Kelley said something early on that resonated, "If you don't maintain the past, you lose the past." That became my motivation, to bring the past to life.

The bridge still exists between the Baltimore and Indianapolis Colts. As a Baltimore native who has been back several times, I realize the Colts will always be a touchy subject there for so many. Aside from the Mayflower chapter, hopefully old Baltimore Colts fans can appreciate the part of the team's legacy that applies to the days when they sat in old Memorial Stadium. And hopefully for Indianapolis Colts fans who enjoy Lucas Oil Stadium, the link between the past and present provides understanding.

There should be a book that connects the greatness of Johnny Unitas to Peyton Manning as well as invaluable coaching contributions from Weeb Ewbank to Tony Dungy. Hall of Famers Gino Marchetti and Raymond Berry still have so much to say and are incredibly insightful. People should remember running backs Lenny Moore, George Taliaferro, and Edgerrin James. And, yes, Chuck Pagano and quarterback Andrew Luck have already accomplished enough in one season to be connected to that rich history.

After 15 years of covering the Colts as a sportswriter and later as a blogger, I had to make sure this book gave fans more because they are as well-read as ever. Fans might disagree with how the chapters are ranked and say I'm out of my mind—and it wouldn't be the first time—but you turn the pages knowing this was produced for you. Argue amongst yourselves about what should be where. After countless hours pounding the keyboard in the wee hours of the morning, it became apparent the ranking was as difficult as any step

in the process. It changed at least two dozen times. But I would have paid to take this literary journey.

From the time I set up shop in my basement, where the floor would be covered in books, media guides, magazines, archived articles, and other background information, this adventure came down to tracking down interesting people. It's more the Colts' history and the fans' than mine. I was fortunate to write about it. If I never type another word as long as I live, I'm proud to present this to fans.

It's been exhausting but exhilarating. After about two months of doing my best to crank this out and keep it real, this book is hopefully the most profound way to say to everyone, "Thank you."

1 "He's the Horseshoe."

The Indianapolis Colts endure as one of the NFL's finest franchises because of one rather unusual individual. Growing up with *his* football team made the man curious and inquisitive, fiercely competitive yet genuinely sincere, stylish and yet sometimes just downright silly, an overgrown kid with a tremendous heart.

That's Jim Irsay.

"Everybody else comes and goes," said Tom Zupancic, former longtime Colts employee. "He's the horseshoe."

The 53-year-old Colts owner started as a wide-eyed, 12-year-old ball boy making $5 per week and just happy to be in an NFL locker room. His ascendance through the decades would take him through every departmental layer of what would one day be his organization.

Sure, Irsay hates to lose, but his team had to mean more than that. When a staffer mentions the "heart behind the horseshoe," it starts with Irsay's expectation for everyone to impact the community. That includes having players eager to interact with the public. He's a man of conviction who at 17 had the guts to board a preseason bus and apologize to the entire team for the irrational behavior of his reactionary father, Robert. In the serenity of his musical world, his passionate, poetic soul has a rhythm that reminds us that life still has to be fun.

Some might remember Irsay's early days as a rather young general manager in 1992 when disgruntled running back Eric Dickerson snickered, "He deserves to be a general manager as much as Daffy Duck does."

By 1999, Irsay had become the owner when he phoned Dickerson to invite the Hall of Famer to return to town and be

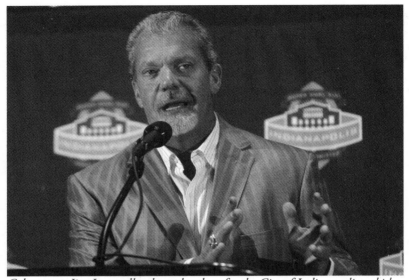

Colts owner Jim Irsay talks about the plans for the City of Indianapolis to bid for the 2018 NFL Super Bowl during an announcement in Indianapolis on Wednesday, July 18, 2012. Irsay said he expected competition would be stiff for the city to be awarded a second Super Bowl, but he is completely behind the new bid. The NFL won't pick the host city for the game until 2014.
(AP Photo/Michael Conroy)

recognized as the first former Indianapolis Colts player inducted in Canton, Ohio. Irsay left a message on the answering machine: "This is Daffy Duck calling, give me a call back." Dickerson cracked up. "I heard that, and you can't believe how hard I started laughing," he said. "I still have it on my answering machine."

Dickerson showed up. Irsay wore goggles just like the running back once did as he presented Dickerson with a framed jersey.

That's the man some still call Jimmy, a free spirit who didn't see the point of holding a grudge. While known these days as Jim or Mr. Irsay, his eventual rise in NFL stature never included distancing himself from the public. While the playbook for quirky, wealthy men typically includes seclusion, Irsay went the other way. Check out his Twitter account, with more than 221,000 followers keeping an eye on him, whether he's quizzing on obscure music lyrics or offering a contest to give away tickets. One trivia-triumphant follower won a car.

Irsay obviously recognized the shortcomings of his father, who didn't always connect with people.

"I know he's learned from his father's mistakes," said Colts chief operating officer Pete Ward, 55, who started as an intern in 1981 and rose through the ranks to become Irsay's right hand.

"Bob Irsay didn't know anything about football or people," said Robin Miller, 63, who covered the Colts from 1984 to 2001 as a columnist at *The Indianapolis Star*. "Jim Irsay knows a lot about people, and he's learned a lot about football."

It's simple math. The Colts were 153–226–1 in the regular season with Robert as owner. They're 157–99 with Jim. In the playoffs, Robert was 2–6 while Jim is 8–11 with a Super Bowl XLI ring. Jim's franchise set NFL records with 115 wins in a decade from 2000 to 2009 and seven consecutive 12-win seasons.

"I'm proud of what Jimmy has become," said retired Colts linebacker Barry Krauss, 56. "He's changed the face of the franchise."

One of the more important lessons learned has been to let people do their jobs. Former coaches Tony Dungy and Jim Mora testified to that. When the team won, there weren't any extra suggestions on how to make it better. When the team lost, Irsay reaffirmed belief in his people. Dungy had to encourage Irsay to become a locker-room visitor because the owner didn't want to give the wrong impression. He doesn't need the obligatory TV camera shot of himself on the sideline.

Ward says Irsay's promotion to general manager at the age of 25 in 1984 made it easy for skeptics to underestimate his boss. It motivated Irsay to work harder to prove himself. But he started paying attention long before that. Ward shared a camp office with Irsay in 1982 and couldn't help but be nervous. At first.

"The thing that shocked me was he would take time to ask me questions and listen to my thoughts," Ward said. "That just blew me away."

After arriving in Indianapolis, Jim Irsay made an immediate connection in radio appearances on *The Bob & Tom Show.*

"I figured he was just the owner's kid and they would give him a salary and a title," said co-host Bob Kevoian, 62. "I was really amazed at how much he knew. He studied. He really was well-versed in the game."

Others who played for him echo that.

"He knows football," said retired offensive tackle Tarik Glenn. "I don't know how many owners have been around football their whole lives. To have an owner like that is pretty special."

Retired offensive linemen Will Wolford and Joe Staysniak are still part of radio broadcasts. "You line up all the owners in the league and you measure their football intelligence and their ability to run a program," Wolford said. "I think Jim Irsay is on the very, very short list of guys who you want to play for because of the success the Colts have had. It's not an accident. Not at all."

What resonates with Staysniak is Irsay's desire. "I don't think people understand the fire that he has to win," Staysniak said. "It's fun to follow him on Twitter, that's one part of Jimmy Irsay. I'm sure he has fun doing that, but the football side of Jimmy Irsay, he wants to win and win badly."

This intensity was most evident in the weight room. Tom Zupancic, called "Zup" during his days as strength and conditioning coach and in the front office, loved working out with his boss. He can still visualize it now. The clanging sound of weights being slammed. Dire Straits singing, "Money for Nothing," on the boom box. Slap the belt on. Get serious. Ammonia tabs flying. Smack the hands and spray that powder in the air.

"He's a guy who could squat 700 pounds one day, and then he could be training for a marathon the next day," said Zup, 57. "He was obsessive about working out. He worked out as hard as any player."

Taking Care of Dungy's Dad

Tony Dungy's 2002 began with the death of his mother, Cleomae, on January 3. Nineteen days later, he was hired as the Colts' head coach.

Owner Jim Irsay noticed how Dungy's father, Wilbur, who had a Ph.D. and was a science professor at Jackson (Michigan) Community College, attended Colts road games.

"He should ride on the plane," Dungy recalled Irsay saying. After that, Wilbur did.

"That was just his idea," Dungy said of Irsay. "He had a seat for my dad for every away game. And he didn't just do it for the head coach. He did it for others, too."

And Irsay has put in the same effort with the public. When hearing of a fan in need, he didn't hesitate to ask executive assistant Cathy Catellier to send tickets and money. People don't realize how often this happens because Irsay prefers that these things not be publicized. Again, it's not about drawing attention to himself.

"As much as Jim wants to win, and believe me, he wants to win as much as the coaches and players, his heart goes so much deeper," said Catellier, 62. "He cares about the fans."

When a single mother phoned to thank Irsay for sending money and tickets, Catellier informed, "I just get to be the giver for the angel who did this."

Seriously, what owner has a contest to give away five Super Bowl XLI rings to fans after he finally won his first? Irsay handled "Quest For A Ring" with a flair for showmanship, walking down the steps of Monument Circle decked out in a white tuxedo, blue Colts top hat, and blue vest, toting a blue-and-white cane.

"I look like Willy Wonka Elton, a combination of Willy Wonka and Elton John," Irsay joked.

Wolford recalled a provision added in player contracts to require community participation. Staysniak attests, "We're still working for him." Both men laughed. "There's proof that he's charitable to the core."

Helping Hands

Colts owner Jim Irsay read a newspaper article about the struggles of a church-based community center on the South side of Indianapolis and decided to pay the place a visit. Myra Borshoff, his publicist since 1996, accompanied him.

"The next day, we drove down and walked in and asked to speak to the director," said Borshoff, 65. "People recognized him. He went in and sat across the desk from the director and had a 15-minute conversation."

Irsay heard what he needed and wrote a check.

"I'm not sure of the amount," Borshoff said, "but I think it was $100,000."

That's the same dollar amount then-head coach Tony Dungy donated and Irsay matched in 2006 to support the endowed chair of Dungy's father, Wilbur, who was Jackson Community College's first black professor in 1953. Wilbur, who taught science classes there for 16 years, died in 2004. A year later, the Dungy family had pledged a $1 million endowment to honor him.

When tornadoes ravaged Southern Indiana cities in 2012, Irsay donated $50,000 to the disaster relief effort. A Colts caravan of players, cheerleaders, and employees were dispatched to the area to assist in any way possible.

Longtime publicist Myra Borshoff could share Irsay stories for hours. "What I think is interesting about Jim is he has so many interests," she said. "He's just really curious. He loves music. He sends poetry to people. He's very poetic and he speaks in lyrics, which has always been interesting but a challenge for me. I'm sort of stuck in the '60s, and he's into the '70s, '80s and '90s. I love Google because I often type something in to see to whom it should be attributed."

After Irsay purchased the Jack Kerouac *On The Road* scroll for $2.4 million in 2001, a party was organized at the New York Public Library. Irsay introduced singer Patti Smith, who sang a song she had written for him. The catchiest rhyme was "scroll" with "Super Bowl."

Blues musician Duke Tumatoe, who has written all those "Lord Help Our Colts" songs, visited the team complex one time and ran into Irsay in the hall. They stood there and chatted about guitars for 15 minutes. "Jim is a remarkable man," Tumatoe said. "I'd do anything he asked me."

Those closest to him all say the same thing. That's because he runs a sound organization and is considerate of everyone who makes it tick. When the Colts reached Super Bowls XLI and XLIV, both in Miami, Irsay picked up the tab on tickets, airfare, and hotel expenses for all of his employees.

"Several years ago, I was fired for about 30 seconds and came back as a contracted employee," said longtime radio voice Bob Lamey. "I had a retirement thing I had to deal with, and I was talking to somebody who runs the pension fund for the NFL. At the end of the conversation, she said, 'Can I tell you something? I deal with all the teams in the league, so I didn't say this. Do you know you have the best owner in the National Football League?' I said, 'We all think that.' And she said, 'He does more for his employees than any other owner in the league.' It didn't surprise me. It just surprised me somebody in that position would say it."

Zupancic admires how his old workout partner continues to take care of NFL business. "Every decision he reaches is to make that franchise better," Zupancic said, "to make that horseshoe shine and never let it be in tarnish mode."

2 Peyton Manning's Legacy

The quarterback comparison is uncanny when Hall of Fame defensive end Gino Marchetti turns on the television and watches

Peyton Manning play. It's déjà vu, as if Marchetti is watching his old Baltimore Colts teammate, Johnny Unitas.

"The way he walks, the way he looks, his facial expression behind the facemask," said Marchetti, 87. "I told my wife he looks like, acts like, and throws like Johnny Unitas. That's probably the best compliment I could ever give him."

The NFL's only four-time MVP, awarded while with Indianapolis from 1998 to 2011, Manning didn't like being mentioned in the same breath with a legend for whom he had the utmost respect. He wore No. 18, Unitas wore No. 19, and Manning said that was appropriate "because Johnny Unitas is always one more than me."

Those who watched Manning work with the Colts suggest otherwise. "Greatest all-time ever," said retired Colts tight end Ken Dilger. "The guy never rested during the week. He knew that defense better than everybody. And he knew the offense better than everybody."

"The greatest Colt ever," said Colts radio voice Bob Lamey. "That says something because Unitas was pretty darn good. But Peyton did more for a city, the franchise, his teammates, himself. I don't know of anybody, any single player off the top of my head, who has done more for a city. Unitas comes close."

Retired Colts head coach Tony Dungy, who celebrated a Super Bowl XLI title with Manning as game MVP, understands why the quarterbacks are compared. Manning's on-field command as a field general and seemingly effortless ability to run the two-minute no-huddle offense made him a throwback to an era when three-time NFL champion Unitas redefined the position.

"He's like Unitas," Dungy said. "In that era, those guys did so much. So much of it was on the field, Unitas with the audibles and the two-minute drill and calling the plays. Then you had a whole generation of quarterbacks who were like [Joe] Montana and [John] Elway who were great, but it was like, 'Give me the plan and I'll execute it.' With Peyton, he was a throwback of being responsible

Colts quarterback Peyton Manning calls out at the line of scrimmage during an AFC wild card game against the New York Jets on January 8, 2011, in Indianapolis. (AP Photo/Nam Y. Huh)

for the success and taking that responsibility on his shoulders.

"He did more for our offense than any quarterback in this era. I'd have to put Peyton at the top."

Manning received a series of suggestions from offensive coordinator Tom Moore, then surveyed the defense and chose the play with the best chance for success. That Manning knew every player's responsibilities on each play was essential in hurry-up mode.

"He's one of the greatest leaders of all time," said Bob Kravitz, *The Indianapolis Star* columnist. "He was a football culture unto himself. He challenged coaches and challenged teammates in ways that no other player ever has. Peyton became the ultimate coach on the field, which is especially impressive in an era of advanced offenses and advanced defenses."

Manning has set so many NFL and team records, it would take several pages to list them. He's the Colts' all-time leader in wins and every major passing category. The record-holding 12-time Pro Bowl selection, counting last season in Denver, has completed 5,082-of-7,793 passes for 59,487 yards with 436 touchdowns, 209 interceptions, and a career passer rating of 95.7. He and wide receiver Marvin Harrison are the most prolific passing duo in league history with 953 completions for 12,756 yards and 112 TDs. Known for his comebacks, Manning had a league-record seven fourth-quarter comeback victories in *one season*, 2009.

When honored with his fourth NFL MVP award in 2009, he reiterated his disdain for being mentioned with the game's greatest players. "I'm really not comfortable with being drawn into comparisons with other athletes," Manning said. "I certainly would think all of those athletes would echo my sentiments of being thankful and grateful for the supporting cast they've had around them. I think they would realize, as I certainly do, that this wouldn't be possible without the help of so many people."

Retired center Jeff Saturday, with whom Manning shares the distinction of most quarterback-center games in league history at 170, remembered how much effort No. 18 expended on a weekly basis. "We used to call him 'Coach Manning' and used to bust him up about how hard he worked," Saturday said. "He showed up early. He left late. He led by example. He never expected you to give anything that he wasn't going to give himself."

When Marv Levy accepted an invite from Colts president Bill Polian to visit the team complex, the retired Buffalo Bills coach saw firsthand how Manning went about his business. "His preparation, that man never thought he had it made," Levy said. "I was blown away. His work ethic was beyond belief. And it was consistent work ethic."

Jim Mora, Manning's Colts coach from 1998 to 2001, remembered a fierce in-game intensity. "Everybody respected Peyton," Mora said, "but I tell you what, he was a fabulous competitor. Nobody I've ever been around has wanted to do more of what it takes to win. He worked at it. He does what it takes to win. And because of that, he infects the people around him."

Manning's distaste for losing was evident from the beginning. He completed 21-of-37 passes for 302 yards with one touchdown and three interceptions in his NFL debut, a 24–15 loss to Miami on September 6, 1998, at the RCA Dome. Afterward, he sharply said, "I don't care what league you're in. When you lose, you hate it."

Dungy was credited with helping Manning become more conscious of knowing when and when not to take chances. The quarterback had a gunslinger mentality, but eventually realized a third-and-20 pass into tight coverage when ahead wasn't the smart play. His interceptions dropped from 19 in 2002, Dungy's first season, to 10 in each of the next three years, then nine in 2006.

"No. 1, he was special in wanting to prepare and wanting to win and wanting to be coached," Dungy said. "He had to buy into things, and he certainly did. You can't overestimate what [former quarterbacks coach] Jim Caldwell did. If you check Peyton's numbers before Jim got there and after Jim got there [in 2002], it's dramatic. The biggest thing was going in and convincing him, 'We're still going to be explosive. We're still going to move the ball. We're still going to score points. But the key to winning a championship is taking care of the football.' It took a little while for him to buy into that, that you could take care of the football and still be explosive."

Dungy said his proudest Manning moment was when the quarterback threw a league-record 49 TD passes with just 10 INTs in 2004.

Then there's Manning off the field. No athlete has ever impacted Indianapolis like him. "For my money, [Basketball Hall of Famer] Oscar Robertson and the tragically underappreciated [Negro League baseball star] Oscar Charleston are the best athletes to come from Indianapolis. Peyton Manning is the best to play for it," said Phil Richards, beat writer for *The Indianapolis Star*. "Still, if you want a read on Manning's true impact, look at Lucas Oil Stadium and the Peyton Manning Children's Hospital. They wouldn't exist without him.

"Manning raised millions. Whatever it took. When St. Vincent needed help with its Gala, its biggest annual fundraiser, Peyton called his pals. Bob Costas emcees. Kenny Chesney plays. The grants arm of Manning's PeyBack Foundation has distributed more than $4 million to kids programs, and it's still giving."

Former Indianapolis Mayor Bart Peterson said, "An appropriate accounting of [Manning's] contributions would have to reach the conclusion that he made Indianapolis a better place to live."

"That's the rarest of athletes and the true measure of the man," Richards said.

Colts director of media content Craig Kelley says Manning is the most unique person he has ever been around. "His encyclopedic memory was truly something to witness," Kelley said. "Peyton's recall for detail and his ability to process what he saw often made me think if there were a football version of the movie *A Beautiful Mind*, it would have to be made about him.

"There are race horses, and then there is Secretariat. Peyton is Secretariat."

3 "Johnny U."

When one of the most important games in NFL history ended, most eyes understandably followed the football. More than a half century later, fans can still check it out on the Internet. Running back Alan Ameche slams into the end zone for the touchdown that decided the Baltimore Colts' 23–17 overtime victory over the New York Giants in "The Greatest Game Ever Played" on December 28, 1958, at Yankee Stadium.

MVP Johnny Unitas drove the Colts to a tying field goal in the final seconds of regulation and the winning score in the first sudden-death overtime in NFL playoff history. But at the moment of victory—a finale watched by an estimated 45 million on television, thus skyrocketing NFL popularity—the quarterback didn't so much as raise his arms. There wasn't any reaction. He just turned and walked away.

"That's the way he was, all the way around," said his son, John Unitas Jr., 56.

"Johnny U." operated at a different level, almost always without emotion in the most pressure-packed situations.

"What my father got emotional about was his children or animals," Unitas Jr. said. "He really enjoyed his children and didn't like harm being done to animals."

Unitas had a 20-acre farm with cattle and horses. He enjoyed mixing feed for his cattle and selling livestock. After a long day, there was nothing like a Michelob beer. And he enjoyed actor John Wayne. "My father could watch westerns all day," Unitas Jr. said.

One of the quarterback's secrets was working boxing bags to enhance reflexes and coordination. At 6'1" and 194 pounds, Unitas wasn't a mobile quarterback nor did he possess the NFL's strongest

Johnny Unitas (19) gets away a pass as the Minnesota Vikings' Gary Larsen (77) reaches out to grab him during first-half action in Minneapolis, Minnesota, on September 19, 1966. This pass was incomplete, but Unitas completed four touchdown passes later in the game, giving him a career total of 214 and breaking the touchdown pass record of 212 held by Y.A. Tittle. The Colts downed the Vikings 38–23. (AP Photo)

arm. But he was a consummate field general who called his own plays and understood teamwork and consistency, working on weaknesses more than strengths and sticking to a philosophy referred to as K.I.S.S.—"Keep It Simple Stupid."

"Neither one of us had a silver spoon in our mouths," said Hall of Fame wide receiver Raymond Berry, who caught a record 12 passes for 178 yards and one TD in the 1958 title game. "We started off in the same place. We had several things in common, the first being a love of football. Another was worth ethic. There's no question John and I were both the same way about football. We worked at it."

Admirers could walk up to Unitas in a restaurant or bar and engage him in conversation. At home, he didn't dwell on football.

"He didn't talk about his career, football, any of that stuff unless you asked him," Unitas Jr. said. "He didn't care about the awards or accolades. He just liked to be an average Joe. And he always remembered names. That was one of his things."

Unitas Jr. shared another passed-on lesson, "It's what you do when other people aren't looking." That's the same philosophy former Colts coach Tony Dungy shared when he advised that the true nature of a star could be determined by how that player treated the water boy.

Those enamored with statistics can log onto www.johnnyunitas.com, a site run by his son, to check out the Unitas numbers as well as videos and other information. When Unitas retired in 1973, he had set NFL records for pass attempts (5,186), completions (2,830), passing yards (40,239), touchdown passes (290), 300-yard passing games (26), and most consecutive games throwing a scoring pass (47). That streak stood for 52 years until New Orleans' Drew Brees surpassed it in 2012. Unitas was enshrined in the Pro Football Hall of Fame in 1979. His No. 19 Colts jersey was retired.

Where he ranks among the all-time quarterbacks inevitably sparks an age-old debate. NFL Films' Steve Sabol once asked Unitas about it. "'I am the best,'" Unitas Jr. recalled his father saying. "He thought he was the greatest. He knew."

Retired Buffalo Bills coach Marv Levy, who took four teams to Super Bowls, was working in the college ranks when Unitas and Berry rose to prominence. "Boy, he blew me away, he and Raymond Berry," said Levy, who got his first NFL job as Philadelphia's kicking teams coach in 1969. "People always ask me who the greatest quarterback was, and I can't say who was the best, but if you mention two or three, he gets mentioned."

Unitas Jr. helped his father take advantage of the legend's popularity in signed sports memorabilia. The asking price climbed to $15,000 per autograph session with a 500-piece maximum per signing. "If my father was alive today," Unitas Jr. said, "he'd probably command $25,000 per appearance, maybe more."

On September 11, 2002, Unitas called his son to discuss a New Jersey memorabilia buyer offering a lot of money for old helmets, jerseys, and anything the Hall of Famer was willing to sell. But Unitas was adamant. He wouldn't part with any of his keepsakes. The father told his son he was going for an afternoon workout. Unitas was on a treadmill when his heart gave out. He was 69.

"My father was my best friend," Unitas Jr. said.

Hall of Fame quarterbacks Bart Starr and Joe Namath eulogized Unitas on Fox News' *On The Record with Greta van Susteren* TV show. Namath, remembered in NFL lore for leading the New York Jets past the Colts in a stunning Super Bowl III upset, idolized Unitas and wore No. 19 in high school as a tribute. "I just loved him," Namath said.

Starr, who won Super Bowls I and II with Green Bay, studied Unitas extensively. "I think his tight end [John] Mackey said it best," Starr told van Susteren. "He said when you got in the huddle with [Unitas], it was like being in there with God."

4 Moving Out on the Mayflowers

Long before the lights were shut off for the final time at the Baltimore Colts complex on March 28, 1984, the marriage between the city and NFL team had become a dysfunctional relationship.

Colts owner Carroll Rosenbloom had lost patience with city officials about an antiquated Memorial Stadium. Rosenbloom had threatened to move Colts games out of the stadium if improvements weren't made. By November 1971, he had no interest in negotiating with the city and vowed the team would not return to the stadium.

Before that played out, Rosenbloom swapped the Colts for the Los Angeles Rams with Robert Irsay in 1972. Irsay's arrival, in all likelihood, saved the city from Rosenbloom trying to move the franchise. That possibility gets ignored because Irsay made himself an easy target for critics. He could be intolerant by nature and prone to alcohol-induced rants. When he later insisted he wasn't moving, Irsay still checked out options elsewhere.

Bert Jones, quarterback from 1973–81, reiterated his disdain for Irsay to *Sports Illustrated* in a 1986 story: "He lied and he cheated and he was rude and he was crude and he was Bob Irsay."

Mike McCormack was head coach for a 2–14 implosion in '81. One of the worst moments described in the *S.I.* 1986 story was when Irsay called plays from the coach's booth during a 38–13 loss to Philadelphia on November 15, 1981. "[Irsay] couldn't have told you how many players there were on the field, never mind what plays we had," said Jones, who alternated snaps with Greg Landry. "All he was trying to do was embarrass the coaches and the players. When he told me to run, I threw. When he told me to throw left, I ran right."

General manager Joe Thomas drew the ire of fans and media. He traded quarterback Johnny Unitas and got rid of other name players, including Tom Matte and Bill Curry. The latter learned of his trade via a collect telephone call. An impatient Thomas went through five head coaches in five years. He fired head coach Don McCafferty after a 1–4 start in 1972, although the coach had won a Super Bowl two years earlier and was 10–4 in '71. Thomas lost a power struggle with head coach Ted Marchibroda and was fired after the '76 season.

The team managed to produce winners with Jones leading the way in 1975, '76, and '77, but losses piled up after that. The Colts were 68–104–1 in their Baltimore years with Irsay. Relocation rumors became constant as early as eight years before the move. Jacksonville, Memphis, and Phoenix were mentioned. The team had stopped selling out in '71, a year after winning Super Bowl V, and attendance continued to slide.

"When I got to Baltimore, it just seemed like there was a disconnect between the community and the Baltimore Colts," said linebacker Barry Krauss, who was drafted in 1979. "It just seemed like nobody wanted to support the Colts anymore. There was a great tradition there, and I wanted to be a part of it. It just wasn't working."

Punter Rohn Stark, drafted in the second round in '82, was taken back. "It was embarrassing," Stark said. "We had no following. The city didn't deserve a team, in my opinion."

The Colts' last game at Memorial Stadium was on December 18, 1983, and drew a total attendance of 27,934 as the team finished a 7–9 season with a 20–10 win over Houston. "After that game, my car was literally running in the parking lot, and I was packed and ready to get out of Baltimore," Stark said.

During the home game before that, the Colts drew 35,462. Three other games that final season failed to eclipse 40,000. Maximum seating capacity was listed as 60,020. As far back as the last Baltimore winner in '77, the Colts sold out half of eight games, and the last was a playoff loss.

"It was a tough situation back then because Irsay was trying to get a lease in a better stadium," said Pete Ward, hired in '81 and now chief operating officer. "I think you could say he gets all the blame, but it wasn't all his fault."

Memorial Stadium was outdated. Irsay visited other stadiums and saw luxury suites and the latest amenities.

"The bathrooms, some worked and some didn't and some were overflowing," Krauss said. "The paint was peeling off the walls."

Ward added, "The clock wouldn't work. It was an old antiquated locker room."

The lease was up after 1983. The first word Ward heard had the Colts headed to Arizona. "Irsay says the team's moving to Phoenix," he recalled general manager Ernie Accorsi saying in January. "Better start packing."

That destination leaked to the media. "Somewhere over the next couple of hours, Bob Irsay changed his mind," Ward said. "He flew into the airport that night, and Accorsi called a press conference. I went to it. They interrupted local programming and went live with the famous press conference from the Baltimore airport."

It was an ugly moment for Robert Irsay, who was described by some in attendance as being in an alcoholic haze. He slurred some of his words and angrily lashed out at reporters. Excerpts were replayed in ESPN's 2009 documentary *The Band That Wouldn't Die*. Even current Colts owner Jim Irsay, Robert's son, concedes in the documentary that the press conference was regrettable.

That was in January. Two months later, one action led to a historical reaction.

On March 27, a chamber in the Maryland State Legislature passed a law to empower the city to seize the Colts under eminent domain. Informed of this development, Robert Irsay wasn't going to be boxed in. The Mayflower moving vans were dispatched to the complex the next day.

"My feeling was that he was just trying to position himself for a better deal with Baltimore," Ward said. "So it was a shock to me when Jim called me into his office and said, 'At 10:00, there's going to be 14 trucks coming. My dad says we're moving to Indianapolis. You need to be here to be in charge of the trucks.'

"That was an all-nighter. It was secret for about two hours. It didn't really break until about midnight."

Krauss was in his apartment, which overlooked the team complex. Teammate Pat Beach phoned. "Look outside," Krauss recalled Beach saying as the Mayflowers rolled in. "We're moving."

"Oh my gosh," a stunned Krauss remembered saying. "Is it really true?

"Nobody really believed Bob was going to do it, and Bob did it."

Krauss didn't know what to do. He called Jim Irsay. "If you want to play for the Colts," Krauss said he was told, "you better head to Indianapolis."

Equipment manager Jon Scott, who joined the Colts as an intern in 1979 and is still with the team today, was alerted the night before in a call from Jim Irsay.

"We're mo-o-o-ving," Irsay said slowly.

Scott, who had previously worked at Arizona State, asked, "Phoenix?"

"No-o-o," Irsay said, again deliberately for effect. "Ind-y-y-y."

Scott asked how much time he had to prepare.

"Tomorro-o-o-w," Jim Irsay said.

Scott was told to not say a word to anyone.

"But you need to start packing," Jim Irsay said.

"I just started packing as best I could," Scott said. "I packed until 3:00 in the morning, got a couple hours sleep, and then they needed some people to go to Indy early on Mr. [Bob] Irsay's private plane."

Reporters awaited their arrival. Cameras seemingly followed them everywhere. Scott recalled checking into a Holiday Inn.

"I just remember everybody following us with the cameras, we get on the elevator, and the doors shut," Scott said. "I looked at Jim and said, 'This must have been how The Beatles felt coming over from Liverpool.'"

When Robert Irsay arrived in Indianapolis, he sent a message to his former city. "At the big welcoming press conference in the Hoosier Dome, Bob Irsay has been quoted as telling the crowd, 'It's not your team, it's my team,'" Ward said. "He has been rapped for that many times, but it was taken way, way out of context. He was referring to the State of Maryland and eminent domain."

Robert Irsay proved he could do what he wanted with his team. Indianapolis provided a new dome stadium and a favorable lease. Baltimore mourned.

"These folks died a thousand deaths," Hall of Fame running back Lenny Moore said.

John Ziemann, director of Baltimore's Legends Sports Museum, admits Memorial Stadium was shot. "But Irsay lied so many times," Ziemann said, "about having no intention to move the team while having discussions with other cities." Then the Colts did end up moving.

"The next day the sun came up, commerce was moving in Baltimore, nobody died," Ziemann said. "But for a major part of us, our heart was taken away in those Mayflower trucks. We didn't even have a chance to save our team. We tried. Every time Mr. Irsay wanted 10 things, then he would come back and want more. We did more, he came back with more. He kept on adding and adding and adding. And he was playing one city against us, Arizona against us, Indianapolis against us.

"We hated Robert Irsay. We hated Indianapolis. We hated [Indianapolis mayor Bill] Hudnut. There's no two ways about it. They took something away from us that belonged to us, and they had no right to do that. No right at all."

After 29 years, Ziemann suggests the wounds have healed. He has nothing but positive words to say about Jim Irsay. It's the same with a lot of other former Colts. They liked Jim. They hated his father.

Baltimore eventually landed another NFL team in a similar circumstance. Owner Art Modell lost money in Cleveland in large part due to an outdated Municipal Stadium and brought the Browns to Baltimore in 1996. They became the Baltimore Ravens.

A year later, on January 14, 1997, Robert Irsay died.

"The scar will always be there," Ziemann said. "The wound has healed, but the scar will always be there, and you can't erase the history of what was done to us."

David Frick, then Indianapolis deputy mayor, handled nego-tiations for the Colts move. "I always believed Robert Irsay would not have left Baltimore if the city didn't force him to leave," said Frick, now 68 and semi-retired. "He didn't want to have a big legal fight for years and years and years. Irsay thought if he didn't get out of town right away, he was going to be there for years."

Michael Chernoff, Irsay's chief counsel who negotiated the move with Frick, uttered the memorable quote about the eminent domain action, "They not only threw down the gauntlet, but they put a gun to his head and cocked it and asked, 'Want to see if it's loaded?' They forced him to make a decision that day."

Now 77 and living in Glencoe, Illinois, Chernoff stands by that statement. "That was absolutely accurate," the attorney said. "I said it, and I meant it. We just didn't give the mayor [Don Schaefer] a chance to pull the trigger."

In a succinct summation he has said before, Chernoff repeated, "Move it or lose it."

5 "Our Super Bowl"

The Indianapolis Colts say it's *the* game they will always remember. Not the Super Bowl XLI win, but the 2007 triumph that got them there.

They didn't seem to have a chance, down 21–3 in the second quarter to a familiar nemesis, the New England Patriots, in the AFC Championship Game on January 21, 2007, at the RCA Dome. The Colts had lost to the Patriots in the 2003 and 2004 postseasons.

"I remember walking in at half, now it's 21–6, we thought Reggie [Wayne] got interfered with in the end zone at the end of

Running back Joseph Addai (29) breaks away from New England Patriots defensive tackle Richard Seymour during the AFC Championship Game on Sunday, January 21, 2007, in Indianapolis. (Photo/Ed Reinke)

the first half and they didn't call it so we got a field goal," said then-head coach Tony Dungy, now 57 and retired in Tampa, Florida. "We're walking in and I still felt good about things. I harkened back to '03 when we were way down to the Patriots at home. Bethel Johnson ran the kickoff back on the last play of the first half and we're just way down to those guys. It was a Thanksgiving weekend game. We ended up getting the ball to the 1-yard line and couldn't get it in on fourth down and we lost that game.

"I'm thinking of that whole scenario and what I'm going to say, 'We're going to be okay.' And you know how they have the TVs in the hallway? I look up and the monitor says something like, 'No team has ever come from more than 10 points down at halftime in the championship game.' And I'm thinking, *Why do they have to show that now?*"

Dungy Savors Every Last Moment

This was one time when Tony Dungy couldn't answer enough questions. And the Colts' head coach set his mind to responding to every single one of them after the 38–34 comeback victory over New England in the AFC Championship Game on January 21, 2007, at the RCA Dome.

"I remember Craig Kelley, he was worried about me after the game," Dungy said of the team's vice president of public relations. "I'm talking to everybody. Craig is like, 'One more question. One more question. Coach has got to go.'"

Actually, Dungy was in no hurry. The Colts had finally reached the Super Bowl after so many playoff disappointments.

"I said, 'No, Craig, I've stood up here for years and answered questions after a playoff loss, and I took every single one of them," the coach said. "'You're not going to steal this moment from me now. We can stay in here all night if we want to.' I talked to everybody. I remember being in there forever."

Family and friends waited patiently. He finally emerged to celebrate. They went to the Marriott to pick up children, then it was time to extend this late evening into the early morning. "We took about 30 people to Palomino's," Dungy said. "The guy said, 'We'll

Dungy sensed his locker room had energy. He told them to keep their poise and reminded his players that they were getting the ball first in the third quarter and a touchdown drive would make it a one-score game. He promised this one would come down to the end, just like the 38–34 home loss in 2003.

Center Jeff Saturday had told the team, "This is our time," in a speech the night before, but even he was having doubts when the Patriots took the big lead.

"I'd like to tell you that I was saying 'our time' as we were down by 18 points," Saturday said during a March radio show. "Tony Dungy stuck with it a long longer than I did. I bailed out, 'What are we doing?!' But he held strong. We went to the locker room and he kept saying it, 'It's our time. It's still our time.' That kind of motto solidified us that night."

keep it open as long as you want.' We stayed in there until almost 5:00 in the morning, just talking about things, the fact we were going to the Super Bowl, what it was going to be like, my wife and her side of the family, our kids, the cousins. It was just one of those special times."

When fired by Tampa Bay on January 14, 2002, management was convinced Dungy couldn't get the Buccaneers to the Super Bowl due to a conservative offense. His teams reached the playoffs in four of six seasons and he had a 54–42 record, but wild-card blowout losses to Philadelphia in back-to-back Januarys spelled the end. While he quickly landed a job with the Colts, Dungy watched his old team win Super Bowl XXXVII the next postseason with head coach Jon Gruden. Buccaneers players credited Dungy for building that championship team.

"You think back to 20 some years of trying to get there," Dungy said, including his time as an NFL assistant.

He cherished that time at the restaurant. "That's one memory I'll never forget, and I'm grateful to those guys for doing that, all the cooks and the service people, they just stayed and said, 'There's no time limit,'" Dungy said. "We almost watched the sun come up. It was one of the best meals and one of the best evenings I've ever had."

The Colts drove 76 yards for a touchdown on that opening possession with Manning scoring on a one-yard run. Another 76-yard drive culminated in Manning throwng a one-yard TD pass to Dan Klecko. Marvin Harrison caught the two-point conversion pass to tie the game at 21. After the Patriots took the lead, the Colts countered with a 67-yard march. Dominic Rhodes fumbled near the goal line, but Saturday recovered for the touchdown. Tied again. The teams traded field goals; the Colts' score came off a 59-yard drive.

The Patriots kicked another field goal to lead 34–31. The Colts went three-and-out, but a defense that had struggled much of the game came up with a stop. The Colts got the ball back at their 20 with 2:17 remaining and one timeout. They didn't waste time. Manning hit wide receiver Reggie Wayne for 11 yards, then two plays later found tight end Bryan Fletcher for a 32-yard gain. A 14-yard pass to Wayne had 12 yards tacked on for a roughing-the-passer penalty. Time for running back Joseph Addai. He ran for 5 yards, then 3. Just like in 2003, the Colts were near the goal line late. Third-and-2 at the Patriots 3-yard line. Addai took the handoff and saw nothing but open space thanks to Saturday's pancake block on defensive tackle Vince Wilfork. Addai scooted in for the go-ahead touchdown.

The Colts scored 32 second-half points on a defense that had not allowed 27 points in a game all season. Manning played one of the best halves of his career with 15-of-23 pass completions for 225 yards and one TD.

But there was still time, one minute remaining, for Patriots quarterback Tom Brady to work his magic. Manning couldn't watch. He sat on the bench, head down, and he prayed. The Patriots reached the Colts' 45. A sellout crowd of 57,433 screamed and stomped. The RCA Dome shook. Then, inexplicably, Brady made a mistake. Cornerback Marlin Jackson intercepted a pass at the Colts' 35 and started to run, then realized he just needed to get down after a six-yard runback.

"I thought for a [moment], *What am I doing?*" Jackson said. "*If I go down, we're going to the Super Bowl.*"

The celebration commenced with 16 seconds remaining. One kneel down and the confetti flew.

"One thing I remember about Marlin's play is two guys setting high jump records for themselves, Peyton Manning off the bench and [offensive coordinator] Tom Moore," Colts radio voice Bob Lamey said. "Peyton was sitting there with his head in his hands because he knew Brady could do anything. Tom was kind of doing the same thing. I just happened to look that way when the play was over, and they were both jumping up and down because they knew. That probably was individually the best play that I've ever seen from the Colts only because of what it led to. If he didn't catch the

Water Bottles and a T-Shirt

RCA Dome director Mike Fox had enough on his mind during the AFC Championship Game when the Indianapolis Colts defeated New England 38–34 in January 2007. If the home team won, the trophy presentation would be on the field. If the visiting team prevailed, the ceremony would be in the locker room.

"The whole second half of that game, I'm in the corner behind the end zone," Fox said. "Archie Manning is in that same corner. He's all by himself. There was no one there but him. He's so far back, nobody can see him."

The father of quarterback Peyton Manning agonized as the game intensified.

"The guys I was working with, some kind of knew him and some didn't. I just told them, 'Look, you leave that guy alone. You don't go near him. You don't talk to him,'" Fox said. "In the fourth quarter, the game was so close, he was sweating and it was humid in there. I really started worrying about him from a physical standpoint. I went and got a couple bottles of water and walked up to him and said, 'Here, Dad, you probably need these.'

"That wasn't Archie Manning, this great quarterback, the father of two NFL guys. This was just a dad watching his kid play the most important game of his life. It reminded me so much of myself when I watch my kids play sports."

When the Colts prevailed on Marlin Jackson's interception with 16 seconds remaining, Fox spotted Colts senior executive vice president Pete Ward in that Southeast corner.

"Pete is about as dull as the day is long, and I say that as a compliment," Fox said. "Three-and-13 or 13-and-three, he's the same guy. I ran up to him and jumped on his back and said, 'Can you believe this?!'

"I get off of him and he says, 'This is pretty cool.' That was it."

Reebok's Eddie White threw Fox an AFC Championship T-shirt.

"I've never worn it," Fox said. "I've got it hanging in my closet. That was a really good day."

ball, who the hell knows, and we've had a lot of dropped interceptions over the years. Marlin was a good player, but he will forever be known for that interception."

Dungy had faith in his defense. He sensed someone would make a play. "It was the greatest feeling," Dungy said. "I knew somehow we were going to stop these guys. Once we scored, it never dawned on me that we wouldn't win the game. When Marlin caught that ball and the dome kind of exploded, you could sense the energy and the excitement for the city, knowing we were going to the Super Bowl."

Dungy couldn't have been more prophetic about his halftime promise. The Colts had that chance in the end and capitalized. The final score was the same as that 2003 Patriots game, only this time the home team won 38–34.

"The greatest football game I've ever been a part of," Saturday said. "No question."

"Obviously, we had to win another game, but that was it," Dungy said. "That was our Super Bowl."

6 Super Bowl XLI

Indianapolis Colts offensive left tackle Tarik Glenn came out of the Dolphin Stadium locker room for Super Bowl XLI warm-ups, scanned the stands, and took it all in. This was it, the goal for every NFL player from the time they're old enough to know what a football is.

"It was raining, but what was awesome is when we went out for pregame warm-ups and saw the stage for the Super Bowl," Glenn said six years later of the big-game atmosphere on February

4, 2007, in Miami. "It was a lot grander than anything we had ever experienced before. It was a surreal moment for me. 'I'm playing in one of the biggest events you can.'"

Head coach Tony Dungy, who still has his home in Tampa, Florida, advised players not to worry about rain. "Then, of course, it rained," Dungy said. "I had told the guys, 'Hey, I live in Florida. If it's going to rain, it's going to shower fast and furious and then it's going to be done. But there's no way it's going to rain and rain and rain.' And of course Peyton [Manning] wants to practice with the wet balls and dunk them. We did all that. And sure enough, it rained.

"I remember the first quarter not even feeling it. That's how much I was into the game. When we turned and went to the other end for the second quarter, and we had a little break, I was walking and I said, 'Man, I am all wet.' That was the first time I really realized it had been raining. [Equipment manager] Jon Scott got me a jacket, and I put it on. From then on, I was cognizant of it. But I was so into the game it took me a whole quarter to really realize it was raining."

It didn't take long for Dungy to make his first mistake. Well, he goofed the day before the game when he overruled special teams coach Russ Purnell and said if the Colts lost the toss they would kick off to dangerous Chicago Bears returner Devin Hester.

"Yeah, that was me, too," Dungy said with a chuckle. "All week Russ Purnell had said, 'That's the only real threat they have. If we just keep the ball away from him, we're going to be fine.' That was our plan all week. Then Saturday, I was just thinking, *We've got to be the aggressors on this.* So Saturday night, I said, 'I hope we lose the toss because we want to kick off and we're going to kick it right down the middle, we're going to kick it to Devin Hester and when we pound him, they'll know that we mean business.'"

Dungy paused and laughed about what transpired. Colts kicker Adam Vinatieri called "Tails," and it was heads. The Bears wanted

Edge's Night Out

Head coach Tony Dungy wanted his Colts players to have some fun before getting serious in their February 2007 preparations for Super Bowl XLI at Miami.

Fun should be Edgerrin James' middle name. The team's all-time rushing leader, who departed a year earlier in free agency, is from nearby Immokalee, Florida. Dungy gave permission for players to join Edge for a Monday night out. If anyone knows about enjoying the night life in South Beach, among other places, it's Edge.

"'Edgerrin has got you guys on Monday,'" Dungy told the team. "'There's no curfew. I don't want to know where you go.'"

The coach laughs about it now, six years later.

He had sought advice from former Super Bowl coaches on how to handle the week. Mike Holmgren advised the team should arrive as late as possible because there's so much hype. Get there too early and players would be consumed by that build-up before the end of the week and just want to get the game played. Players received the previous weekend off and departed on Monday. Then the Edge plan went into effect.

"'Edgerrin has promised me he's going to keep everybody out of jail,'" Dungy recalled telling the players. "'I don't even want to hear

the ball. Hester broke the opening kickoff 92 yards for a touchdown, the earliest lead in Super Bowl history. It took 14 seconds.

"Sure enough, it was one of the dumbest decisions ever," Dungy said. "That was all on me. It kind of got things going on the wrong foot. But again, like our team did all year, they just didn't get concerned about little disappointments or little problems."

The Colts had learned their lesson and would avoid Hester with squib kicks the rest of the game. But the Bears had seized the early momentum. And it continued when Manning was intercepted in the Colts' opening series. Manning atoned with a 53-yard touchdown pass to wide receiver Reggie Wayne. The Bears botched the coverage as cornerback Charles Tillman thought he had safety help from Danieal Manning. Wayne was all alone.

about it. Monday is your night, and then Tuesday, media day, we'll start to go back to work.'

"That's the way we started it. To this day, I don't know where they went or what happened or who stayed out late, who came in when. No one got in trouble, and we started the week on Tuesday. That was a big enjoyable part for me, to let him have a hand in how our Super Bowl week went."

James enjoyed himself, but then again, that's his daily objective in life. "We just had fun," he said. "At the end of the day, nobody walked away with a bad taste. Everybody had fun. Not to go into details, but at the end of the day, it was all having fun, responsible fun.

"It didn't surprise me because everybody understands the type of person I am and what I'm about. All my life and most of my career, you always have to fight for steps. I've always been aware of everything that's going on and make sure I'm in good company. When somebody is around, I'm going to make sure they're with good company. Just livin' life, man, having fun."

The Colts defeated Chicago 29–17, and owner Jim Irsay gave James a Super Bowl ring for the two-time NFL rushing champion's seven years of dedicated service.

The Colts made another mistake as sure-handed holder Hunter Smith fumbled the extra-point snap. The fumbles didn't stop. The Bears gave up the ball on the kickoff, but the Colts gave it back on offense. Bears running back Thomas Jones ripped off a 52-yard run to the Colts' 5 against the NFL's worst rushing defense. Three plays later, Rex Grossman threw a four-yard TD pass to Muhsin Muhammad to make it 14–6, Bears.

As the rain continued, so did the turnovers. Colts safety Bob Sanders, also known as "The Eraser," knocked Bears running back Cedric Benson silly. Dwight Freeney fell on the fumble, but the Colts didn't capitalize. Four turnovers and counting. Vinatieri kicked a 29-yard field goal. It started raining harder. Yet the Colts drove to a go-ahead touchdown as Manning hit wide receiver

Marvin Harrison for 22 yards and tight end Dallas Clark for 17. Dominic Rhodes ran three times from the Bears' 11, the last from one-yard out for the score. The Colts were up, 16–14. That's the way it stayed for the first half, although there were two more turnovers as Colts tight end Bryan Fletcher coughed up a fumble before Grossman returned the favor by dropping a snap on the next play. Vinatieri missed a 36-yard field goal wide right to end the half.

The Colts dominated time of possession in the third quarter but settled for Vinatieri field goals of 24 and 20 yards and a 22–14 lead. The Bears' Robbie Gould kicked a 44-yarder to trim it to 22–17, Colts. Through three quarters, the Colts had the ball for 30 minutes, 51 seconds to the Bears' 14 minutes, 9 seconds.

Then came the game's pivotal play. Grossman pump-faked and tried to throw to a spot, but Muhammad had not turned around. Colts cornerback Kelvin Hayden, inserted for an injured Nick Harper in the second quarter, saw the ball the whole way, leaped, and intercepted it. He came down ever so close to the sideline, then followed a Colts caravan of blockers for a 56-yard touchdown return.

"I was right in front of it," Dungy said. "And you know how they have extra officials, the emergency guys? [Referee] Buddy Horton was on our sideline and right next to me. We were talking while they were going. 'You saw this, Buddy? His foot didn't hit the line, did it?' And he said, 'No, I would have called 'em in. I think it's good.' You're sitting there for what seems like forever waiting on it."

Instant replay confirmed Hayden had stayed inbounds. The touchdown stood, 29–17 Colts, and 11:44 remained in the final quarter.

"When they said, 'The play stands,' we pretty much knew that was it," Dungy said. "That was the game."

Grossman threw another interception. Wide receiver Bernard Berrian had a step deep, but the ball hung up forever and Sanders sped over to catch it. The Colts ground it out from there. Rhodes finished with 113 yards rushing on 21 carries. Running back

Joseph Addai caught a Super Bowl–record 10 passes for 66 yards. Manning was MVP after he completed 25-of-38 passes for 247 yards with one touchdown and one interception.

At the final gun, Dungy received two Gatorade baths. Freeney and Booger McFarland had the first container, Jeff Saturday and Glenn the second. Manning raised a clenched fist in triumph.

"I wanted to be on a team that won the Super Bowl," Manning said afterward. "To me, that's what it's always been about. In years past when our team has come up short, it's been disappointing. But somehow, some way, we have found a way to learn from some of those losses. We're a better team because of it."

"Now we're world champions!" owner Jim Irsay shouted from the on-field stage after receiving the Vince Lombardi Trophy.

Later in the locker room, a euphoric Irsay lifted up the trophy again and shouted, "Right here! Right here!" The room erupted.

"That's what you live for as an owner," Irsay said amid the din.

The Colts returned home to celebrate their first Super Bowl championship in Indianapolis. It was freezing outside, but fans lined the streets.

"One of my fondest memories was when we got back and saw the town shut down," Glenn said. "The people in the streets, everybody was wearing blue and white. I was just amazed at how the city came together."

7 "The Greatest Game Ever Played"

The 1958 Baltimore Colts are synonymous with what became known as "The Greatest Game Ever Played," a watershed moment that launched the NFL into a curious nation's living rooms. When the Colts outlasted the New York Giants 23–17 in overtime for the championship on December 28, 1958, at Yankee Stadium in the Bronx, an estimated 45 million people tuned in on television. Imagine the numbers if the game wasn't blacked out in New York City.

Chris Schenkel, who called the action, opened a 2011 ESPN *SportsCentury* documentary with the pronouncement, "This game was the game that changed professional football forever." Pat Summerall, the Giants' kicker who would become a sports announcer, said in the same ESPN retrospective, "It captured the imagination of everybody in the country."

The ripple effect added to the mystique. But some of the Colts who played that day, as well as the Giants' Frank Gifford, would attest it really wasn't the "greatest game."

"I really don't think it was, but the way it ended up made it the best game," said defensive end Gino Marchetti, 86 and living in West Chester, Pennsylvania. "And it was in New York. Anything in New York is magnified.

"I would call it the most important game ever played."

Lenny Moore said the greatest game the Colts played that season was against San Francisco when they rallied from a 27–7 halftime deficit for a 35–27 home win to clinch the Western Conference title. The victory allowed head coach Weeb Ewbank to rest starters the final two weeks, both road losses, that dropped the Colts to 9–3.

The Colts' future Hall of Famer list had Johnny Unitas, Marchetti, Moore, Raymond Berry, Jim Parker, Art Donovan, and Ewbank. The Giants' Canton, Ohio–bound contingent consisted of linebacker Sam Huff, halfback Frank Gifford, wide receiver Don Maynard, offensive tackle Roosevelt Brown, defensive end Andy Robustelli, and defensive back Emlen Tunnell.

"Just look at the cast," said Berry, 80 and living in Murfreesboro, Tennessee.

Don't forget two recognizable names on the other sideline. While Jim Lee Howell was the Giants' head coach, he had Vince Lombardi as offensive coordinator and Tom Landry as defensive coordinator. Both assistants would become Hall of Fame head coaches, Lombardi with Green Bay and Landry with Dallas. Lombardi is for whom today's Super Bowl trophy is named.

"You've got two legends in NFL history coaching the New York Giants," Berry said. "I'm glad we didn't know what we were up against."

The Colts led 14–3 at halftime on an Alan Ameche two-yard TD run and a Unitas 15-yard scoring pass to Berry. The Giants stuffed Ameche in a goal-line stand to seize momentum, and scored two touchdowns, the latter a Charlie Conerly 15-yard TD pass to Gifford, to take a 17–14 lead in the final quarter. Late in the game, Gifford ran right on a third-and-4 play and the ball was spotted inches short. Marchetti made the tackle but fractured his right ankle in the pileup. Gifford maintains to this day he reached the marker.

"I know I made the first down. There was never any doubt in my mind," he said in the ESPN documentary.

Berry and Marchetti disagree. "I don't think he got it," Marchetti said. "When I hit him, he was two or three yards from the first down. Then he went inside, and I made the tackle."

"His version of where the ball was placed and where he thought he got to, I don't think he was accurate," Berry said. "I've looked at the film. I don't think there's clear-cut proof that it happened the way Frank said it happened."

On fourth-and-inches at their 40-yard line, the Giants punted with about two minutes remaining. That set the stage for Unitas. Ameche, mentioned in a 2008 *Baltimore Sun* story, recalled what the quarterback said in the huddle. "John is not one to make speeches," Ameche said, "but he said, 'We've got 80-some yards to go and two minutes left to do it in. Now we find out what stuff we're made out of.'"

While the hurry-up, two-minute drill is commonplace today, it was a relatively new strategy back then. Unitas ran it to near perfection. He completed a key 11-yard pass to Moore to convert one third down.

"This was an area where it really showed the importance, the expertise, the full understanding of what to do and how to do it and when to do it of Johnny Unitas," said Moore, 79 and still residing in Baltimore. "That was the beginning of other teams picking up and establishing what they now call the two-minute drill. Unitas did it automatically. It wasn't even in our game plan. Nobody figured it was going to be a sudden-death overtime. Johnny called his shots. I tell you, that's what he was all about. He knew everything that was going on."

Three consecutive completions to Berry gained 62 yards. Berry finished with 12 catches for 178 yards and one touchdown. The dozen catches are still a Championship Game record. "He and Berry got together," Ewbank told ESPN. "They were just unstoppable."

Berry mentions another factor in the Colts clicking late. "It was a perfect-weather day in late December for our style of attack because we had to throw the ball," Berry said. "We had told [Unitas], 'You need to throw the ball and throw it a lot.'"

Bob Lamey, who became the Indianapolis Colts' longtime radio voice, grew up a Berry fan and listened to the game in Texas. He recalled legendary New York public address announcer Bob Sheppard said later of the call, "'The most boring day I had behind the mic. All I said in the second half was, 'Unitas to Berry. First down.' It was a very subtle way to compliment both of them."

Steve Myhra kicked a 20-yard field goal with seven seconds remaining to force the first overtime game in NFL playoff history. Credit NFL commissioner Bert Bell's institution of overtime rules prior to this game.

On December 28, 1958, Baltimore Colts fullback Alan Ameche advances through a big opening provided by his teammates to score the winning touchdown in overtime against the New York Giants during the NFL Championship Game at Yankee Stadium in New York. The Colts' Lenny Moore gets a good block on the Giants' Emlen Tunnell (45) at left. Colts quarterback Johnny Unitas (19) is at right along with the Giants' Jim Patton (20). The Colts won 23–17.
(AP Photo/File)

"We started hearing about overtime for the first time," Berry said. "Good grief, nobody knew about overtime. It's no wonder the game raised an eyebrow. It was an explosion of football."

Moore didn't have any idea what was supposed to happen next. "Nobody knew," he said. "Not even the referees. They weren't even sure how they were going to conduct it."

Unitas called "Tails" on the coin toss. It was heads. The Giants got the ball first but punted. Unitas went to work from his 20. He called 13 plays in the 80-yard drive. Many were for Ameche, who caught an eight-yard pass on third-and-8 from the Colts' 33. The back went up the gut for 22 yards. Berry caught two passes for 33 yards, the latter a 12-yarder for a first down at the Giants' 8. Ameche ran for one yard. Tight end Jim Mutscheller caught a six-yard pass.

Mutscheller and Moore threw the key blocks to open a gaping hole on the final play. Ameche, in an NFL highlight that would be replayed forever, lowered his head and slammed into the end zone for that last yard. He gave that game ball to a fan before a teammate retrieved it. That ball would be shared by teammates. Marchetti said he ended up with it for about five years, then he gave the ball to the National Italian American Sports Hall of Fame for display when he was inducted.

Unitas was MVP after he completed 26-of-40 passes for 349 yards with one TD and one INT. Ameche ran 14 times for 65 yards and two scores. Gifford, who ran for 60 yards on 12 carries, attributed the bad spot on his infamous third-down rush to chaos surrounding Marchetti breaking his ankle. Expressing amazement about several books written on the game, Gifford told *The New York Times* in 2008, "When you think about it, it was a lousy game."

To mark the game's 50th anniversary, Gifford came out with *The Glory Game: How the 1958 NFL Championship Changed Football Forever*, written with Peter Richmond. In his opening chapter, Gifford writes, "On December 28, 1958, the National Football League grew up. From Madison Avenue to small-town living rooms, fans began to pay attention to our weekly battles on their small-screen televisions. On that long Sunday afternoon, a nation began to recognize the unique appeal of a sport in which any one play could bring extraordinarily athletic feats or grimace-inducing collisions. Or both."

Berry understands why Gifford was so adamant about making that first down, which would have enabled the Giants to kill the clock.

"To be in a game like that and lose it," Berry said, "it's got to be hard to live with."

Berry still gets asked about "The Greatest Game Ever Played." "The fact that people still talk about it today says a whole lot," Berry said. The Hall of Famer sounds like he's describing a game from yesterday. "Well," he said, "I've had more than 50 years to think about it."

8 Gino Marchetti

As a member of the NFL's 50th and 75th Anniversary teams, Gino Marchetti has been called the greatest defensive end to ever play the game. But the humble Baltimore Colts Hall of Famer doesn't care for such absolute distinction.

"One of," said Marchetti, 86, who lives with his wife, Joan, in West Chester, Pennsylvania. "I'll take that any day. You can't compare eras."

It was a different time when he played for the Colts from 1953–64 and again in 1966. Tackles and sacks weren't an official stat. So how did the 11-time Pro Bowl selection come to be known as one of the best players? Colts Hall of Fame wide receiver Raymond Berry laughs for about five seconds when asked if his teammate is deserving of the time-honored reputation.

"You could line up a bunch of right tackles and I could tell you what you would get from them," Berry said. "It was a nightmare for them. He would throw them aside, flip them, whatever. I'm sure they lost sleep for three nights after trying to keep him off their quarterbacks."

Aside from the 6'4", 244-lb. end being the complete package, a blend of unique strength and speed with powerful hands and an understanding of leverage, Berry mentions Marchetti's unmatched competitive spirit.

"I think about him in a locker room before a game," Berry said. "You ever been to a zoo and you see a lion going back and forth? That was Marchetti. He was always pacing like a caged animal. He was just non-stop."

Marchetti admits he was wired differently. Still is to this day. Intense at the drop of a hat. Impatient to the point of needing to move around. In retirement, he attended a Colts game at Memorial Stadium. He got so worked up watching, he couldn't remember where he parked. So Marchetti headed to the locker room to hang out, waited until the fans filed out and the cars disappeared, and that's how he found his vehicle.

On one road trip, he had developed a 102-degree fever. Trainer Ed Block insisted on rooming with him to monitor the player's condition.

"The next day we get up and we're eating breakfast and Ed said, 'You know, Gino, if I could figure out a way to calm you down the night before a game, I could add two or three more years to your career,'" Marchetti recalled Block saying.

Ted Marchibroda, a backup NFL quarterback from 1953–57, started his NFL coaching career as an assistant in 1961. He would later coach the Colts in Baltimore after Marchetti's playing days and in Indianapolis.

"There was no question, in his day he was the most outstanding defensive end," said Marchibroda, now 82 and living in Weems, Virginia. "Even at this particular time, he's one of the best defensive ends in league history. He was on some great teams with some great players, but he stood out even among those guys."

How much so?

Gino Marchetti at the team's summer training camp at Western Maryland College on July 18, 1960. (AP Photo)

"He and Johnny Unitas were neck and neck," Berry said when asked who was the greatest Baltimore Colt. "That's how dominating a defensive player Gino was. We had Unitas on offense and Marchetti on defense. That equates to two world championships."

And Marchetti says the Colts should have won the title in 1957 before the championships in 1958 and 1959. "We lost three games in about three minutes of playing time," he said. "You have to learn how to win. That phrase gets used a lot, but I don't think people realize how true it is."

Marchetti reminisces more about the good old days now, something he didn't take time to appreciate decades ago. He mentions some of his favorite teammates, especially the guy who lined up next to him, Hall of Fame defensive tackle Art Donovan.

"I think a lot about Artie," Marchetti said. "We were side by side all those years. It all means more to me now than when I was playing."

Number crunchers who prefer statistics to validate greatness need only to know that Marchetti sacked Detroit quarterback Bobby Layne eight times in one home game. And he said those stats weren't kept by the team the way they are today, when the nearest defender to a quarterback scrambling out of bounds behind the line gets credit for a sack. The way Colts head coach Weeb Ewbank scored it, a defender in that situation was listed as getting blocked when that happened. The player had to make the tackle.

One year, Marchetti remembers being shown one of Ewbank's statistical breakdown charts. The defensive end was credited with disrupting the quarterback 60 times in a season. That total wasn't necessarily sacks, but any play in which the pass rusher disrupted the passer. And it was in a 12-game regular season.

"I was double-teamed a hell of a lot," Marchetti said. "One time, Coach George Halas had me triple-teamed the whole game against the Chicago Bears. And hey, listen, they held me a lot in those days, too."

9 Wave 'Em Down the Field

Forget the statistics. Indianapolis Colts wide receiver Marvin Harrison often accomplished the unimaginable.

Granted, the combination of speed, route-running precision, great hands, and an indefatigable work ethic produced 1,102 catches in 13 seasons. But if you want to inspire some entertaining water-cooler conversation, wonder aloud which of his grabs was the greatest.

There was the time he reached back behind his body to haul in a pass with one hand at Denver. And who could forget the ball he tipped back to himself and caught before getting

Brush with the Law

If Colts wide receiver Marvin Harrison isn't a first-ballot Hall of Famer next year, it's because of a shooting in 2008.

Convicted drug dealer Dwight Dixon accused Harrison of shooting him after an altercation outside a Philadelphia establishment Harrison owned and operated. Dwight Dixon sued Harrison, who denied involvement.

The law determined from a ballistics test that the gun that shot Dixon belonged to Harrison, but authorities couldn't determine who pulled the trigger. Dixon died in 2009 after being shot several times while parked in a car two blocks from Harrison's sports bar.

both feet just in bounds to score a touchdown in a win at New England? And there was the pass tight end Ken Dilger deflected that Harrison reached back and snagged in the back of the end zone for a score.

Eventually, someone will inevitably assert that those catches were a distant second to what Harrison did at Tennessee on December 7, 2003. When Peyton Manning unloaded the deep pass, it appeared to be overthrown. Harrison kept running. At the last possible moment, the receiver leaped forward, reached out his right hand, caught the nose of the ball, and all in one motion while falling, tucked it away with that one hand.

"He got it! What a circus catch!" Colts radio voice Bob Lamey exclaimed. "Holy mackerel! What a catch by the great one, Marvin Harrison!"

While everybody else was catching their breath, trying to believe what they just saw, Harrison jumped up as if it was business as usual and looked back at his teammates. He waved at them to come down the field and join him after the miraculous 42-yard grab that set up the Colts' final score in a 29–27 win.

"He's sick. He's a freak," said former Colts cornerback Ray Buchanan, then with Atlanta, which faced Harrison the next week. "We might have to check his DNA. He might be an alien."

Maybe the 6', 178-lb. receiver's secret was his sweet tooth.

"He really loved Tastykakes," Dilger said of the popular cupcake produced in Philadelphia. Harrison once had a Tastykakes stand next to his locker. "I never saw a guy eat so much junk food. He had everything, and he still had no body fat, just a freak of nature."

Dilger and Harrison were locker neighbors for six seasons. "Inside the locker room and on the field, he was one of my all-time favorites," Dilger said of Harrison, who was selected with the 19th overall pick in 1996. "We would chat about everything."

Harrison rewrote the Colts record books with those 1,102 catches—third in league history to Jerry Rice's 1,549 and Tony Gonzalez's 1,242 through 2012—14,580 receiving yards, and 128 TDs. He set the NFL single-season reception record with 143 in 2002. Manning and Harrison own several league marks for a passing combination including touchdowns (112), completions (953), and passing yards (12,756).

"If you look at that 1996 draft, there were three wide receivers taken ahead of him and we had him as our No. 1 wide receiver," said Bill Tobin, the Colts' director of football operations that year. "But the national people and all these people who were making their lists, they didn't have him where we had him.

"His route-running, he could uncover, he had sneaky fast speed, he was so smooth, he didn't [use] a lot of effort to run fast. He was deceiving."

Toward the end of Harrison's career, he rarely granted an interview. His last season was in 2008, but he didn't announce his retirement. It had to be presumed.

The Colts inducted Harrison into the Ring of Honor on November 27, 2011.

In the days leading up to becoming the eighth inductee, Harrison was remembered by his former team. "I think he started it all, really," said defensive end Dwight Freeney. Manning recalled his first throw to Harrison. "When I threw my first pass at the preseason game in Seattle, it was a four-yard pass and he ran 48 yards for a touchdown," Manning said in remarks distributed by the Colts. "I said to myself, 'All you have to do in the NFL is just throw four-yard passes to Marvin Harrison, and he runs for a touchdown.'"

Colts vice club chairman Bill Polian spoke of Harrison's preference to keep a low profile during a 2011 radio show. "The big joke [around the team complex] was that he could disappear in plain sight," Polian said. "There were people taking bets about whether or not he would actually be in the team picture at the [2007] Super Bowl; and he was, and we didn't know where he went after that."

In a team video, center Jeff Saturday said, "Marvin was a perfectionist. He doesn't talk at all. He shows it all." Manning said in the video, "It's truly an honor and a privilege to say I played quarterback with Marvin Harrison." The tribute included head coach Jim Caldwell sharing a time when Harrison said, "75 and counting," in reference to how many passes the receiver had caught in practice without a drop.

In a halftime ceremony, Colts owner Jim Irsay praised the wide receiver's quiet excellence, his diligence in practice, and his precise nature of running pass patterns in setting the standard for others to follow. "All the great acrobatic catches, all the greatness and happiness that he's brought to all Colt fans and Indiana, we're really proud to call him our own," Irsay said.

Harrison's name was unveiled on a Lucas Oil Stadium façade. He took the microphone and, as expected, kept it short and sweet. "Thank you, thank you, thank you very much," he said. "To the city of Indianapolis, to all the fans here and the Irsay family, I just want to say thank you. It's truly an honor to be a part of the Ring of Honor. Words can't describe how I feel right now. So thank you very much."

Irsay took the microphone and yelled, "Canton, Ohio, awaits this man!"

Harrison and retired Colts head coach Tony Dungy are eligible for the Pro Football Hall of Fame in the next vote before Super Bowl XLVIII.

10 Raymond Berry

Sometimes questions don't get answered. Wide receiver Raymond Berry had his share of them early in his career. He didn't understand why Baltimore Colts owner Carroll Rosenbloom hired Cleveland Browns assistant Weeb Ewbank as head coach in 1954.

"I wish I got a chance to talk to Carroll before he died about Weeb," Berry said. "I wish I could have asked him, 'What in the heck were you thinking?' He spotted something, and he hired a great coach. Then Weeb decided to keep both me and John Unitas for some reason. He saw something. We didn't know anything. We just played the game when we got the chance to play."

The Colts selected Berry in the 20th round of the 1954 draft. He decided to return to Southern Methodist University for his senior year, then he joined the Colts in '55 and started what would be a Hall of Fame connection with Unitas in '56.

"Our careers are linked to Weeb Ewbank," Berry said. "Carroll Rosenbloom saw something in Weeb Ewbank in the same way Weeb Ewbank saw something in me and Johnny Unitas, and it didn't make any sense."

Halfback/quarterback George Taliaferro, who played for the Colts in 1953 and '54, surmised Rosenbloom's decision had something to do with Ewbank's mentor in Cleveland. "What he saw in Weeb Ewbank was Paul Brown," Taliaferro said of the Hall of Famers. "And Paul Brown was an absolute genius."

While with the Browns, Ewbank oversaw quarterback Otto Graham connecting with the likes of Mac Speedie and Dante Lavelli in an evolving pass attack, and the coach brought one of their preparation secrets to Baltimore. After practice, Ewbank didn't schedule anything for players so quarterbacks and pass catchers could spend extra time working on routes and developing chemistry.

"In a normal two-hour practice, you go out and watch the receivers and you watch how many times the No. 1 quarterback throws to the No. 1 receiver," Berry said. "You may come up with five, six, seven, or eight on a good day. You know how many pass patterns you can get done in 15 minutes after practice? At least 15 to 20. You get more done. That's where it developed. It was like clockwork."

Nobody put in more time after hours than Berry.

"You've never seen a player work as hard as Ray Berry," said Taliaferro, who was often enlisted to throw extra passes to the wide receiver before he spent his last NFL season in Philadelphia.

Berry chuckled when told of Taliaferro's compliment. "There wasn't any reason for that except I had to," said Berry, who laughed at his own explanation.

An obsession with preparation also meant hours of film study. "John wasn't big on that, but I spent hours with that movie projector," Berry said. "I was off board. I probably wasn't operating with a full deck. That was my M.O. It was just in my DNA. There's a lot to be said for hard work."

Berry retired with an NFL-record 631 receptions for 9,275 yards and 68 touchdowns. He was inducted into the Hall of Fame in 1973, and his No. 82 jersey was retired.

Unitas and Berry were convinced the extra work carried over to games. It was especially evident in that 1958 Championship Game

Hall of Fame Colts

These Colts are enshrined in the Pro Football Hall of Fame in Canton, Ohio.

Inducted in 1968, defensive tackle **Art Donovan**: 1953–61; All-Pro 1954–57; five Pro Bowls; jersey No. 70 retired.

Inducted in 1972, defensive end **Gino Marchetti**: 1953–64, '66; member of NFL's 50th and 75th Anniversary teams; All-Pro and Pro Bowl selection 1956–64; jersey No. 89 retired.

Inducted in 1973, wide receiver **Raymond Berry**: 1955–67; 631 catches for 9,275 yards and 68 TDs; retired as NFL's all-time receptions leader; named to NFL's 75th Anniversary team; All-Pro 1958–60; selected for six, played in five Pro Bowls; jersey No. 82 retired.

Inducted in 1973, offensive guard/tackle **Jim Parker**: 1957–67; All-Pro and Pro Bowl 1958–65; played in 139 consecutive games; jersey No. 77 retired; died 2005.

Inducted in 1975, running back/flanker **Lenny Moore**: 1956–67; retired ninth all-time with 12,451 combined yards; club's career rushing leader with 5,174 yards on 1,069 carries with 63 TDs; caught 363 passes for 6,039 yards and 48 TDs; NFL records for TDs in 18 consecutive games and rushing scores in 11 consecutive games; All-Pro 1958–61, '64; seven Pro Bowls; jersey No. 24 retired.

Inducted in 1978, head coach **Weeb Ewbank**: 1954–62 with Baltimore; led Colts to World Championships in 1958 and '59; 59–52–1 record in nine seasons with Colts; coached New York Jets to win over Colts in Super Bowl III; only coach with NFL and AFL championships; died 1998.

Inducted in 1979, quarterback **Johnny Unitas**: 1956–72; owned numerous league records including passes attempted (5,186),

when the wide receiver caught a record 12 passes for 178 yards and one touchdown in the Colts' 23–17 overtime victory over the New York Giants.

"There is a confidence factor that begins to surface in the heat of a game," Berry said. "When the heat is on and the battle is at its peak, the quarterback will go to the receiver he has the most confidence in. All of this was at work on December 28, 1958."

passes completed (2,830), passing yards (40,239), three seasons with 3,000 passing yards, 300-yard passing games (26), touchdown passes (290), consecutive games with a TD pass (47); only Colt to play on 1958–59, '70 championship teams; NFL MVP three times; All-Pro 1958–59, 1964–65, and '67; 10 Pro Bowls; NFL's 50th and 75th Anniversary teams; jersey No. 19 retired; died 2002.

Inducted in 1990, linebacker **Ted Hendricks**: 1969–73; four-time All-Pro; eight Pro Bowls; 25 career blocked kicks; NFL's 75th Anniversary Team.

Inducted in 1992, tight end **John Mackey**: 1963–71; second Hall of Fame tight end inductee; 331 catches for 5,236 yards and 38 TDs; All-Pro 1966–68; five Pro Bowls; NFL's 50th Anniversary Team; died 2011.

Inducted in 1997, head coach **Don Shula**: played for Baltimore 1953–56; coached Colts 1963–69; NFL's winningest head coach (328–156–6); formerly Colts winningest head coach (71–23–4); led Colts to winning records each year and to Super Bowl III.

Inducted in 1999, running back **Eric Dickerson**: 1987–91; 5,194 yards rushing on 1,258 carries with 32 TDs for Colts; 1988 NFL rushing champion with 1,659 yards; set NFL record with 2,105 rushing yards in 1984 (with Los Angeles Rams); retired with 13,259 career rushing yards, second in NFL history; All-Pro 1983–84, 1986–88; six Pro Bowls.

Inducted in 2011, running back **Marshall Faulk**: 1994–98; 5,320 rushing yards on 1,389 carries with 42 TDs; 297 catches for 2,804 yards and nine TDs; 8,124 combined yards with Colts; retired with 12,279 rushing yards and 100 TDs; 767 receptions for 6,875 yards and 36 TDs; 19,154 combined yards; All-Pro 1994–95, 1998–2001; seven Pro Bowls including rookie MVP.

"You get one chance to play professional football, the body will only last so long, and I get to play 12 of my 13 years with Johnny Unitas. Figure out what kind of deal that is for a receiver."

It was after "The Greatest Game Ever Played" that Berry experienced an epiphany.

"I'm over in the locker room, sitting in my stall," he said. "I remember for the first time, it dawned on me, *Where in the world did I get the abilities to go out there and play like that? Where did I get that physical skill and drive?*

"In that locker room, for the first time in my life, I started to see the package that I was dealt and I was just gifted. It wasn't just the physical, it was the mental. And it was the motor. I was just non-stop."

Finally, he was able to answer one lingering question for himself.

11 More from Moore

Lenny Moore thanks God and Raymond Berry.

"Oh, what a beautiful, beautiful human being," Moore said. "You're talking about one of the greatest human beings I have ever met in professional football circles, Raymond Berry."

One future Hall of Famer to another, Berry approached Moore in the early days of the Baltimore Colts. The wide receiver saw so much more in the talented halfback/flanker.

"Raymond was the guy who turned me around," Moore recalled. "He was telling me, 'Lenny, I've been watching these films, and we need more of you in our offense.' I'm thinking, *What in the hell is he talking about?*"

Berry explained in great detail how Moore could improve his skills. When going out for a pass, Moore needed to be in sync with quarterback Johnny Unitas. It started with understanding the importance of footwork, Berry advised, planting with an outside foot when making cuts to bring Moore closer to the hand-eye coordination required to catch the football.

Teammates used to laugh as they headed up the hill to the locker room while Berry and Unitas stayed out after practice.

Baltimore Colts Hall of Fame running back Lenny Moore (24) is met by Detroit Lions defensive end Darrius McCord (78) during a game at Tigers Stadium on October 20, 1963. The Colts defeated the Lions 25–21.
(AP Photo/NFL Photos/Ben Liebenberg)

Curious about what Berry had told him, Moore stayed after one day. And it changed his football life.

"Raymond said, 'Do a 12-yard angle out. And I want to see your footwork,'" Moore said. "So I did a 12-yard angle out to the sideline. And he said, 'You know what I noticed? You were kind of leaning more to cutting on your inside foot than your outside foot.' I didn't know what the hell he was talking about. 'What do you mean, man?' 'You're throwing yourself off. In other words, you're throwing yourself off on your hand-eye coordination to John. When John gets that ball from center, it's going to be one thousand one, one thousand two, one thousand three, then boom! He's ready to turn and throw and hit you. You've got to have the same pattern going on in your mind as you do your footwork.'

"Boy, he was 100 percent correct."

Moore continued to stay after. They got on the same page.

"Johnny looked over at me and he used to call me 'Sput,' short for Sputnik," Moore said. "He'd say, 'What do you got, Sput?' And I said, 'Well, I can do a slant in, I can do a slant in takeoff, I can do a slant in takeoff sideline.' And he wouldn't call it. We'd go on.

"Then he would say, 'Is it still there?' And I'd say, 'Any time you're ready, my man. It's there.' We might go a whole quarter and he wouldn't call it. But he was calling it when it fit exactly into the situation we had going, knowing that's what he needed to call at that particular time. That's how Johnny Unitas was."

Moore was named to seven Pro Bowls. He retired in 1967 with 12,449 all-purpose yards and 113 TDs.

Berry retired as a player the same year as Moore. And Berry's continual pursuit of knowledge and insight into the game would propel him to an NFL coaching career, which included a trip to Super Bowl XX as New England's head coach.

He speaks of Moore today with as much conviction as he did that day on the practice field. "When we're talking about Lenny Moore, we're talking about one of the greatest athletes to ever set foot on a football field," Berry said. "You don't find many athletes who can combine speed, power, great hands, and an ability to run the football the way he could. And beyond that, he was a total team player."

Carry the Ball

While in college, Lenny Moore had the opportunity to meet Cleveland running back Marion Motley. Their link went beyond playing the same position. Both were black in a time of racial discrimination.

"I went up to his hotel room. They were going to play the next day," Moore said. "I had a chance to sit down and really talk with him. He said, 'Somebody has to be here and we've got to carry the ball. And you make sure when you come in and you're a part of this, you continue to carry the ball much further than we are able to carry it. We're carrying it in order to open up the doors for guys like you.'

"Oh, yeah. Never, ever forgot that."

Moore still talks to another black former running back, George Taliaferro, who played for the Baltimore Colts in 1953–54.

"I congratulate Taliaferro. I've talked to George often," Moore said. "'How in the hell did you do it?' He was doing it because there were people like myself and other folks coming up behind him. I had the opportunity to talk to baseball great Jackie Robinson. I said, 'How did you do it, with your limitations?' Mainly, they didn't know themselves other than they needed to hang in there, they needed to get tough and go through it in hopes of down the line, the tension and the pressure and all the other things would lift so it would make it easier for guys like myself."

Motley, who died in 1999, was inducted into the Hall of Fame in 1968. When Moore made it in the NFL and encountered some of the same discrimination, Motley's words truly sunk in.

"*Now I know what he's talking about,*" Moore remembers thinking. "Thank God for those guys, man."

Both of their jersey numbers were retired, Moore's No. 24 and Berry's No. 82. Berry got the Hall of Fame call in 1973. Moore's bronze bust was added two years later.

"God is the one who blessed me with the talent that I wasn't even sure I had," Moore said. "Raymond could see it. Other than that, I never would have got involved to the depths of how I got involved unless Raymond pointed it out."

12 "Let 'Er Rip," "Captain Comeback"

One month after coming up five yards shy of possibly winning Super Bowl XLVII on February 3, 2013, Jim Harbaugh was asked which was worse—losing that game to Baltimore as San Francisco head coach or coming up short as the Indianapolis Colts quarterback in a down-to-the-last-play AFC Championship Game on January 14, 1996?

"Both were bitter life disappointments," Harbaugh said. But then he alluded to an upside easy to overlook. "They're kind of tied into life's major accomplishments, life's finest hours."

A new era of Colts fans should be required to research NFL history on Harbaugh when he was "Captain Comeback" and understand what the 1995 Colts were able to accomplish. That's when the Colts truly arrived in Indianapolis, 11 years after the franchise relocated from Baltimore.

They were supposed to be an afterthought that season, just like before. But the Colts improbably erased 21-point deficits to win two 27–24 road games, first at the New York Jets and then in Week 6 at previously undefeated Miami in overtime. They knocked off defending Super Bowl champion San Francisco 18–17 at home. Twelve of their 16 games were decided by a touchdown or less. They needed the last game to make the playoffs and rallied to a 10–7 home win over New England.

"I remember at the time, marveling week after week how we would be in games and win games, and it could be a different guy," Harbaugh said. "It could be Marcus Pollard. It could be Marshall Faulk. It could be Kirk Lowdermilk, Will Wolford, Trev Alberts, Jeff Herrod, Ray Buchanan won games for us, Brian Stablein or Ken Dilger. You could look at all of those guys and say that was the game their contribution won the game for us. Game ball."

Harbaugh names more names, many fans didn't know.

"Everybody was involved in it. It wasn't just one person," he said. "Great decisions made by the coaches, great decisions made by the front office, [vice president of football operations] Bill Tobin, ownership, just everybody making good decisions and a team that was focused on each other and winning. We had a great strength coach, Tom Zupancic, he had an unbelievable impact on the team. Jon Scott in the equipment room with 'Frog' [Mike Mays], [trainer] Dave Hammer, [director of public relations] Craig Kelley, it was such a bond. You go to do interviews, and just to see the excitement and how much fun [Kelley] was having. Everybody in the building had that fun and excitement. 'Aw man, this is awesome. This is cool.'"

Harbaugh led the NFL with a career-high 100.7 passer rating, far exceeding his 77.6 average in 14 seasons. The Colts (9–7) were the AFC's fifth seed. As head coach Marchibroda used to say to Harbaugh, that's when they really "Let 'er rip."

A 35–20 win at San Diego was the Colts' first postseason victory since arriving in Indianapolis. As a franchise, it was the first playoff win since 1971. Rookie backup running back Zack Crockett wasn't even born then. He ran for a club playoff record 147 yards on 13 carries. Harbaugh threw two TD passes.

"San Diego apparently thought they would win just by showing up," said Wolford, a Pro Bowl left tackle. "We absolutely blew them out on both sides of the ball."

Next stop—Kansas City. The road warriors accustomed to playing home games indoors at the RCA Dome were subjected to a game-time temperature of 11 degrees with a wind chill factor of minus-9 degrees—the Gatorade was frozen in sideline cups—yet prevailed 10–7 at Arrowhead Stadium where the top-seeded Chiefs had not lost all season.

"We're just a bunch of ragamuffins out there—that's what everybody says," Harbaugh told *The Indianapolis Star* after the game.

Fans identified with the blue-collar spirit of this team and their grandfatherly 64-year-old head coach. Thousands greeted the Colts at the airport after playoff games.

"The connection with the fans was genuine love," Harbaugh said. "You felt loved by the city and vice versa. It was just an amazing time."

The Colts headed to Three Rivers Stadium to face the Pittsburgh Steelers.

"Not too many people had an idea we would be there," Marchibroda said. "We had as much character as any team I've ever been associated with. I don't think we had the talent to go that far, but character goes a long way."

The decided underdogs took a 16–13 lead when Harbaugh threw a 47-yard touchdown pass to Floyd Turner early in the final quarter. The Colts still led when they got the ball back and had a chance to convert a third-and-1 play at their 31-yard line with 3½ minutes remaining. Running back Lamont Warren took the handoff and had room to run, but Steelers cornerback Willie Williams tripped him up. Williams was unsure of his responsibility on the play, so he blitzed. Instead of taking more precious seconds off the clock, the Colts had to punt.

"He wasn't supposed to be there," said Mike Chappell of *The Indianapolis Star*. "If he isn't, Warren runs for 20 yards."

"Unbelievable," said Dilger, a rookie tight end.

"Lamont Warren was at this last Senior Bowl, and we talked about it," said Tobin, now a Cincinnati Bengals scout. "When the hole opened up, he said it was like the sea parted. The guy got him by the tip of his toe, at the top of his foot."

Too many plays fit that oh-so-close category. The Steelers' Kordell Stewart caught a second-quarter touchdown pass that would be disallowed by instant replay today because he stepped out of bounds first. Colts linebacker Quentin Coryatt dropped a sure interception with the Steelers driving late for a go-ahead score. The Steelers converted a fourth-and-3 pass for a first down on that drive. Cornerback Ashley Ambrose bit on a double move to allow wide receiver Ernie Mills a 37-yard pass reception to the Colts' 1-yard line that set up a Bam Morris TD run for a 20–16 Steelers lead with 1:34 remaining.

"Any one of four or five plays in the second half," Chappell said, "If the Colts make the play, they win."

That includes the final play. The Colts drove to the Steelers' 29 with five seconds remaining. Harbaugh lofted a high pass into the end zone. Bodies collided. Wide receiver Aaron Bailey had the ball hit his chest, then he disappeared into a pile. Some thought he caught it for a game-winning touchdown.

"I replay it in my mind all the time," said Colts right guard Joe Staysniak. "I was blocking, I had a guy on me, I remember looking back at Jimmy and he's launching it. As I remember it, I'm running stride for stride underneath that ball. Must have been the shadow, because I wasn't even close. But I remember being down there and asking Aaron, 'Dude, did you catch it? Did you catch it?' He said, 'No.' I said, 'Well, shut up then. Don't tell anybody.'"

"I don't know how the referee saw it come out," Bailey said in the locker room afterward. "I grabbed the ball, put it underneath me, and tried to put on my act, as if I caught it. I guess I'm a lousy actor."

Wolford knew it was incomplete from one official's reaction.

"A ref from the back came flying in, and you could just tell the way he was waving it off that he saw it, that it was incomplete, and he was right," he said.

In his foreword to Terry Hutchens' 1996 book, *Let 'er Rip*, Harbaugh wrote, "We ended up one play, you pick it, from going to the Super Bowl."

The Steelers lost to Dallas in Super Bowl XXX. Wolford, Staysniak, and Marchibroda believe the Colts would have upset the Cowboys. The AFC Championship Game loss at Pittsburgh marked the final time Wolford, Staysniak, and Marchibroda were with the Colts.

"You really never came down after that game because that ended up being my last game as a Colt," Staysniak said. "I never came down from it. I'm still thinking we're playing, we've still got a quarter to go."

"That loss hurt me more than any other loss, not so much that we lost but how we lost," Marchibroda said.

As Harbaugh reminded, it wasn't all for naught. An unforgettable playoff run introduced Indianapolis to what the NFL could be all about.

"I know people have told me, 'You started it all, Ted, with that season,'" Marchibroda said.

13 Manning or Leaf?

Bill Polian's most important Indianapolis Colts' draft pick as president had to be his first.

Contrary to how it played out, it wasn't a no-brainer early on to select quarterback Peyton Manning over quarterback Ryan Leaf with the first overall choice in 1998. Early on, there was debate. Manning had completed a stellar four-year college career at Tennessee. He was considered NFL-ready. But Leaf's stock rose considerably after a strong junior season at Washington State. Some thought he had the stronger arm and greater potential.

Best Draft Picks

An educated guess on the Colts' best all-time selections in the NFL draft.

1. QB **Peyton Manning**, No. 1 overall, 1998—The NFL's only four-time MVP makes this the easiest choice. His passing numbers rewrote the team's record book. Think fans are grateful this wasn't Ryan Leaf?
2. WR **Marvin Harrison**, first round, 19th overall, 1996—He set an NFL single-season record with 143 receptions in 2002 and retired with 1,102 career catches, second to Jerry Rice. Harrison and Manning top many all-time combination lists, including TDs (112), completions (953), and passing yards (12,756).
3. RB **Edgerrin James**, first round, fourth overall, 1999—Speculative talk centered around RB Ricky Williams, but the Colts stuck to their scouting reports and surprised some fans with the selection of Edge. It was a great pick from day one. James led the NFL in rushing his first two years and finished as the Colts' all-time leader with 9,226 yards.
4. OLB **Robert Mathis**, fifth round, 138th overall, 2003—Quite possibly president Bill Polian's best value pick. The undersized pass rusher has 91½ career sacks, 16 behind franchise leader Dwight Freeney, who was not re-signed after 2012.
5. DE **Dwight Freeney**, first round, 11th overall, 2002—No pass rusher demanded more attention than "Free," who drew double- and triple-teams yet still finished his Colts career with a franchise-record 107.5 sacks. He teamed with Mathis to provide a Pro Bowl pass-rush tandem that was second to none.

Polian weighed the pros and cons admittedly more than necessary.

"It was just too important a decision not to do everything possible to make sure you were 100 percent comfortable with the choice," Polian told *The Indianapolis Star* during his first season with the Colts. "We were not going to leave any stone unturned. We probably turned over too many rocks and chased too many ghosts."

A *Newsday* poll of 20 NFL general managers favored Leaf over Manning: "The overwhelming consensus: Manning may have the more recognizable name, but Leaf clearly is the preferred quarterback among league executives. Fourteen of the 20 polled said they would draft Leaf over Manning, citing the Washington State quarterback's stronger arm, better mobility, and more promising long-term prospect as a franchise-caliber player."

Polian said the scouting department was initially split 50–50. Eventually, the scouts started leaning toward Leaf. Polian, head coach Jim Mora, offensive coordinator Tom Moore, and quarterbacks coach Bruce Arians evaluated both and liked Manning.

"The coaches, almost to a man, pretty much leaned toward Peyton," Polian said. "Tom was the biggest supporter, but Bruce was in that camp, too. I was probably leaning toward Peyton, but I have to admit I had some strong-arm concerns, which turned out to be incorrect. The intangible part, that was Peyton by a very wide margin."

When it came time for personal workouts, Manning shined.

"Tom and I stood together at the workout and were astonished at his arm strength," Polian said of the April 1 session in Knoxville, Tennessee. "He threw a tight, hard ball. It wasn't even the most catchable ball. He rifled it. Tom put him through a workout where he asks the quarterback to throw flat-footed. Peyton just rifled it out there. There wasn't a question in our mind after that about arm strength."

Leaf surprised for the wrong reasons the next day in Pullman, Washington, where Polian and Moore again watched together.

"We looked at each other and kind of raised our eyebrows," Polian said. "There was a marked difference in the velocity and spin rate of Ryan's ball versus Peyton's."

Manning showed up for his pre-draft interview prepared, yellow pad in hand. Leaf reportedly missed his interview due to a medical exam, but it bothered Mora that Leaf didn't contact the team.

Quarterback Peyton Manning of Tennessee holds up an Indianapolis Colts jersey while flanked by Colts owner Jim Irsay (left) and NFL Commissioner Paul Tagliabue on Saturday, April 18, 1998, in New York after being chosen by the Colts as the No. 1 pick in the draft. (AP Photo/Adam Nadel)

When Manning returned to Indianapolis for a final medical check-up, he pressed Polian for an answer on what the Colts were going to do. Polian said he would inform Manning of the decision later in the week before the quarterback departed to attend the draft in New York City.

"He told me, 'If you pick me, I guarantee you that we will win a championship and we'll have a great program here,'" Polian recalled Manning saying. "If you don't, I'll come back and I'll kick your butt."

Polian then added, "He didn't say 'butt.'"

The rest, as they say, is well-known history. Manning became the NFL's only four-time MVP. That's the same number of games Leaf would win in four years with San Diego and Dallas.

Worst Draft Picks

An educated guess on the Colts' worst all-time selections in the NFL draft.

1. QB **Art Schlichter**, first round, fourth overall, 1982—He never won a game in three seasons. And after playing in just three games as a rookie, the league suspended him for gambling in 1983. In three years with the Colts, he appeared in just 13 games with three TD passes and 11 INTs.
2. QB **Jeff George**, No. 1 overall, 1990—He possessed one of the strongest arms, but the hometown hopeful was unable to live up to the largest rookie contract in league history at that time. He won 14 of 49 starts after the Colts gave up a lot to acquire the pick to select him.
3. LB **Trev Alberts**, first round, fifth overall, 1994—Injuries reduced his career to just three seasons, 29 games, seven starts. He had just four sacks and one interception.
4. CB **Leonard Coleman**, first round, eighth overall, 1984—Not exactly the way to make a splash with the Colts' first pick upon arriving in Indianapolis. He refused to sign as a rookie and bolted to the United States Football League. He reported a year later, but played just three years. Three of his four career interceptions as a Colt came in one game.
5. OT **Tony Ugoh**, second round, 42nd overall, 2007—The Colts gave up a future first-round pick to move up to get him. But he never could replace retired Pro Bowl LT Tarik Glenn. Cut in the 2010 regular season's first week, he bounced around with no success and then retired in the 2012 off-season.

Manning won a championship, Super Bowl XLI, in 2007. Leaf was out of the league by 2002 when he retired at the age of 26. Leaf is mentioned on many lists as the greatest draft bust in NFL history. Manning is considered one of the finest field generals in the game's history for his master of the no-huddle offense and calling his own plays after a series of checks at the line of scrimmage.

Manning is still playing with Denver. He led the Broncos to a 13–3 season and the AFC's No. 1 playoff seed. While Denver got knocked off by eventual Super Bowl champion Baltimore in the AFC Divisional playoff round, Manning was named NFL Comeback Player of the Year.

14 Why Release a Legend?

Many Indianapolis Colts fans still have a difficult time accepting the unfathomable. Perhaps they never will. The sight of quarterback Peyton Manning in a Denver Broncos uniform elicits the resigned refrains of, "How can this be?" or, "It's just not right."

It's complicated. That's the only way to explain how the NFL's only four-time MVP could end up somewhere else after a glorious 13-year career, not counting a 2011 season that was lost after four neck surgeries in about 19 months.

Some fans will be forever convinced owner Jim Irsay made an unforgivable mistake in releasing Manning on March 7, 2012. They say this even after the Colts were reborn with rookie quarterback Andrew Luck and shocked the league with 11 wins in 2012. After all the NFL records, the glory years with so many wins, and invaluable charity contributions to the Indianapolis community, Manning was gone? And then he returned from his year hiatus to be named NFL Comeback Player of the Year in Denver?

His career was thought to be in jeopardy from those neck procedures, the last of which occurred in September 2011. Doctors advised Irsay of what he knew for himself, that the legendary quarterback would be a tremendous risk. Trading him wasn't an option. That would have accelerated his salary cap hit to about $38 million for a team that already faced cap issues. If Manning stayed, the Colts would have to ante up a $28 million roster bonus. Because

Manning knew he was hurt when he accepted the five-year, $90 million deal in 2011, he insisted on the "out" clause after one year to protect the team if he didn't come back. That provision would eventually lead to his release. Four more years in an NFL contract has never seemed to carry so much weight. Irsay could afford to take the financial risk, but what about his Colts? Where would the franchise be if the 36-year-old Manning couldn't fulfill that contract and the team didn't have a franchise quarterback?

The new collective bargaining agreement meant Luck would come at a fraction of the price. His *entire* four-year contract was for $22 million. And Luck has been considered the best quarterback prospect since, well, Manning, or maybe even John Elway in 1983. When distancing himself from emotion, Irsay realized the future of his franchise would be best served by making a decision he really didn't want to make.

"It was absolutely the way the chessboard was aligned with me and Peyton," Irsay said in an exclusive February interview with Bob Kravitz, *The Indianapolis Star* columnist. "Sometimes people don't listen to Peyton's own words. 'It's not Peyton Manning, it's not Jim Irsay, it's circumstances, and that's why it's happening.' He understood we had to draft Luck; we weren't going to trade him for picks. And he understood the cap-room situation where if he'd stayed, there would have been no Reggie Wayne, no Winston Justice, no Samson Satele, I'm not sure about Robert Mathis. We couldn't have kept anybody. I mean, our offensive line would have been even worse than it was.

"The worst thing you can imagine would have been to see (Manning) struggling with a team completely deprived of talent, being 1–6 or something like that, and then calls for Andrew to come in and play over Peyton. I could see it happening. The cap situation was that dire."

Kravitz had more than a front-row seat to this playing out. He was talking on a regular basis to Irsay and Manning. Nobody was more privy to what these two men were thinking and why they sometimes made statements which couldn't be described as anything other than posturing themselves with the public.

"It was like talking to two people who knew they needed a divorce but didn't have the heart to tell the other that they wanted out of the marriage," Kravitz said. "I felt like a divorce lawyer. I think they both knew in their heart of hearts it had to happen. It was a difficult, emotional decision, and yet it was the easiest decision an owner could ever make.

"The Colts knew his whole health history and were concerned he could stay healthy long-term. They had significant health concerns about him at the time, and they had to say good-bye."

And Kravitz said Irsay was "sold on Andrew Luck."

The owner made life as easy as possible on new general manager Ryan Grigson and head coach Chuck Pagano. Any time they were asked about Manning's future, Grigson and Pagano basically said Irsay was handling it.

"He didn't want them to be caught in the slip-stream," Kravitz said.

Fans couldn't help but be caught up in the speculation. When Super Bowl XLVI hit town in February 2012, the media circus turned into a he-said, he-said between Irsay and Manning for much of the week. Manning made it clear he had no intention of retiring. Irsay reiterated there was more to this sensitive subject than the public was aware, and that it was complicated. A short time later, news that Manning had undergone a fourth surgery came to light.

Manning and Irsay kept talking to Kravitz.

"I think they both trusted me with their message, which was weird because I was saying Peyton had to go and Peyton was calling me Andrew Luck's agent," the columnist said of Manning's needling of Kravitz in the locker room after a season-ending loss at Jacksonville.

The team called a press conference to announce Manning's release.

"I know Peyton and I have had numerous conversations over the months," Irsay said in the televised farewell. "We always kept trying to come back to the circumstances that were before us. We tried to put each other in each other's shoes and try to realize what the situation was for the franchise, what it was for Peyton. In the end, those circumstances were too difficult to overcome, circumstances that dictated to us, to the franchise, that really were unavoidable."

Manning stepped to the lectern.

"I sure have loved playing football for the Indianapolis Colts. For 14 wonderful years, the only professional football I've known is Colts football," he said. "Our team won a lot of games here, I've played with so many great teammates here, and I've been part of a great organization here, an organization and an owner who I respect and continue to respect.

"I've been a Colt for almost all my adult life. But I guess in life and in sports, we all know that nothing lasts forever."

He paused, his voice overcome with emotion as he said, "Times change, circumstances change, and that's the reality of playing in the NFL."

Manning concluded, his tone continuing to waver.

"I haven't thought yet about where I'll play, but I have thought a lot about where I've been," he said. "And I've truly been blessed. I've been blessed to play here. I've been blessed to be in the NFL.

"And as I go, I go with just a few words left to say, a few words I want to address to Colts fans everywhere. Thank you very much from the bottom of my heart. I truly have enjoyed being your quarterback."

15 Tony Dungy: Faith, Family, Football

Speaking engagements provide former Indianapolis Colts strength and conditioning coach Jon Torine an opportunity to enlighten athletes and coaches on his area of expertise. He often utters a favorite line about one of his former NFL head coaches.

"When the Dalai Lama is confused," Torine says, "he calls Tony Dungy for answers."

Dungy was known for his stoic nature when he walked the Colts sidelines from 2002 through 2008. His unflappable demeanor set an example for his players. They respected him, and after four years of playoff frustration, he finally reached the NFL's summit and won Super Bowl XLI.

The first black coach to win a Super Bowl is proud of the accomplishment and of what his teams were able to achieve, but he always preached life priorities to players. Football couldn't be the most important thing in life. Dungy ranked it third, behind faith and family.

His devout Christian beliefs were understood, although he didn't beat everybody over the head with his Bible. Just like on the sideline, Dungy subscribed to setting an example for others, walking a path in hopes that others would join the journey. His best-selling 2007 memoir, *Quiet Strength: The Principles, Practices, and Priorities of a Winning Life,* chipped away at stereotypes, including the notion that football coaches had to be profane screamers to ensure maximum effort.

Dungy's family values were evident from day one.

"When I think of my legacy, more so than even the Super Bowl, I think about going in there for a staff meeting and saying, 'We do want this to be a family place. We're going to win, but it's got to be a place where everybody enjoys coming. And you can never be afraid to bring your family, bring your kids, they're going to be a part of this, too,'" said Dungy, who resides in Tampa, Florida, where he and his wife, Lauren, have had seven children.

"I remember the first time I brought my kids. They were being kids. We were in the offensive room, and coaches could hear the noise outside. [Running backs coach] Gene Huey said, 'What's that? What's going on?' And [assistant] Clyde [Christensen] said, 'You'd better get used to that. That's the Dungy kids.' It was like the first time anybody had heard that in the building. But from then on, I think the atmosphere was a little different. I remember [equipment manager] Jon Scott telling me, 'In the equipment room, we've got guys now that really enjoy coming to work.' That probably meant more than anything, winning but creating that family atmosphere, creating a place where people liked to come to work."

Dungy made a difference in the community with endeavors that included All Pro Dad, Family First, Big Brothers/Big Sisters and the Boys and Girls Club. The role model took time to call on those less fortunate. He was a popular choice for speaking engagements.

The Colts won 85 regular season games under Dungy, the most for any coach in franchise history. His "Do what we do" mantra that players always repeated didn't excite others at times, especially after crushing defeats, but the team always stayed the course. Players had the utmost faith in him, and many in Him—so many of them Christians whose work week included Bible study.

The Indianapolis Star beat writer Phil Richards says his favorite Dungy triumph was one of the least celebrated, a regular season finale on January 1, 2006, the coach's first game back on the sideline after 18-year-old son James had taken his own life on December 22, 2005.

"The Colts were 13–2, resting key starters for the playoffs, and had most of the rest of their regulars out by the time the Arizona

Coach Tony Dungy looks on from the sideline during the third quarter of an game against the Buffalo Bills in Indianapolis on Sunday, November 12, 2006. Indianapolis defeated Buffalo 17–16. (AP Photo/ Darron Cummmings)

Cardinals lined up on second-and-goal from the Indianapolis 2 with 1:18 to play," Richards said. "Three times the Cardinals tried to ram it in. Three times Colts backups stoned them to preserve a 17–13 victory. After the last, safety Mike Doss snatched the football, sprinted to the sideline, and presented it to Dungy.

"It was a moment suffused with feeling, a group of caring men reaching deep to tangibly express their affection for their stricken coach. I'll never forget it."

As the Colts celebrated a 29–17 Super Bowl XLI triumph over Chicago in Miami, Dungy stood on the stage and said, "We did it the Lord's way." Just a year earlier, after losing his son and seeing the No. 1–seeded Colts upset in the playoffs by Pittsburgh, Dungy's methods had come into question. Tampa Bay had fired him after the 2001 season because of the perception he couldn't achieve the ultimate. Frustrated fans and reporters were suggesting the same in Indianapolis.

A year later, his conviction was validated.

"It felt so special for the city. You're probably 15' high," he said of being on that Super Bowl postgame stage. "It's just mostly the Indy people there celebrating. You look out over the stadium and you see all our players. And, of course, what [owner] Jim [Irsay] had done, he brought everybody, everybody that worked in the building and their spouses. You see everybody, players and staff, just a mass of Indy people down on the field. I remember thinking, *We finally did it.*"

He thought of his father, Wilbur, who had passed away on June 8, 2004. About five months before that death, when the Colts lost the AFC Championship Game at New England on January 18, 2004, Dungy had emerged from the locker room to see Wilbur.

"I remember walking out and my dad saying, 'Just continue to do what you do. There's going to be a lot of people that are going to tell you that you have to change this or that. You don't have to. You'll get these guys,'" Dungy recalled. "I thought about that, definitely, my mom [Cleomae, who died in 2002], my dad, and James. I thought about all the people that kind of had a hand in it.

"I remember thinking, *How did I get from Exchange Playground in Jackson, Michigan, to the Super Bowl and up on this podium?* There were so many hands involved and so many things the Lord had to orchestrate. It just felt so good being there and saying, 'You know what? The city of Indianapolis, and the whole state really for one day, we've come together and we've won a championship.'"

Exchange Playground used to be Dungy's world where he learned how to play sports. On return trips in later years, he couldn't believe the special place was so small.

"From there to Miami and the Super Bowl was a long, long ways," Dungy said.

16 "Lassie" Leap in Super Bowl V

Jim O'Brien realizes he could stump today's generation of NFL fans with this trivia question: Who kicked the first game-winning field goal in Super Bowl history?

"Most people wouldn't know," said the man known 42 years ago as "Lassie."

Baltimore Colts fans might get it. Yeah, it was him.

He was 23 then, a rookie straight-ahead "toe" kicker thrust into the kind of pressure situation every athlete dreams about. O'Brien's 32-yard field goal with five seconds remaining lifted the Colts to a 16–13 Super Bowl V victory over the Dallas Cowboys on January 17, 1971, at Miami's Orange Bowl.

"Yeah, I knew it," O'Brien said of the kick. "I hit it really well. By the time I looked up, it was going through the goal posts."

Lassie let loose with an enthusiastic leap. He had some athleticism. In addition to also playing wide receiver, the 6' kicker could dunk a basketball. "Some white people could jump," he said with a chuckle. "I just knew I made it, and then it sunk in slowly after that, that we had won a Super Bowl."

Colts defensive lineman Billy Ray Smith Sr., whose 14-year career ended with that win, had nicknamed O'Brien "Lassie" because the kicker's brown hair could be seen below the helmet.

"They were of an older era," O'Brien said of veterans. "They had their hair cut really short. Mine was a little longer, but not by today's standards. You could see the name on the back of my jersey. You can't see the names on some of these guys today. My hair just stuck out of my helmet a little bit, but he thought I looked like a dog."

Most of those Colts had suffered a humiliating loss to the New York Jets in Super Bowl III on this same field. "They were still upset about that game," O'Brien said. "The closer they got back to the Super Bowl, the more they thought about it and getting some retribution."

Don Shula had coached the Colts in Super Bowl III. After an 8–5–1 season in 1969, he took the Miami Dolphins' job. His replacement, Don McCafferty, had been with the franchise since 1959. Players appreciated his even-keel demeanor and called him "Easy Rider."

The Colts finished the regular season 11–2–1 and captured the AFC Eastern Division crown, then they dispatched Cincinnati 17–0 and Oakland 27–17, both playoff games in Baltimore, to set up a Super Bowl V matchup against Dallas (10–4). *Sports Illustrated* would call it the "Blunder Bowl." The Colts committed seven of the game's 11 turnovers. The Cowboys were penalized a Super Bowl–record 10 times for 133 yards.

"I didn't look at it as a comedy of errors," O'Brien said. "I looked at it as a very defensive game where the defenses created a lot of mistakes by the offenses. There were a lot of misadventures. And the game was played at 1:00 on AstroTurf, so it was hotter than hell."

Now a construction company manager in Thousand Oaks, California, O'Brien's memories are vivid about his 15 minutes of fame. But his entrance fit the game's sloppy theme.

After the Cowboys had kicked two field goals, the Colts pulled even on a couple of lucky bounces as a Johnny Unitas pass deflected off the hands of intended receiver Ed Hinton was tipped by Cowboys defensive back Mel Renfro and fluttered to tight end John Mackey, who turned it into a 75-yard touchdown. Out trotted a nervous O'Brien, whose hesitation on the extra-point kick enabled the Cowboys to block it.

Unitas threw two interceptions and lost a fumble. Dallas converted the latter into a Craig Morton seven-yard TD pass to running back Duane Thomas for a 13–6 lead in the second quarter.

When the Colts got the ball back, Unitas suffered a rib injury while throwing a pass that Renfro intercepted. Earl Morrall, who received his share of blame for the Super Bowl III loss, replaced Unitas.

The Colts fumbled the second-half kickoff. The Cowboys drove to the Baltimore 1-yard line. Just when it looked as if Dallas would build a 14-point lead, Pro Bowl linebacker Mike Curtis dislodged the football from Thomas and the Colts recovered on their own 1-yard line. The turnover was controversial because Cowboys center Dave Manders emerged from the pile with the ball.

The score didn't change until the final quarter when safety Rick Volk returned an interception 30 yards to the Dallas 3. Running back Tom Nowatzke scored two plays later on a two-yard run. O'Brien drilled the extra point this time to tie it at 13.

Curtis came through again, intercepting a Morton pass after it went through the hands of running back Dan Reeves and returning it 13 yards to the Cowboys' 28. Two plays later, O'Brien had the opportunity he had envisioned for years.

"I practiced that kick from the time I was in high school," he said. "I would pretend I was kicking a winner in college. I'd finish every practice with a 45-yarder. Then when I was in college, I practiced the kick like I was in the NFL."

He just stuck to his routine.

"If you start thinking about it," he said, "only bad things can happen."

It would be 31 years before another kicker would join O'Brien for such heroics. New England's Adam Vinatieri drilled a deciding 48-yard field goal on the final play of Super Bowl XXXVI. Two years later, Vinatieri did it again for the Patriots, this time from 41 yards out with four seconds remaining. Vinatieri now kicks for the Indianapolis Colts.

McCafferty became the first rookie NFL coach to win a Super Bowl. The only other one to do it since is San Francisco's George Seifert in 1990.

O'Brien's career lasted just four years. He got clocked by a beer bottle in a bar misunderstanding, and one of the lenses from his glasses scratched the cornea of his right eye. His career field-goal percentage was 55.6 percent, which wouldn't keep a kicker employed these days.

But he made the most important kick of his life.

"It was an honor to be put in that position," O'Brien said, "and to be able to come through for my teammates."

"Edge"

Retired Indianapolis Colts tight end Ken Dilger remembers those five-gallon buckets Edgerrin James brought into the locker room after losing 2001 World Series bets to teammates Sam Sword and Rodregis Brooks. The fan favorite known simply as "Edge" paid in pennies—50,000 for Sword and 10,000 for Brooks. Congrats and good day, gentlemen.

"He was always a character at heart," Dilger said. "He was fun to play with, one of my all-time favorites. They called him 'Stress Free' for a reason. He'd come out for a practice and didn't really seem to care about anything. He just ran the ball hard. Always a smile on his face."

Eight years after his last Colts game, the franchise's all-time leading rusher laughs about the pennies.

"With me it's like, it's not what you do, it's how you do it," Edge said. "The penny thing, it was one of those things where, okay, I lost the bet and I honored the bet, but then I wanted to get a joy out of the way I lost. If I'm going to go out, I'm going to go out in style. I went out in style with that one. They had to carry

Edge-Speak

When Edgerrin James did interviews, you just never knew what he was going to say. The Indianapolis Colts running back could always be counted on for a laugh.

"The ad people want me to clean up my grammar, my speech, my look, my image. But I've got a saying, 'It's real easy to be me; it's too hard to be someone else.'"
—2000, about why he didn't want to get
rid of his gold teeth and dreadlocks

"I only went to college for 2½ years, but I think I know the meaning of the word 'voluntary.'"
—2001, after being criticized for not participating
in the team's voluntary off-season program

"I'll be a tourist, full time. Just do whatever. You know tourists. They don't know where they're going, but they're having a good time."
—2003, on plans after he retires from the NFL

"The closest I'm going to get to Tokyo is Benihana."
—2005, on his reluctance to accompany
the team to Japan for a preseason game

those big buckets and go through all of that, do all of that work for that money. I caught 'em off guard."

The cool dude with dreadlocks definitely had his own style. He burst onto the scene in 1999 and won back-to-back NFL rushing titles. But it wasn't just about running for yardage. Edge was unselfish and didn't complain about a shortage of carries in a pass-happy offense. He took pride in destroying blitzing linebackers with a crushing block. The guy was smart, too, a necessity in the Colts' complicated offense. He so endeared himself to fans and media with such unfiltered expression, Edge is still admired to this day.

"Edge's greatest gift is the one he gives so freely," said Phil Richards of *The Indianapolis Star*. "You always walk away from him feeling good."

"Edge is a classic," Colts radio voice Bob Lamey said. "He meant more to this franchise than people think. In the early days, when Marshall [Faulk] was leaving, we needed somebody to step in and fill the void. Edgerrin not only stepped in and filled the void, he did it with class and he did it every day."

"I loved Edgerrin," said Jim Mora, his coach from 1999 to 2001. "His teammates loved him. Great guy, one of the best people I've ever been around. Tough, durable, really good receiver out of the backfield. And I'll tell you one thing about Edgerrin, he was really smart. He was a very unselfish football player. He could do it all."

The Colts added Edge, who ran for 9,226 of his career 12,246 yards for Indianapolis, to the Ring of Honor in a 2012 halftime ceremony. He received a standing ovation when he walked off the field.

"I always loved the Colts fans. I knew they were the best fans in the world," Edge said, thinking back. "I grew up in the NFL and as a person from the first day I stepped out as an Indianapolis Colt. When I got to Indianapolis, the way everybody embraced me, I understand a lot of people didn't know me, but little bit by little bit, being in the community and being around and getting a grasp of what is going on around that city, you actually become a part of that city. When I got back there for the Ring of Honor, it was just a reminder."

Owner Jim Irsay gave the running back a Super Bowl XLI ring even though the running back didn't play on that team and was with the Arizona Cardinals.

"It's one of those things where he didn't have to do it but it showed your work was appreciated," Edge said. "We understand the business side of things. I understand the fact that I wasn't there, but I always stayed in touch with everybody. When Mr. Irsay gave me the ring, that just made it mean a little bit more. That's a ring that I will never let anybody else get. I will always hold it and

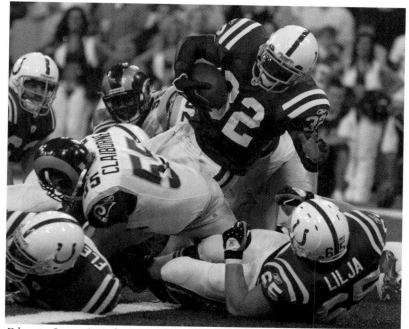

Edgerrin James (32) dives into the end zone for a touchdown during the second quarter against the St. Louis Rams in Indianapolis on Monday, October 17, 2005. (AP Photo/Darron Cummings)

seriously. It's bigger than other peoples' rings. This right here is something that has so much sentimental value."

When Edge was selected with the fourth overall pick in the 1999 NFL Draft, some were convinced the Colts should have taken Heisman Trophy running back Ricky Williams out of Texas. Edge credits Colts president Bill Polian's eye for talent. Because the University of Miami Hurricanes split carries, Edge's numbers didn't stand out. But turn on the film and his talent was undeniable.

"Mr. Polian and the rest of the Colts organization, they understood what they needed for that offense," he said. "It's not who's the best runner. They needed somebody who could do both. And for me, because I had to block a lot and do other things, I don't think Ricky had to do all of that stuff. The fans and everybody else, they see somebody run around all day, but they don't understand all of the other things you have to do.

"And the Colts offense, it's not easy. It's tough to be a running back in that offense. You have to be smart. You have to be tough. You've got to do a lot of blocking. Then you get to run the ball, but it kind of fits in after the passing."

Edge wishes he could have run for more yards and is hopeful his Colts mark will stand forever.

"Hopefully nobody ever breaks that record," he said. "The way the NFL is going now with the two-back systems, it don't look like nobody will be sticking around for seven or eight years anyway. It's one of those things, man, where I've got something to hang my hat on, like I did do pretty good when I was there."

Considering his roots in Immokalee, Florida, "pretty good" is a gross understatement. Conrad Brunner, senior writer for 1070-AM. com, recalled being sent to the Sunshine State in December 1999 when he was covering the Colts for *The Indianapolis Star.* Just getting there was an adventure. Brunner and a photographer had to maneuver through "Alligator Alley."

"It's not just hype. The fences were 10' high on the interstate. Then we got on a two-lane road in the morning and it's alligators everywhere. For the first time in my life, I saw a sign for a 'Panther Crossing.' You're traveling into a whole different world.

"Then you pull into Immokalee and it's a humble little town. It's hard to imagine anyone coming from there. When you go to the town and see where he came from, it gives you an appreciation of who he is. It would have been real easy to never amount to anything."

Edge warned Brunner beforehand about running into a local known as "Ice Pick" Willie. Sure enough, after stopping on the side of the road, Willie stepped out seemingly from nowhere with an ice pick. He wanted the photographer's equipment and might have ended up with it had a deputy sheriff not stopped by. Willie

Taking a Taxi to Camp

Yancy Jackson pulled Yellow Cab No. 42 to a stop in a parking lot at Rose-Hulman Institute of Technology in Terre Haute, Indiana.

Welcome back to training camp, Edgerrin James.

His driver's license suspended, the fun-loving running back with a flair for the unusual opted for a cab ride from Indianapolis in 2002. That's about 70 miles, quite the expensive fare, about $150.

"It was a time where I lost my license and it was in the paper," James said 11 years later of his memorable arrival. "It was this big deal, and I'm like, 'People always lose their license.' I understand that you're in the spotlight and it was a dead time from a media standpoint. Okay, my license got suspended. If you want to make a big deal out of it, let me go ahead and go out in style with it."

Wide receiver and fellow Floridian Reggie Wayne joined him. "I made sure me and Reggie rolled over there, and we actually had us a chauffeur," James said.

Asked how his buddy lost his license, Wayne said, "I guess he's got the need for speed."

Tight end Marcus Pollard approached to ask the driver for his autograph. "You've made this man famous," Pollard said of Jackson.

James hollered back, "Hey, don't take my ride. He drives the speed limit and everything."

suddenly became friendly. When told of the run-in after the Colts won at Miami 37–34 a few days later, Edge smiled and laughed.

He's still smiling and laughing. Nobody needs to ever worry about Edge.

He cracks up about some of his memorable quotes, including the time he explained skipping voluntary off-season minicamp with, "I only went to college for 2½ years, but I think I know the meaning of the word 'voluntary.'"

"That's when I was riding that boat. I was hanging on that bus. Those were in the 'Stress Free' times," he said of his boat. "Some year, I'll probably look back on all of that stuff. Man, I'm so busy living life right now, I don't really get a chance to step back and reflect on that stuff."

All you need to know about Edge, everyone already knows. Life is always about having fun.

"Man, every day. Fun. Fun. Fun," he said. "I wish I was in the reality thing. I would show people how to live. Every day. My day is not complete unless I find something fun to do, no matter what it is."

18 ChuckStrong

The Indianapolis Colts were fortunate to have Chuck Pagano as their head coach.

As Baltimore's defensive coordinator, if the Ravens would have defeated New England in an AFC Championship Game in January 2012, it's possible the Colts wouldn't have waited around at least two more weeks to hire him. But the Ravens lost, which meant owner Jim Irsay and general manager Ryan Grigson interviewed Pagano.

Such opportunities don't come around often. The 51-year-old Pagano, who grew up in a football family with his father a successful Colorado high school coach, jumped at the chance to lead his own team. It didn't matter the Colts were 2–14 the previous year and faced salary cap limitations that eventually led to the release of tight end Dallas Clark, running back Joseph Addai, middle linebacker Gary Brackett, and safety Melvin Bullitt. And the Colts then parted with four-time NFL MVP quarterback Peyton Manning due to concerns about the passer's four neck surgeries in 19 months.

Pagano hit the Colts complex running in establishing a can-do mentality in the locker room. Players wore T-shirts with a "Build The Monster" slogan as well as an NFL ranking that suggested the

Colts were dead last in 32nd. It's the classic us-against-them bunker mentality, an age-old motivational technique, but the players bonded.

Grigson supplied the expected direction when he selected quarterback Andrew Luck with the first overall pick in the 2012 NFL Draft. The new GM's first draft would prove to be deep, too, with tight ends Coby Fleener and Dwayne Allen, wide receiver T.Y. Hilton, and running back Vick Ballard. Each player made immediate contributions.

But the honeymoon didn't last long. The Colts lost two of their first three games, including a heartbreaking 22–17 home setback to AFC South rival Jacksonville on wide receiver Cecil Shorts' 80-yard TD reception with just 45 seconds remaining.

As discouraging as the start would be, it couldn't prepare them for the stunning subtraction of Pagano from the mix. The franchise was floored to learn its coach was diagnosed with leukemia on September 26. His form of cancer, acute promyelocytic leukemia, required a hospital stay for the first of three rounds of chemotherapy, then out-patient treatment. The team hoped to have him back by the end of the season. Offensive coordinator Bruce Arians, who might have been finished in the NFL until Pagano phoned to offer him a job, was named interim coach at the request of his sidelined head coach.

Just when it seemed the rebuilding project was falling apart, an amazing transformation occurred. The Colts came together for their hospitalized coach. The ChuckStrong mantra was everywhere—on a Lucas Oil Stadium banner, T-shirts, and blue bracelets. Colts fans on Twitter typed #ChuckStrong in tweets. Players, including Luck, shaved their heads in support of their coach, who had lost all of his hair. Two cheerleaders were shaved bald during a game.

"There's no doubt it galvanized the team," said Will Wolford, a retired Colts left tackle who supplied color commentary on radio broadcasts. "They're sitting at 1–2 with Green Bay coming to town. Now, you could go the other way. But one thing this team didn't do—when guys made mistakes, they didn't rip each other. They remained a team all through everything. Maybe that's because with Coach Pagano and what he was going through, what's really important was to just come out, play hard, see if the scoreboard takes care of itself, but don't place too much importance on it because at the end of the day, our head coach is battling for his life. Let's not get too serious about this or only worry about your own statistics."

The Colts rallied from an 18-point deficit to stun Green Bay 30–27 at Lucas Oil Stadium. Irsay took the game ball to his coach in the hospital.

Pagano's wife, Tina, informed him of how everybody had committed to being ChuckStrong, a twist from the previous ColtStrong slogan.

"I had no idea," Pagano said, reflecting on the outpouring of community affection. "It's overwhelming when you think about it today. You look back on it, so much of that was going on that, at the time going through what I was going through, it was being relayed to me through my wife who was sitting there hour after hour, reading the mail, opening cards, bringing that stuff to me, going through my phone, and answering texts.

"When they did the ChuckStrong picture out here with the shaving of the heads, and what this city did, I mean they didn't know me. I look back on it, and it is overwhelming. For this city, the organization, the fans, the people of this state, for them to embrace me and my family the way they did and to support us the way they did, and this team, watching them play week in and week out.... Unbelievable."

He of course thought first of his family, Tina and three daughters and three granddaughters, who were counting on him to stick around. "That, and then along with everything else, there was no way I wasn't walking out of there," Pagano said. "No way."

A 35–9 loss at the New York Jets brought the Colts plummeting back to reality after such an inspiring upset of the Packers. They regrouped and held off Cleveland 17–13 at home. Irsay informed the team afterward that Pagano had been released from Indiana University Simon Cancer Center.

"I was more thrilled about that than the win," said Luck, who quickly lived up to his billing as a talented NFL-ready quarterback.

The Colts endured 19–13 in overtime at Tennessee on a screen pass in which Ballard epitomized the team's determination with a leap to the goal line, his body inverted, to hit the pylon. The win snapped a 10-game road losing streak.

A 23–20 home win over Miami couldn't have been more special. Pagano spoke before and after the game. His postgame speech couldn't have been more uplifting—not just to the team and organization but to people everywhere who were facing cancer.

"I mentioned before the game that you guys were living in a vision and you weren't living in circumstances," Pagano said. "Because you know where they had us at the beginning, every last one of 'em, but you refused to live in circumstances and you decided consciously as a team and as a family to live in a vision. That's why you bring things home like you brought home today. That's why you're already champions and well on your way.

"I've got circumstances. You guys understand it. I understand it. It's already beat. It's already beat."

The Colts avenged a previous defeat with a 27–10 triumph at Jacksonville. At 6–3, the NFL's feel-good story of the season had a new twist. Pagano's Colts were playoff contenders. Once again, a humbling loss stifled momentum as the team fell apart 59–24 at New England. But the Colts bounced back for a 20–13 home win over Buffalo. A road trip to Detroit came down to the final play when Luck threw a 14-yard TD pass to Donnie Avery as time expired for a 35–33 victory. The Colts had scored 14 points in the final 2:39 to prevail.

A 27–23 home win over Tennessee kept the Colts in AFC South Division title contention for one more week, but they lost 29–17 at Houston the week after. The team that didn't lose two games in a row continued that trend with a 20–13 win at Kansas City to clinch what was once thought to be the impossible, a playoff berth.

Pagano's cancer was deemed in remission when he returned to work the next day in an emotional press conference. He arrived early, at about 5:00 AM. He said it was the second-best day of his life, the first was when he married Tina on July 1, 1989.

"Getting to pull up, drive in, get out of my car, the key fob worked," he said. "I was beginning to question whether it would or not."

A Pagano office light that Arians said would remain on until the head coach returned was finally switched off at day's end. The Colts were not about to rest starters and play it safe in his return. They defeated Houston 28–16 at Lucas Oil Stadium.

An 11–5 regular season was rewarded with a playoff trip back to Baltimore, where Pagano faced off against his former employer. Before the game, a disoriented Arians had to be hospitalized with a brief illness. The Colts lost 24–9 to the eventual Super Bowl champions.

That conclusion couldn't overshadow what ChuckStrong meant to a team, an organization, the city of Indianapolis, and fans. Irsay, who first became connected with the team in 1972, had never seen anything like it.

"Out of the 41 years and everything else, wow, what a year, one of the most special years in the history of the 90-plus years of the National Football League, not just the Colts," the owner said. "If you would have asked most of those people, 'What would happen if the coach gets a life-threatening disease and misses most of the season?' they would have probably said, 'Welcome to the club of 0–16.' The next thing you know, you're winning 11 games. I mean, 11 games I don't know what to say. People quietly kind of acted like on the national front, 'Oh well, the Colts surprised some people,' as opposed to how they won 11 games.

"If you went to those people in July, they would have said, 'You are out of your mind! Out of your mind! Winning 11 games with what happened to Chuck Pagano? Just out of your complete mind!' I don't think it quite got emphasized enough."

Pagano had said from the day he was introduced that his pursuit of winning a Vince Lombardi Trophy was predicated on building relationships.

He certainly built more than he ever could have imagined.

"I kind of went to extreme measures to build relationships," he said with an appreciative smile.

19 Chuck Pagano Game Ball

Chuck Pagano would prefer not to go back in time. Words aren't enough to express gratitude. Sometimes it takes tears and uncontrollable emotion.

The intense Indianapolis Colts head coach is overcome by both when he starts to talk about owner Jim Irsay walking into Pagano's hospital room on October 7, 2012, at the Indiana University Health Simon Cancer Center.

That was the first time Pagano had to watch his Colts on television since being diagnosed with leukemia on September 26. Instead of overseeing practices, watching film, conducting team meetings, and finalizing game plans, he had been sentenced to a purgatory of chemotherapy.

Then in walked Irsay, an overjoyed owner with a game ball.

About one hour earlier in a jubilant Lucas Oil Stadium locker room, after the Colts had rallied from an 18-point halftime deficit to upset Green Bay 30–27, Irsay thrust that game ball into the air and shouted he was taking it "right down the street!"

"Mr. Irsay came walking through that door," Pagano said, seeing it again in his mind. "Wow." The coach has to pause for a moment. He wipes away tears and exhales loudly, then composes himself.

It's been five months since that day. Pagano is almost back to full strength. Those three rounds of chemotherapy are in his rear-view mirror, the cancer in remission.

Everything had happened so fast. His world turned upside down. Then the Colts launched their ChuckStrong movement with that victory in an overnight sensation that captivated not just Indianapolis but an NFL nation.

"That means the world to me," Pagano said of how he and his wife, Tina, and family were embraced nine months after this city became their new home.

"Without it, you don't know where you would be. Everybody I talked to, those still going through [cancer] right now, just one phone call, you know what I mean? Sometimes that's all, one text, one email, one phone call, one letter. Unless you do it, you never know if it's going to make a difference or not."

The Colts had lost their coach during the bye week and were 1–2. Offensive coordinator Bruce Arians—at Pagano's request— was named interim coach. The Packers, seven-point road favorites, built a 21–3 halftime lead.

Wide receiver Reggie Wayne, re-signed in the off-season and now a team leader in his 12th season, was furious and let his team-mates know it. No player was closer to Pagano. They had shared four years together at the University of Miami from 1997 to 2000. The inspired receiver wore orange gloves, the color for leukemia awareness, against the Packers. And he put them to good use.

Cornerback Jerraud Powers started the comeback with an interception of quarterback Aaron Rodgers. Rookie quarterback Andrew Luck opened a 39-yard scoring drive with an 18-yard pass to Wayne and finished with an eight-yard TD strike to rookie tight end Dwayne Allen. Adam Vinatieri added a 50-yard field goal. Luck engineered a 58-yard drive and handled the last three yards himself for a touchdown run, then ran over to a ChuckStrong banner behind the end zone and slapped it. The Packers clung to a 21–19 lead when the Colts' two-point pass failed.

At the outset of the final quarter, Colts outside linebacker Dwight Freeney sacked Rodgers to force a punt. Outside linebacker Robert Mathis followed suit with a sack to foil Green Bay's next possession. The Colts started a go-ahead scoring drive with a Luck 26-yard pass to Wayne. Vinatieri kicked a 28-yard field goal. Colts 22–21.

"Oh man, Reggie was definitely ballin'," said former teammate and close friend Edgerrin James, who watched on TV. "That's the thing, when you have somebody like Reggie out there, and he shows the guys this is what it takes, not only talking and going back on what you've done in the past, but going out there and representing right then and there at a crucial time, it was big for the team and for the organization."

Moise Fokou and Cory Redding sacked Rodgers to force another punt. After a Colts three-and-out, the Packers needed two plays to cover 49 yards as Rodgers threw an eight-yard TD pass to James Jones. Just 4:30 remained when the Colts started at their 20. Wayne caught four passes for 60 yards, including a 15-yarder on third-and-12, when Luck somehow broke free from outside linebacker Clay Matthews and unloaded a high pass that his receiver snagged in traffic. Luck delivered another key play with a seven-yard scramble on third-and-7 for a first down at the Packers' 4.

Luck knew where the ball had to go. As did Wayne. Everybody including the Packers knew.

"He is the heart and soul and leader of the offense," Arians said of Wayne. "Andrew will take that torch one day, but right now it's definitely Reggie's."

The receiver ran an inside slant. Luck fired a quick pass. Wayne hauled it in and absorbed a defender's shot at the 2-yard line. As two more defenders converged, he stretched the ball over the goal line for a four-yard TD pass. A sellout crowd of 67,020 serenaded the hero with, "Reg-gie! Reg-gie! Reg-gie!"

"I told him after the game he's the best player I've ever played with," Luck said.

Donald Brown's two-point run gave the Colts a 30–27 lead. When the Packers' Mason Crosby missed a 51-yard field goal wide right in the final seconds, it was time to take that game ball to Pagano.

"Great human being, great coach, great personality, great husband. He identifies the word great," Wayne said of his coach. "To be able to come out and just do it for him, I said to myself I was going to lay it all on the line."

After all he's been through, Pagano hasn't forgotten Wayne's numbers. "Thirteen catches, 212 yards with the winning touchdown?" Pagano said. "Are you kidding me?"

The yardage ranks second in the franchise's 60-year history.

Colts radio voice Bob Lamey was in the locker room for Irsay's speech. "I had an unbelievable feeling walking out of that building, having beaten a team like Green Bay, having seen the scene and hearing Jimmy in the locker room," Lamey said. "I guarantee you, if he could have, Jimmy would have run all the way to the hospital."

That game ball is now on the mantle in Pagano's office at home.

"We talk about the proper state of mind. We can, we will, we must by any means necessary get the job done," Pagano said. "It doesn't matter what it has to do with in your life, whether it's trying to win a football game, trying to overcome circumstances, dealing with anything. That's got to be your mind-set."

"And that was Reggie's mind-set. When they had guys draped on him and he needed to keep his balance and keep his knee off the ground and stretch that ball out, that's will. That's will. That, you can never repay."

20 "The Immaculate Tackle"

The Indianapolis Colts were the best team in the NFL in 2005—for 13 games. Each foe had been vanquished by at least a touchdown in an unprecedented, unblemished run...then it all came crashing down tragically in a series of gut-wrenching events that plunged an organization into the deepest depths of grief.

"There were such high expectations," Colts offensive left tackle Tarik Glenn said eight years later.

The Colts finally lost 26–17 at home to San Diego, but the real shocker came four days later on December 22 when head coach Tony Dungy's 18-year-old son, James, took his own life. Instead of closing out an impressive season and setting their minds on the playoffs, the Colts organization filed into Idlewild Baptist Church in Lutz, Florida, six days later to hear their leader give an emotional 20-minute eulogy. Football is of no significance when the man these players respected and admired stands in front of a casket and says, "Parents, hug your kids each chance you get. Tell them you love them each chance you get. You don't know when it's going to be the last time."

"You'll never know how much of an impact that had," Glenn said of James' death.

Dungy missed one game and returned. The Colts closed out the regular season 14–2. But another unexpected, off-the-field twist would eventually play a role in this team's fate. Police were dispatched to the home of cornerback Nick Harper, who had been stabbed in his right knee with a filet knife by his wife, Daniell, in a domestic dispute the day before the Colts were to face Pittsburgh in the playoffs. Colts president Bill Polian, in a written statement, said Harper's wound was 1" deep, ½" wide, and required three stitches.

Harper played the next day when the sixth-seeded, nine-point underdog Steelers visited the RCA Dome for an unforgettable AFC Divisional Playoff game on January 15, 2006. The Colts had pounded Pittsburgh 26–7 on *Monday Night Football* at home during the regular season, but they didn't play like a No. 1 seed in the rematch. Pittsburgh jumped out to a 14–0 lead on two Ben Roethlisberger touchdown passes in the first quarter and seemed in command with a 21–3 advantage entering the final quarter. Colts quarterback Peyton Manning faced constant pressure from the Steelers' "Blitzburgh" 3–4 defense.

"In the end, when I reflect back on that game, emotionally as a team we were in a bad place. It was so disappointing," Glenn said. "The majority of that game is emotional. You play with passion. The emotional aspect translates to the physical. And from my perspective, we could have been better at making adjustments in that game. We kept doing the same things and expected different results."

Just when all seemed lost, the Colts snapped out of it with a furious 15-point rally. They got the ball back for a desperation drive, but Manning was swarmed on a fourth-down sack at his own 2-yard line with 1:20 remaining. Game over.

Well, not so fast.

The Steelers handed off to their battering ram of a running back, 252-lb. Jerome "The Bus" Bettis, to score a game-ending touchdown. But as Bettis neared the goal line, Colts middle linebacker Gary Brackett's helmet smacked the ball free. Harper, the stitched-up defender, scooped it up and started running.

"I was just trying to run as hard as possible to get to the end zone," Harper said, "and find a clearing where there's no defenders and I can score."

He had one man to beat, the slow-footed Roethlisberger. Instead of continuing to sprint to his right, Harper cut inside to the left. The Steelers quarterback stumbled then lunged, and his outstretched right arm tripped up Harper. A picture of the memorable shoestring stop would later adorn Steelers T-shirts with the words, "Immaculate Tackle," a spin-off of the Steelers' infamous "Immaculate Reception" playoff win over Oakland in 1972.

The Colts still had a chance to pull it out and drove into field-goal range, but kicker Mike Vanderjagt wasn't even remotely close on a 46-yard attempt as the football fluttered way wide right. The Steelers celebrated a 21–18 upset.

"Handling success takes maturity," said Glenn, who retired before the 2007 season. "We were beating people so bad, we didn't handle playing somebody a second time and understand the magnitude of the playoffs with everybody so desperate. It was a hard lesson to learn."

Dungy was never one to make excuses, as the sign read in the Colts complex locker room: "No excuses, No explanations."

"People say, 'Well, did that take a little away from us?'" Dungy said of his son's suicide. "I don't think it did. I think it was just a matter of what's kind of happened the last eight or nine playoff runs. Someone gets hot at the end and things just go right for them. That was Pittsburgh that year."

But Dungy agreed with Glenn that the Colts were unsettled emotionally. "I think that was certainly part of it," the coach said. "We were rocked as an organization for a couple of weeks there. It happens. It's just so hard to say. We basically were kind of a month without going at football full blast. You have those emotional things that happened. It was a time you can't prepare for and you have no blueprint in how you're going to do it. You don't know how to come out of it. It was just uncharted waters, really."

The Colts were that team to get hot the next postseason and exorcised their demons with a Super Bowl XLI victory over Chicago. But the 2005 team is still considered the best of those glory years.

"I think it was," said running back Edgerrin James, whose last Colts game was the playoff loss. "There's a lot that goes into winning games. You have to be clicking on all cylinders at the right time. We had some distractions. You try to mask them, but you can't really hide them. Sometimes your body actually does things differently than what you try to force it to do.

"As far as that team, that was a complete team. That team had everything. Everybody went out and worked hard. We didn't have no issues. Everybody got along. It seemed like we had everything together, but we just didn't get it done."

Dungy doesn't have any doubt about the 2005 squad, either. "Yeah, the '05 team was the best," he said. "In '05, it was almost like we practiced and we'd go out and just execute everything like in practice. It was just stunning. I had never been around a team that had really done that. It was offense, defense, special teams, young guys, veterans, new guys, everything just kind of clicked. That was a very, very good football team."

Safety Bob Sanders spoke after the game of how the players so desperately wanted to win to ease Dungy's pain. "I would have done anything to be able to get this one for him, and then the next one, and then go to a Super Bowl and win," Sanders said. "It would have been a year like no other. Coach Dungy is like a father to all of us. A guy like that, a man like that, you want to do anything for him to make him and his family feel good."

21 One and Only Guarantee

Any victory guarantee is a cliché because it will never top Joe Namath. Nobody beats "Broadway" Joe who made "The Guarantee."

In the days leading up to Super Bowl III on January 12, 1969, at Miami's Orange Bowl, the New York Jets' playboy of a quarterback wasn't about to play the role of understated underdog. The Jets supposedly didn't belong on the same field with the Baltimore Colts, who some considered to be the greatest professional football team of all time.

The prevailing question leading up to this American Football League vs. National Football League clash pertained to the necessity of this annual postseason game. The NFL champion Green Bay Packers had dispatched Kansas City 35–10 and the Oakland Raiders 33–14 in the previous installments of these showdowns. The Packers' first win drew a crowd of 61,946, which meant about 40,000 empty seats at Los Angeles Memorial Coliseum. The Packers' second win drew 75,546 at the Miami Orange Bowl. Those games weren't known as Super Bowls then. The Colts-Jets clash was the first to be called a Super Bowl. The Packers' wins the previous two years were retroactively added to the Super Bowl legacy.

The Colts had finished the regular season 13–1, they then defeated Minnesota 24–14 at home and Cleveland 34–0 on the road for the NFL title. Depending upon the oddsmaker, the Colts were 17- or 18-point favorites against the Jets, who were 11–3 during their regular season and edged Oakland 27–23 for the AFL crown.

If any athlete embodied the spirit of his generation, it was Namath, an outspoken rebel in a time of anti-establishment protests. He spoke his mind. He lived life in the fast lane. Three days before the game, Namath started talking. In response to a heckler at a luncheon, he made the infamous boast, "We're going to win Sunday. I guarantee you." Sometimes old TV clips show Namath smiling as he soaks up the sun by a hotel pool. It was at this setting he told *Sports Illustrated*, "We're a better team than Baltimore."

He also took shots at Colts quarterback Earl Morrall, the NFL MVP inserted into the lineup at the start of the season because John Unitas had an elbow injury. "Earl Morrall would be a third-string quarterback on the Jets," Namath told *S.I.* "There are maybe five or six better quarterbacks than Morrall in the AFL."

If anything is obvious from what transpired, it's that the Colts didn't take the Jets seriously enough. Overconfidence is the logical explanation for how the NFL champions played in what would be regarded as one of the greatest upsets in sports history. Or perhaps Namath was just spot on about the Jets being better.

The Colts made mistakes from the outset. Morrall would end up throwing three interceptions before being replaced by Unitas. The Jets relentlessly pounded away with Matt Snell, who finished with 121 yards. Snell's four-yard TD run gave the AFL champs a 7–0 lead in the second quarter. Late in the opening half, the Colts tried a flea flicker. Wide receiver Jimmy Orr was wide open near the end zone. The video highlights show Orr frantically waving his arms. But Morrall didn't see him. The pass went elsewhere and was intercepted.

If there was any doubt as to which team was going to win this game, it was all but eliminated in a one-sided third quarter. While the Jets didn't score touchdowns, they managed to cash in with two field goals and dominated time of possession. The Colts ran just seven plays and gained but 11 yards.

Unitas entered and eventually engineered the Colts' only scoring drive late in the final quarter. But it was too little, too late.

The Jets walked off the field 16–7 winners. Namath, an obvious fixation for the cameras, jogged to the tunnel and wagged his right index finger in the air. The Jets were No. 1. The MVP completed 17-of-28 passes for 206 yards. The Colts had been so concerned with receiver Don Maynard, they failed to effectively cover George Sauer Jr., who caught eight passes for 133 yards.

Morrall was just 6-of-17 for 71 yards with the three interceptions. Unitas completed 11-of-24 passes for 110 yards with one interception.

"Do I look back? Yeah, you look back," Morrall told *The New York Daily News* in 2010. "That's where the 'ifs' come in. If this would've happened, if that would've happened…the things that make a difference. And yeah, it's difficult. But it's there and it's not going to change. When big games come like that, there are lots of areas you could point to that would change the outlook. Whenever we played the Jets after that, I don't think I was ever on the losing team again.

"But it was their day in the sun."

The victory was also especially sweet for Jets head coach Weeb Ewbank, who had led the Colts to back-to-back NFL titles but was fired after 1962.

"You never go against Weeb Ewbank," said Colts Hall of Fame wide receiver Raymond Berry.

Berry had retired after the 1967 season and was an assistant with the Dallas Cowboys in 1969. Because he was connected with so many involved in Super Bowl III, he watched the game and reviewed the film with keen interest.

"It was classic Weeb Ewbank," Berry said. "It was their ability to execute a few simple plays. He didn't burden his athletes [with complicated strategy] so they could play at maximum."

22 Super Bowl XLIV

Big games lost are remembered for the pivotal plays that weren't made. Super Bowl XLIV had at least three that Indianapolis Colts fans wish could be brainwashed from existence.

Just mention the names. That's enough to evoke memories.

Hank Baskett. He's the special-teams guy who didn't recover the onside kick to start the second half.

Pierre Garcon. He's the wide receiver who dropped a third-and-4 slant pass in the second quarter when it looked as if he could run to the ocean with the Colts ahead 10–3.

Tracy Porter. He's the New Orleans cornerback who jumped Reggie Wayne's route to intercept a Peyton Manning pass and return it 74 yards for a Super Bowl–clinching touchdown.

Saints 31, Colts 17.

Three years after the Colts had celebrated a Super Bowl XLI triumph on this same Miami field, they suffered the indignity of losing an NFL title game on February 7, 2010. Broach the subject with fans or the team today and it still stings. The Colts were five-point favorites and almost everybody's pick to win. The Saints were riding a wave of emotion for a spirited city still recovering from the effects of Hurricane Katrina five years earlier.

Down 10–6 at halftime, Saints coach Sean Payton was convinced his team could change momentum with an onside kick to open the second half. Some would say that was beyond crazy. If the Colts recover…

"They go down and score and it's a blowout," said Bob Kravitz, columnist for *The Indianapolis Star.*

The football bounced to Baskett, who took one step forward. Perhaps it was instinct. But it was a mistake. Until that moment, the wide receiver was known more for whom he married in 2009, former *Playboy* model Kendra Wilkinson.

Not anymore.

The ball bounced off Baskett's facemask. A scrum ensued. It seemingly took forever to determine which team had the ball. At different moments, an official signaled for each team. The Saints came away with it then drove to a go-ahead touchdown for their first lead.

"The game revolved around the onside kick," Colts radio voice Bob Lamey said. "Hindsight being what it is, if Hank Baskett stays right where he is, we win the Super Bowl and nobody ever remembers that. He took a step forward and it hit him up high."

Baskett didn't return to the Colts and played only one more season. His dubious distinction is almost unmatched. *Almost.*

"He's right up there with Mike Vanderjagt," Kravitz said of the former Colts kicker who sparked a national spat when he criticized Manning in 2003.

Garcon, whose 19-yard touchdown catch provided a 10–0 lead in the first quarter, had a chance to build on a touchdown advantage when he dropped the quick slant pass just inside Saints territory. He had already beaten one defender, and a hard-charging safety didn't appear to have the best angle at bringing him down. But he had to make the catch first. Instead of the Colts scoring on that play or eventually converting the third-down pass into points, they punted.

After the onside kick, the second half is remembered as much for Saints quarterback Drew Brees carving up the Colts' defense with a quick-hit, dink-and-dunk passing attack. Colts defensive end Dwight Freeney, who played with a torn ligament in his right ankle, had thrown down Brees for a one-armed sack in the second quarter. That play aside, the Colts' pass rush was non-existent. Brees was named MVP after he completed 32-of-39 passes for 288 yards and two TDs.

Sour Notes for New Orleans Natives

The Colts had just lost to the New Orleans Saints 31–17 in Super Bowl XLIV at Miami. Craig Kelley handled public relations, and he walked head coach Jim Caldwell into an interview tent first then quarterback Peyton Manning.

"We got done with Peyton and it was just the worst professional moment you've ever had," Kelley said.

Worse than losing an AFC Championship Game?

"No, this was the worst," Kelley insisted. "You want to play for the marbles as often as you can in life."

Worse than losing your marbles over 1–15 in '91?

"This was tougher because there are only so many title Sundays in somebody's life," Kelley said. "Some people never have one. We've had two so far."

The Colts had prevailed in a Super Bowl XLI trip to this stadium three years earlier. But losing to the Saints struck a deeper chord. Kelley grew up in New Orleans, as did Manning. Kelley's family had Saints season tickets for 29 years, and he started his professional career with the team. Manning's parents, Archie and Olivia, still had a house in the Big Easy.

"I remember walking out of the tent to the busses. All the interviews were done, and I wasn't going to let anybody else get Peyton," Kelley said. "As we walked, the celebration music inside the stadium was Dr. John's version of 'Iko, Iko.'"

That would be Dr. John, the Rock 'n' Roll Hall of Fame inductee and Grammy Award winner.

"I'm a New Orleans native and so is Peyton, and you can't help but love the city's music," Kelley said. "I'm thinking, *Neither of us ever wants to hear this song ever again.* It took me months before I wanted to listen to it. To this day, I can't look at the Saints' logo and not think about the worst professional day in my life. It's not their fault. We didn't play well enough when it counted the most."

Despite their mistakes, the Colts were still in it as Manning drove the offense into scoring position. But everything went terribly wrong on a pass intended for Wayne, who had aggravated a right knee injury during Friday's practice. The replay showed Wayne wasn't himself. The receiver known for running precise routes chopped his feet to make the cut inside. It's unknown if Wayne actually cut off the route or Manning threw the ball where he thought Wayne would be. But Porter was there instead.

"I just kept thinking Peyton was on his way to establishing himself as one of the greatest of all time," Kravitz said. "Then boom! Here comes Tracy Porter."

Neither Manning nor Wayne took the blame for what went wrong on the third-and-5 throw that basically ended the game with 3:12 remaining.

"Porter made a great play," said Manning, who completed 31-of-45 passes for 333 yards with one touchdown and that interception. "That's all I can say about it."

"He did a good job of jumping the route and pick-six," said Wayne, who had five catches for 46 yards. "That's what they've done all year."

Lamey is among those who thought Wayne played hurt. But the old adage reminds us that injuries aren't used as an excuse. "I'm still convinced, and I've never asked him because he wouldn't tell me the truth anyway, but I just believe Reggie was hurt more in that game than we thought," Lamey said. "He didn't get to a couple of passes early in the game, and those are passes he usually puts in his back pocket."

To a man, the Colts credited the Saints.

"In the biggest game of the year," center Jeff Saturday said, "we got outplayed."

Lamey is hopeful another Super Bowl trip in the future will distance everyone in Indianapolis from this nightmare. "You lose in the Super Bowl, people say, 'Well, at least you got there,'" he said. "But that's not the goal. When you get there, you want to win the game. New Orleans played a little better. They made the plays to win the game, but that was a weird Super Bowl from a lot of viewpoints.

"I just hope this team gets back, and I believe it will some day, so our lasting memory of the Super Bowl is a good one."

23 "Reg-gie! Reg-gie! Reg-gie!"

It's as if Indianapolis already had the chant down pat from when Indiana Pacers' star Reggie Miller stimulated NBA fans with his game-changing play.

Miller retired in 2005, about the same time Indianapolis Colts wide receiver Reggie Wayne was coming into his own, no longer just the other guy across the field from Marvin Harrison.

Colts fans are still yelling, "Reg-gie! Reg-gie! Reg-gie!"

Wayne's returning to the team instead of landing elsewhere as a free agent last season further solidified his popularity with fans and in the locker room. Wayne became a leader for rookie quarterback Andrew Luck and others from Day 1 at training camp. Who's going to stay after to catch more footballs from the JUGS machine? Yeah, No. 87. If something needed to be said at halftime, Wayne spoke up. And when Luck really needed to convert a challenging third down, that pass usually went to Wayne.

Still, it almost never was. On the verge of leaving Miami to sign with another team for his 12th year last off-season, Wayne kept his promise to call owner Jim Irsay and head coach Chuck Pagano before committing to anything. Wayne stayed put. He suggested a minimum of $3 million was left on the table by re-signing with the Colts, but there are more important things than money. That's one more reason fans and teammates love the guy.

"It's an honor for me to throw the ball to him," Luck said.

Nobody knows Wayne better than his bud from the "U," running back Edgerrin James, who like Wayne played his college ball at the University of Miami. James became the Colts' all-time leading rusher and was ecstatic about sharing the same locker room with Wayne from 2001 through 2005.

"Hey, that's like my brother. He's family to me," James said. "As a football player, I watched Reggie from Day 1, watched his game evolve into being one of the greatest receivers of all time. And then the way he stuck in there with the Colts, I told him I always hoped he could finish his career with the Colts. The rest of us haven't been able to accomplish that. Hopefully, Reggie will be the one to make that happen, and his last game will be in a Colts uniform."

When James was inducted into the Colts' Ring of Honor during a halftime ceremony in 2012, Wayne sprinted from the locker room to stand by his guy.

"I was so happy to have Reggie in my life and have Reggie on the team with me," James said. "To come from the University of Miami to the NFL, that's very rare that you have someone you were actually close to in college play on the same NFL team with you."

Reggie Wayne (87) runs during the first half of an NFL football game against the Houston Texans on Sunday, December 30, 2012, in Indianapolis.
(AP Photo/AJ Mast)

Wayne's knack for speaking his mind attracts reporters. When a writer suggested in 2010 that a receiver never complained of catching too many passes, an amused Wayne said, "I don't even get that in practice, so I damn sure am not going to get that in games."

He takes pride in putting up numbers, not just because it proves his value, but it provides his team the best chance to win. Wayne has caught 968 passes for 13,063 yards and 78 touchdowns. In 18 playoff games, he's contributed 92 receptions for 1,242 yards and nine touchdowns. He's made the Pro Bowl six of the past seven years, the lone exception when the Colts imploded in 2011. They didn't have a decent quarterback to get him the ball.

His return for 2012 training camp set a tone. Wayne arrived at Anderson University in a convoy of three camouflaged Humvees with seven members of the Indiana National Guard. He climbed out in military fatigues.

"Reggie Wayne, reporting for duty!" he said, then he saluted the guardsmen and grabbed his backpack.

Before the Colts ventured to Nashville, Tennessee, to face the Titans on October 28, Wayne addressed the team's need to snap a 10-game road losing streak. A 10–3 halftime deficit meant sending a more intense message.

"I was pissed," Wayne said in a triumphant locker room after the Colts rallied to accomplish their mission with a 19–13 overtime victory. "There was no false enthusiasm on this one. I was pissed because I knew what we were capable of. We should have had a lead at halftime, and we were behind. I felt like we needed a little fire. I had to speak up."

Wayne reveled in how the Colts surprised their critics—and basically everyone else but themselves—with a turnaround from 2–14 to 11–5 last season. Although the ride ended with a 24–9 AFC Divisional playoff loss at Baltimore, the 34-year-old Wayne showed up with nine receptions for 114 yards.

Undisputed *Madden* Supremacy?

The drudgery of 2006 training camp had two of the Indianapolis Colts' biggest stars debating their skills—not on the field, but when playing EA Sports' *Madden NFL* video game.

Defensive end Dwight Freeney, a two-time league champion, insisted he was No. 1. But wide receiver Reggie Wayne said he defeated Freeney the year before at camp and proclaimed himself the undisputed king.

"He's never played me in *Madden* in his life," Freeney said.

"I'm the best, man," Wayne said. "As soon as I pick up those sticks, it's automatically mine. Everybody in that locker room knows about it already."

Evidently not Freeney.

"He knows. He really does," Wayne said, smiling. "He's finished. He's done. Terminated."

Really?

"So he says. Self-proclaimed," Freeney said. "Nothing has changed. Nothing has changed."

The pass rusher didn't even consider the debate amusing.

"Not at all. Not even entertained," Freeney said matter-of-factly. "It's just complete propaganda to try to stir something up. He knows what it is."

After the game, he criticized Ravens linebacker Ray Lewis for a final-second celebration in which the retiring defender took the field on offense as the deep back in victory formation. As the clock ticked down to the end, Lewis had one more opportunity to do his "Squirrel Dance" for fans in a final home game at Baltimore.

"I saw it as disrespectful," Wayne said. "They'd already had a tribute every quarter."

The leader had stood up and spoken for his team once more.

"Reggie Wayne has never been bashful," said Phil Richards, longtime beat writer for *The Indianapolis Star*. "He's an eager and accomplished trash talker, but he's not a rah-rah guy. At least he wasn't one until the young 2012 Colts needed him to be."

"He's talked more this year than he had in all the 11 previous years, and it's helped our team in every way," said Colts outside linebacker Robert Mathis. "He's more a show-you guy than a tell-you guy. He's, 'Follow me. I'll show you.'"

Colts radio voice Bob Lamey said there's nothing like a one-on-one interview with Wayne, just hanging out and shooting the breeze. "He's as good as it gets," Lamey said. "I love the guy. He played in Marvin's shadow for a long time. He never said anything or griped about it. He just goes out and does his job, and he does it better than 99.9 percent of the players in this game. How many times have we seen him take brutal hits, and he bounces right back up? And he never says anything. He just goes back to the huddle and plays again. He's made big play after big play.

"Right now, I've got Marvin and Reggie as No. 1 and No. 1A in no particular order as the two best receivers I have ever seen. [Baltimore Hall of Famer] Raymond Berry was great, but these two guys could do things Raymond couldn't do because of speed."

Wayne has two more years on his contract. Some might suggest he's lost some of his speed on deep routes, but don't tell him that. He still sees himself as the same guy who caught a career-high 111 passes in 2010 or amassed a personal-best 1,510 yards receiving in 2007. Last season's offense allowed him to move around in the slot in three-receiver sets. He excelled as much with experience and smarts as talent.

"The Colts' best move of the 2012 season was taking quarterback Andrew Luck with the first pick in the draft," Richards said. "Second-best? Re-signing Wayne for a 12th season during which he caught 106 passes for 1,355 yards and five touchdowns and went to his sixth Pro Bowl.

"If anyone should be a forever Colt, it's 'Reg-gie, Reg-gie, Reg-gie.'"

"Playoffs?!"

When Tim Bragg hears the word "playoffs," he thinks of former Colts head coach Jim Mora. Bragg asked the question about the Colts' playoff chances on November 25, 2001, that incited one of the most memorable sound bites in NFL history.

If you're a Colts fan, you remember Mora going off: "What's that? Ah—*Playoffs*?! Don't talk about—*playoffs*?! You kiddin' me?! *Playoffs*?! I just hope we can win a game! Another game!"

The Colts had lost 40–21 at home to San Francisco, whose defensive coordinator was Mora's son, Jim L. It was the Colts' third consecutive loss, dropping them to 4–6 in what would become a five-game losing streak that eventually eliminated the team from playoff contention.

Reporters in the interview room could tell Mora was fuming when he arrived. The coach started by saying, "Do not blame that game on the defense, okay?" It was an obvious shot at Colts president Bill Polian, with whom Mora would feud at season's end about replacing two coaches, including defensive coordinator Vic Fangio, thus costing the head coach his job.

Mora bemoaned five turnovers—four of them Peyton Manning interceptions, one returned for a touchdown. Three of the turnovers were with the Colts in scoring position.

"We threw that game," Mora said. "We gave it away by doing that. We gave 'em the friggin' game. In my opinion, that sucked."

His words sizzled.

"The underpinning of it was Mora walked into that press conference already pissed off that Bill Polian had spent the previous two weeks ripping Vic Fangio and the defense and kept kissing

Peyton Manning's ass," said Bob Kravitz, *The Indianapolis Star* columnist. "Jim was just loaded for bear.

"After the press conference, I was walking back to the locker room and Jim grabbed me. We went back into a little room. 'Tell me, Bobby, did I say anything that wasn't 100 percent true?'" Kravitz recalled Mora saying.

And Mora wasn't talking about the sound bite everyone else would be.

"He wasn't even thinking about the 'playoffs' quote," Kravitz said. "He was talking about poking the bear, No. 18, Peyton."

Manning took exception to being called out by Mora, first in front of the team in the locker room and then in the postgame presser. The quarterback responded in a teleconference with Baltimore media and in an interview with *The Star* later in the week.

"He and I have had one-on-one talks before where he's gotten on me," Manning told *The Star*. "I have no problem with that. It's just that it was national television."

Bragg, who had worked eight years for WNDE radio, was with WRTV-6 at the time of his infamous question. He knew Mora's history of blowing off steam in postgame pressers as a coach in New Orleans. "You could tell he was not himself that day," Bragg said. "You could tell he was angry. That was the first time his tone was different."

At that moment, remembering those much-publicized Mora blow-ups with the Saints, Bragg thought, *This might be the day*. In retrospect a dozen years later, he conceded, "It really wasn't a shock that he went off like that."

The Colts had been in the playoffs the previous two years. But now those postseason possibilities were slipping away. Bragg said he wasn't trying to rile the coach in asking about the team's playoff chances.

Mora didn't care for the question. He has said a few times since that his response wasn't a rant. It just sounded like one. "The guy asked me a question, and I responded," said Mora, 78 and living in Palm Desert, California. "But it caught on. I can be walking down the street, and somebody will bring it up to this day."

Bragg said he felt like he was shrinking as Mora gave his answer. He likened it to the 2006 Coors Light commercial, when Mora's outburst was used in a re-staged presser with beer-can-holding party guys acting intimidated. The coach might have had the last laugh on that one. While the hype bothered him at first, he evidently mellowed about it enough to accept a Coors Light paycheck.

"Those Coors commercials, they were great," Mora said.

Mora's son, Jim L., had some fun with it, too. While Seattle's head coach in 2009, the younger Mora admitted his offspring could impersonate their grandfather. "He gets a kick out of it, especially when his grandsons do it," Jim L. said. "I put my 6-year-old on the phone with him two years ago, and he had it down perfect. I think that kind of lightened the moment for him. It was funny."

Bragg, 44, is still in the Indianapolis area as a physical education teacher and coach at Raymond Park Middle School in Warren Township. "I get a kick out of it," Bragg said. "I think it's great to be connected to it. It's a great memory from my radio/broadcasting years."

Mora's retired routine involves working out and playing a lot of golf. He and his wife, Connie, built their dream home in the Canyon View area of Ironwood Country Club in Palm Desert, California.

Mora recently competed in a 200-player, three-day tournament at the country club. He and his partner, former college athletic director Rick Bay, ended up tied with another team for low net.

"We're standing there watching the scores on the board," Mora said. "And someone comes out and says, 'We've got to have a playoff.'"

There was that word again.

"All the people start laughing and are saying, 'Playoffs?! Playoffs?!'" Mora said. "Even I was laughing. It was funny.

"I'm sure when I die, I'll be known for that."

25 "NoiseGate"

Before he became a stadium director in Indianapolis, Mike Fox didn't work as a Metallica roadie with a specialization in boosting audio. However, he did hear his share of loud decibels in college, as a student manager for coach Bob Knight's Indiana Hoosiers men's basketball teams. How could he not?

And Fox has worked in his share of loud gymnasiums as a high school and college basketball referee for three decades, although those ear-piercing moments don't compare to how loud it used to get in the RCA Dome during Peyton Manning's glory years.

But nobody was more surprised than Fox on November 28, 2005, at an accusation that the Colts pumped up the public-address system volume in their packed dome home during a 26–7 dismantling of the Pittsburgh Steelers on *Monday Night Football*.

"NoiseGate" created quite the stir. The over-hyped controversy didn't pipe down for years.

ESPN's Ed Werder attended the game and started the fuss. On a Dallas radio show the next day, he stated his opinion that the Colts violated league rules by pumping in crowd noise. Two days later on an ESPN Radio show, Werder was adamant the Colts jacked up the bass line.

"There is no question this occurs," he told host Dan Patrick. "Where exactly this emanated from and how it is created, I'm not sure. But it definitely exists."

The Colts vehemently denied the accusation. Head coach Tony Dungy called it "an insult to our crowd."

Fox's initial amusement eventually turned to resentment. Don't let a juicy conspiracy get in the way of the facts.

Fox is employed by the Capital Improvement Board, which runs the Colts' stadium. He's never been a Colts' employee. If the Colts ever would have asked him to pump up the volume, he said he would have waved a red flag. It's a good thing Fox spent some formative years with Knight. Those years toughened his skin.

"Oh my God, it did," he said, "for everything I ever wanted to do.

"Any game I referee, I don't care what level, my boiling point never changes. Just keep it even. If I have to call a technical foul, it's just another call. There's 5,000 people in the audience screaming at me, and I don't even notice it."

But NoiseGate did become annoying.

Stories were written about extra microphones near the field. Those were installed by the television crew, as is often the case for national games. Neither the Colts nor the dome had anything to do with those.

"The part that bugs me about that is, first of all, I'm not so sure I would have even known how to do it with my sound and lights guys," Fox said. "And the part that bothers me about it more than anything is that it goes to integrity and my history as a referee and fairness. That just kind of got to me. I was mad."

But teams kept bringing it up.

"It grew legs," Fox said.

NoiseGate gave Jacksonville coach Jack Del Rio material for a few years. He mentioned it before the Jaguars came to Indianapolis.

On November 4, 2007, when the Colts lost 24–20 to New England in a matchup of previous unbeatens, Patriots president Jonathan Kraft complained about the noise issue after the game to Milt Ahlerich, the NFL vice president of security. The NFL, which had investigated previously and found no wrongdoing, issued a statement the next day. "CBS has informed us that the unusual audio moment heard by fans during the Patriots-Colts telecast was the result of tape feedback in the CBS production truck and was isolated to the CBS broadcast. It was in no way related to any sound within the stadium and could not be heard in the stadium," said NFL spokesman Greg Aiello.

The RCA Dome had the smallest capacity in the NFL at about 56,000, and fans were closer to the field than in most stadiums. The back row of seats were just 100' vertically from the ground and 20' below the roof.

"By design, that building like any dome, it's just loud," Fox said. "You go in there when it's empty and clap your hands and that sound bounces around."

Now Lucas Oil Stadium director, Fox looks back at the uproar and takes it a step further.

"I've always had a theory about stuff like that," he said. "I've always thought people who go out and accuse others of doing things like that are probably doing some things on their own because there's a little bit of insecurity to it. I never would have even dreamed of something like that. Somewhere or another, those who accused us of doing that perhaps had known it had taken place somewhere else. That's why they even knew it was a possibility.

"Those of us who run these places, and arenas and convention centers, we never ever want to be in the spotlight. We want to be like a good referee."

After a few years, NoiseGate finally quieted. It's only brought up in Indianapolis these days as a punchline to what was then a not-so-funny joke.

"Yes, it eventually died," Fox said. "To accuse us of actually doing that was ridiculous."

26 "Lord Help Our Colts"

A founding member of what would become REO Speedwagon, blues musician Duke Tumatoe struck out on his own in 1969 and would open for such legendary artists as Muddy Waters, Buddy Guy, and B.B. King.

In Indianapolis, he is known for one song, a catchy tune he suggests has been rewritten about 800 times in a quarter of a century. "Lord Help Our Colts" became synonymous with the NFL team in the mid-1980s.

About three years after moving to Indianapolis in 1980, Tumatoe befriended Tom Griswold, who teamed with Bob Kevoian on *The Bob & Tom Show*, which would become a popular nationally syndicated radio show that mixes comedy with music. Tumatoe wanted to come up with a way to promote the Uncle Slugs blues club at Union Station in '85. Griswold suggested he write a song about the city's new NFL team.

"I, of course, wrote the song in a form that I thought if necessary I could easily update, which turned out to be a real good thing, a smart move," said Tumatoe, now 65. "It went from there. The song was just about what they did."

In the beginning, the refrain was fairly consistent:
Lord help our Colts. Lord help our Colts.
Ple-e-e-a-a-s-s-s-e, Lord help our Colts.
Oh I sing the blues, for the men who wear horseshoes.
Lord help our Colts.

When he started tinkering with the lines, the verse deviated to:
Everybody ple-e-e-a-a-a-s-s-se,
get down on your knees.
Lord help our Colts.

Colts owner Jim Irsay is passionate about music, so the two became fast friends. Tumatoe had agreed to play the Colts' Christmas party in 1986, but when Ron Meyer was hired as head coach after an 0–13 start, the show was canceled. When the team did well the next year, Tumatoe was playing at a fundraiser with some Colts players and cheerleaders. Meyer was there, too.

"He's coming my way and I'm thinking, 'Oh good. This is either going to be real good or real bad,'" Tumatoe said. "He comes up right in front of me and says, 'Good songs this year, Duke.' I go, 'Coach, it was a good year.'"

The songs became a weekly gig on *The Bob & Tom Show*. But sometimes the players didn't care for Tumatoe's lyrics. Defensive tackle Tony Siragusa was at a bar one night and decided to give his two cents.

"He's getting drunk and all of a sudden he starts getting pissed at me about the songs," Tumatoe said. "He turned on me big time. There's times in your life when you've got to decide, 'Am I in this to make a point, or is it time to cut and run?' At that time, I was in good shape and much younger, but this son of a bitch is huge. And he's a football player. He's quicker than me, stronger than me, and twice my size. I'm thinking, *Cut and run, son. Cut and run.*"

That's basically what he did.

"I worked it," he said. "Some other people came in, I found some space, and got away from him.

"We both came from Italian heritage, so we both like talking about stuff. As I told those guys all the time when they would get

Birthday Gift for a Music Lover

What's the perfect birthday gift for a wealthy man who can have anything he wants? Myra Borshoff concedes it takes creativity to find that special something for Colts owner Jim Irsay.

"Over the years, I've found little things that I thought were meaningful," said Borshoff, a publicist for Irsay since 1996. "One time, I hit the jackpot."

Irsay is a music lover, capable of strapping on a guitar and jamming in his office if he so chooses. Borshoff heard him once say he would give up all of his guitars for one Robert Johnson guitar. The Mississippi Delta blues musician and singer died at the age of 27 in 1938, but the guitars he used have fascinated enthusiasts, so much so that many models were designed in tribute to him.

Borshoff was attending a slide show shared by architects from the South when she saw a picture of Johnson's tombstone where fans had left items to honor the music legend. She asked for a copy of the slide.

"Several weeks later, I got an email with the attached slide," she said. "I got a copy of it, put it in a frame, and gave it to Jim on his birthday."

Irsay was impressed. He placed it on the credenza behind his office desk at the Colts complex.

"He was surprised, then he had this big smile and he said, 'This is so cool,'" Borshoff said. "It reminded me that for all he is and does, there's a simplicity to him."

like that, and a lot of guys took umbrage with me, 'You know I never made anything up.' The gig was do something about the game, and the purpose of the show is comedy, light-heartedness, right? What am I going to say? 'The Colts are great. They're really wonderful. They're 0–13, but let's be happy?'"

Right from the start, Tumatoe couldn't resist taking shots at oft-criticized quarterback Jeff George.

Jeff George will be a great one.

That's what everyone has said.

But right now he's 0 and 1,
and he's got an aching head.
Lord help our Colts. Lord help our Colts.
As Cornelius Bennett did tell
Jeff, welcome to the NFL.
Lord help our Colts.

"I think people miss a basic thing about the blues, and I don't understand why they don't get it," Tumatoe explains. "Blues is a light-hearted music. They're stories that make fun of what goes on in your life.

"Don't get me wrong, I'm a football fan. I enjoy these games. I watch them all. But the premise of all these guys getting millions and millions of dollars to play a kids' game is in and of itself not serious. It's a cause to celebrate when they're winning, but it really doesn't affect your life other than it's nice when your team is doing well. And these guys are getting millions of dollars, and these guys are bitching about it when you criticize their performance? I didn't really criticize their performance. I just made it rhyme."

He laughs when adding, "There was probably a lot of slant rhyming."

While he isn't writing new versions these days, Tumatoe is working on a song about Colts quarterback Andrew Luck for next season.

We don't need a four-leaf clover,
We can't be denied.
We don't need a rabbit's foot,
We've got Luck on our side.

Peyton is a hero,
of course that's understood.
But the future is pretty darn bright,
because Andrew is pretty darn good.

Longer "Lord" Version

Some of Duke Tumatoe's "Lord Help Our Colts" songs were more elaborate than others. Here's an extended version:

In 1984, Robert Irsay had a plan
to move the Colts to Indianapolis.
He called the Mayflower moving vans.
Lord help our Colts. Lord help our Colts.

Hooray! The Colts' new home
was called the Hoosier Dome.
Lord help our Colts.

Do you remember Frank Kush?
When Rod Dowhower split his pants?
How about Ron Meyer, Jack Trudeau, or
   Pat Beach,
Clarence Verdin doing an end-zone
   dance?
Lord help our Colts. Baby, Lord help our
   Colts.

There's Barry Krauss,
And I'll make a bet Art Schlichter is a Colt
   you won't forget.
Lord help our Colts. Lord help our Colts.

I got a kick out of Rohn Stark.
Lord help our Colts.
I miss 'The Goose.'
Ple-e-e-a-a-a-s-s-s-e
Lord help our Colts.

Billy Brooks could catch a pass.
I love 'The Creature,' Kevin Call.
And Albert Bentley running the ball.
Lord help our Colts. Lord help our Colts.

Marshall Faulk wasn't too bad, either.
Eric Dickerson had the Colts in the
   playoffs.
Jeff George was a horse's ass.
Jim Harbaugh would have had 'em in the
   Super Bowl,
had he completed one more pass.
Lord help our Colts. Lord help our Colts.

Remember old coach Ted?
'Let 'er rip' is what he said.
Lord help our Colts.

Now with Peyton, Marvin, and Edgerrin,
the Colts are on a roll.
Bill Polian, Jim Mora, Jim Irsay
have 'em all headed to the Super Bowl.
Lord help our Colts. Lord help our Colts.

Yeah, we all need to-o-o
get out for the blue!
Lord help our Colts. Lord help our Colts.

Where's Roosevelt Potts?
Lord help our Colts.
He can play Ray Buchanan.
Ple-e-e-a-a-a-s-s-s-e.
Lord help our Colts.
Good luck to Jeff Herrod.

Everybody please, get down on your
   knees.
Lord help our Colts.

"I don't know if all of that will make the final cut," he said, "but there's nothing negative there."

Tumatoe has reduced his touring schedule to about 100 dates per year. He does woodworking for recreation and teaches guitar. He's been married 33 years, and their six children are grown and have produced grandchildren.

"I've had a great life," he said. "If you get a chance the next time around, pick Duke Tumatoe. It's a lot of fun."

Every now and then, he gets recognized at airports.

With a wink of the right eye, he says, "I've done it all, kid."

27 "No Trim 'Til Colts Win"

A hopeless start to an NFL season can be demoralizing, especially for a fan base with just two winners to cheer about in seven years since the Colts' 1984 arrival in Indianapolis. In 1991, everything completely fell apart.

The Colts started 0–4, outscored by 45 points. As the outlook became increasingly bleak, two local radio stations came up with a catchy campaign to try to offer inspiration. "No Trim 'Til Colts Win" became the rallying cry, promoted by Bob Kevoian and Tom Griswold on WFBQ's *The Bob & Tom Show* as well as WENS radio personalities Audrey Rochelle and Scott Fischer.

While some initially thought the slogan pertained to not trimming facial hair, Kevoian and Griswold knew "trim" could be construed as something else. So did Rochelle and Fischer, who advocated fans should abstain from sex until their team finally produced on the field.

The "trim" euphemism for sex was tied in popular culture to comedian-turned-actor Eddie Murphy in the 1982 movie *48 Hours*. Murphy's jail-sprung character, Reggie Hammond, propositioned a hooker in a police station but was whisked away before he could score by salty cop Jack Cates, played by Nick Nolte. "Do you know how close I was to getting some trim?" Hammond complained.

"Obviously, it's a double entendre, but maybe not so obviously now," Griswold said 22 years later. "That was sort of floating out there. Then the idea was we would not shave, no trimming of our facial hair until the Colts won a game. We did bumper stickers, a billboard. We ended up getting a ton of publicity. We didn't think it would. We did stuff that was stupid because we thought it was funny."

While Kevoian and Griswold refused to shave, Rochelle and Fischer took vows of celibacy. The latter suggested the Colts weren't winning because players were having sex too close to game day.

"My wife said, 'Why just wait for a win?'" Fischer told the Associated Press. "Why not wait for a Super Bowl?"

"For the so-called straight press, the joke was 'No Trim 'Til Colts Win,' Bob and Tom aren't going to shave," Griswold said. "But the subtle, some might think joke was no one is going to have any sex until the Colts win. A lot of our listeners took it that way. I don't want to get too pretentious here, but there's a famous play in which the women refused to have sex with the men until they stopped having a war."

In *Lysistrata*, a 411 BC play written by Aristophanes, the title character persuaded women of Greece to withhold sex from their husbands and lovers as a means of forcing the men to negotiate an end to the Peloponnesian War.

"This now sounds so ridiculously inflated, but that was the gag," Griswold said. "Okay, ladies, you're not allowed to have sex until the Colts win. We actually pulled it off. It was goofy and funny and stupid. And I ended up looking like an idiot with my terrible moustache. It's not good."

Kevoian laughs about how his partner looked at the time. "It was pretty sad and pathetic," he said of Griswold's unshaven appearance. "We were all scruffy. It really was embarrassing. It was just incredible how it changed from no trim to the moustache to no trim from the ladies, either. It became a national story because the Colts were winless."

Part of Kevoian's persona was and still is his thick moustache. So he didn't look nearly as scruffy as his partner. "I had never grown facial hair," Griswold said. "I had never tried. Bob, of course, has a legendary moustache. Bob's moustache is older than most of your readers, I think. Bob has a beautiful, very thick moustache; he literally started growing it the day he graduated from high school. For Bob, it was a matter of kind of making it a Fu Manchu and growing it down. For me, it was a matter of letting it go, which I had never done. Of course, as would happen, the Colts didn't win and I've got this pretty awful facial hair thing.

"What happens is people that don't know you're part of some stunt, they're wondering, 'What the hell is Tom Griswold doing? He looks awful.' I had a couple of formal things I had to do. There's a picture of me in a tux that I still have, and I have this horrible moustache."

The Colts visited Seattle in the fifth game. The Seahawks entered 1–3. It seemed like the ideal time for the Colts to end their skid. Instead, Seattle won easily, 31–3. Head coach Ron Meyer, who had led the Colts to the AFC East division title in 1987, was fired after the Seahawks loss. Rick Venturi replaced him. A return home didn't help. The Colts lost 21–3 to Pittsburgh at home.

The sensationalizing TV show *A Current Affair* visited town to report on the sex strike. The video clip can still be found on the Internet on YouTube. Kevoian and Griswold, both sporting unkempt facial hair, were interviewed on the steps of the Hoosier Dome. The report included an interview with a woman who intended to abstain from consummating her marriage on her honeymoon.

The Colts kept losing. They fell to 0–7 with a 42–6 loss at Buffalo. Two more home games didn't help. The Colts lost 17–6 to the New York Jets and then 10–6 to the Miami Dolphins. The slide had reached 0–9.

"The other aspect of it was, as a Colts fan, God, it was so painful," Griswold said. "Bob and I have been season ticket holders since the very first game at the dome. Oddly enough, it's one of those things that proves what a great city Indy is and what great fans they are. People have a sense of humor. With all of the teams here, people had generally really hung in there through the lean years. It was just kind of a way to keep the whole thing with the Colts up and running and in everybody's consciousness.

"Remember there was a time here when the Colts games weren't all sold out. We did lots of stuff to keep the Colts in the consciousness of the people here in town. We did 'Lord Help Our Colts' songs with [blues musician] Duke Tumatoe. We always had Colts players on the air."

Finally, on November 10, 1991, the Colts rallied for a 28–27 road win over the Jets.

"It was a great day when they won," Kevoian said. "I'm curious to know how many babies were born nine months later."

It would be the team's only win in a 1–15 season that goes down as the worst 16-game record in franchise history. The 1991 Colts redefined offensive ineptitude with just 143 points scored, a dubious franchise record for a 16-game season. The team failed to score a touchdown in nine games. They managed 10 points or less in 12 games. Kicker Dean Biasucci led the team in scoring with just 59 points—15-of-26 on field goals and 14 extra points.

"That was Dean Biasucci's year," said Mike Chappell, Colts beat writer for *The Indianapolis Star*. "It was Dean Biasucci or nobody. The season from hell. It was Groundhog Day, same stuff, over and over."

Adds Biasucci, "We'd get down to the 5-yard line, then the next thing you know, three plays later, I'm kicking a 48-yard field goal."

If nothing else, "No Trim 'Til Colts Win" gave fans another reason to keep track of the team.

"That had people actually staying interested," Kevoian said. "People wanted to know the score that week, like, 'Can we shave or have sex, finally?' I think we kind of helped the team through one of its worst seasons."

28 Giving "Johnny U." a Ride

Craig Kelley was a freshman at Louisiana State University when he first met Hall of Fame quarterback Johnny Unitas. CBS had its network personnel in New Orleans for Super Bowl XII in 1978. As is commonplace for the NFL's greatest spectacle, the week's schedule leading up to the game included several special events.

"They played a benefit football game at City Park in New Orleans," Kelley said. "Everybody was there, Brent Musburger and Phyllis George, who was rather attractive at the time and I'm sure still is. They had all their voices, Tom Brookshier, Pat Summerall. I don't know if Jimmy 'The Greek' was there, I'm sure he was.

"But I went just so I could meet Johnny Unitas. I remember chatting with him that day. I said, 'I came here to meet you.' And he said, 'You mean Phyllis George is here and you came to see me?'"

Kelley, who has worked 28 years in the Colts' front office, laughs about it to this day.

After the Colts' move to Indianapolis from Baltimore in 1984, Unitas was outspoken about how he was not connected to the new city. He wanted his Pro Football Hall of Fame displays removed unless his career was acknowledged as being with the Baltimore Colts.

As fate would have it, Kelley had an opportunity to see Unitas again in 1997. The Colts' director of public relations was asked to donate some items to a benefit for Hall of Fame coach Weeb Ewbank and retired Rams Fearsome Foursome member Lamar Lundy in their hometown of Richmond, Indiana. Kelley learned Unitas would attend. This was a chance for someone connected to the Indianapolis Colts to make peace with Unitas. Kelley asked how Unitas was getting to the airport and was told there was a problem. Unitas was flying out of Dayton, Ohio, and event organizers needed someone to give him a ride.

"I'm your guy," Kelley said.

It would make for a long day of driving, but Kelley was more than up to being a chauffeur.

"I got a throwback Unitas jersey donated and I told my wife that we would drive to Richmond, Indiana, and then we would drive Unitas to Dayton, Ohio, and then drive home," he said. "Katie is the best sport of all time. So on we went."

Perhaps the moment of truth was when Kelley introduced himself.

"I went up to Unitas, who I had never met officially, and told him, 'I'm Craig Kelley, the Colts' P.R. guy,'" he said.

"I won't hold that against you," Kelley remembered a good-natured Unitas saying.

"That's good because I'm your ride to Dayton," Kelley said.

After the event, they congregated at the Kelleys' SUV.

"You never put your wife in the back seat. You never put your wife second," he said. "Unitas sat in the back seat, but he had his head between us the whole way for an hour, just telling us stories."

It was such an unforgettable moment. Unitas was so engaging. If only the drive didn't have to end.

"It was one of the most pleasant rides," Kelley said. "We're all laughing, and he's telling story after story. Before most of the anecdotes, he would hit me on my right shoulder for emphasis. I loved it. We get to the Dayton airport and I had a couple of balls I wanted signed for co-workers. I said, 'Look, I can't account for anything in the past, but if I can benefit your future, please let me know.'"

Unitas acknowledged Kelley's gesture and said, "Thank you." They shook hands. Kelley surmised that would be the end of it. But they would cross paths again one year later. And the experience would be even more memorable.

29 Thanksgiving with Unitas

The Indianapolis Colts visited Baltimore for the first time to play the Ravens in 1998, one year after Craig Kelley gave Johnny Unitas that ride from Richmond, Indiana, to the Dayton, Ohio, airport.

Back then, NFL teams sent a public relations representative to host cities in the days leading up to a game. Kelley planned to fly to Baltimore Tuesday night and spend the rest of the week in town. Before departing, Kelley decided to give Unitas a call.

"John, I don't know if you remember me," the director of public relations began.

"Sure, I remember. You did me a favor," Unitas said. "What can I do for you?"

"As you know, we're coming to town and I'll be in town by Tuesday," Kelley said. "Can I buy you lunch on Friday?"

Unitas agreed and asked Kelley to call when he got to town. That Wednesday, the day before Thanksgiving, Kelley phoned again.

After agreeing on Friday lunch plans, Unitas inquired, "What are you doing tomorrow for dinner?"

"Well, I'm just going to eat here at the hotel," Kelley said.

He was surprised when Unitas responded definitively, "No, you're coming to my house."

The Unitas 20-acre ranch, "A Passing Fancy," was in the country. Kelley was excited as he woke up Thanksgiving morning.

"I wanted the day to be perfect," he said. "I actually got up early in the morning. His farm was about 30 miles away, and I actually drove it to make sure when the time came that I wouldn't get lost. I guess I could have tapped on the door for breakfast."

When the time came to make the drive again for Thanksgiving dinner, Kelley didn't arrive empty handed.

"Of course, I had to bring chocolates for the family," he said.

John Unitas Jr. answered the door.

"I can't believe a Colts person is coming into this house," Kelley recalled Unitas Jr. saying.

"Your dad is very gracious," Kelley said.

The two, who would become friends, chuckle about that front-door exchange these days.

"I met five of his eight children, saw his dog named Bruce, and saw a couple of his cows," Kelley said. "We stood outside while John smoked a turkey. We talked about players he faced and old teammates. He asked me at one point before dinner if I wanted to see his trophy room."

As if there was any doubt.

"Second door on the left," Kelley recalled Unitas saying. "He was so matter-of-fact about it. He wasn't bragging. He was just a point-blank kind of guy.

"An hour later, I was finished looking at it. I've always had a deep appreciation for Colts history and maintaining it however I could that being in John's memento room was something not to be rushed."

There were more moments to be savored.

"He was a little under the weather that day, big John was, but it was a very, very nice meal," Kelley said. "He signed a picture for me. It was just one of those days in your life that you'll never forget, Thanksgiving with the Unitas family in 1998. It was special."

Kelley, reflecting on that day, repeats the word again: "Special."

The signed Unitas picture still hangs in Kelley's office. An NFL journalist once suggested Kelley should have it insured.

"How could that be replaced?" Kelley said.

It can't. Neither could another framed poster hanging in his office. The collage of former Baltimore Colts greats has signatures from Unitas, Raymond Berry, Art Donovan, Gino Marchetti, Jim Parker, Lenny Moore, John Mackey, and Don Shula.

"It took me three years to get those," Kelley said of his impressive array of autographs. "If you don't maintain the past, you lose the past."

When Unitas passed away on September 11, 2002, the Colts had to decide who should represent the team at the funeral. "I heard someone said, 'Let's send Craig. He's the only one John liked,'" Kelley said.

He made the trip to Baltimore's Cathedral of Mary Our Queen. "It was such a solemn day for such a gracious family," Kelley said. "He was the guy. He was Johnny U. Raymond Berry spoke. The Ravens team was there. Ray Lewis was behind me in the pews. I sat with Ted and Ann Marchibroda."

As mourners exited the church, a plane flew by pulling an aerial banner that read, "Unitas We Stand."

"As a P.R. guy," Kelley said, "you're around moments that are just special."

Yes, indeed.

Special.

30 Striking a Deal in Indy

The Hoosier Dome had not yet been completed when two men took an important tour of the facility on February 23, 1984. David

Frick, Indianapolis deputy mayor, brought Baltimore Colts owner Robert Irsay to the downtown venue in what is remembered 29 years later as a seminal moment for an aspiring city trying to land an NFL franchise.

"The old Hoosier Dome had three colors," Frick said. "It had the deep blue seats in the lower deck, the incredible white in the roof, and it had the silver in the upper-deck bench seats.

"I can still remember taking Mr. Irsay into the stadium, walking through the tunnel. He was quiet. Didn't say a word."

Frick asked, "Mr. Irsay, are you okay?"

"You know, these are the Colts' colors," Frick recalled Irsay saying. "It's meant to be."

That first impression evidently resonated.

"At that point, I think he mentally moved from Indianapolis as being an alternative that he could use in a negotiation elsewhere to Indianapolis being a viable option," said Frick, 68, a semi-retired attorney with Faegre Baker Daniels.

There would be extensive negotiations, and Frick didn't need to be reminded of the competition. He considered a Phoenix offer "substantially better." So why did Irsay choose Indianapolis?

"I think there was more of a fit between Mr. Irsay, [Colts chief counsel] Mike Chernoff, and the Indianapolis people than there was with the Phoenix people," Frick said. "Secondly, I think the NFL frankly preferred he moved to Indianapolis. It would be much less disruptive. To have a team on the West Coast would have required realignment, where a move to Indianapolis wouldn't require realignment. We had worked hard to build a relationship with the NFL. The NFL was frankly assisting us to build exposure with NFL owners. We knew enough NFL owners, and the NFL thought we were a good city. The NFL probably nudged, well in fact, I know they nudged Mr. Irsay, 'If he was going to move, move to Indianapolis.'"

Chernoff, 77, of Glencoe, Illinois, acknowledged Irsay liked Indianapolis. "I think that's fair. Absolutely," Chernoff said. "Bob Irsay liked the people. It was terribly important. He's putting his life in the hands of the city in a lot of ways."

The attorney offers another explanation. "If there was no David Frick, there might not have been a move to Indianapolis," said Chernoff, who enjoyed a positive give-and-take with the understated negotiator.

Frick modestly says he just played a role in the move. "There [were] a lot of people involved in that effort," he said. "I was just one of those players."

Chernoff isn't surprised by the humility. "That's David Frick," he said.

Frick reciprocated the compliment. "People forget that the entire negotiation and move process lasted only six weeks, so it was a very action-packed period of time. Because the time frame was so compressed, Mike Chernoff played a critical role in the process," Frick said. "It was clear to me that Bob Irsay trusted Mike completely and Mike brought a professional approach to the negotiation and relocation decision. He wanted to achieve the best deal for the Colts, but he realized that the relationship with the community (not words in a lengthy legal document) was the key for long-term success. Thus, he didn't try to overreach, and he sought ways that both sides could win.

"That approach is rare among lawyers, and I have always believed that the Colts would not be in Indy but for Mike."

Frick also mentioned that his boss, Indianapolis Mayor Bill Hudnut, risked his political future by building the Hoosier Dome before attracting a team. Hudnut's vision was with precedence. His marketing of the city earned Indianapolis the distinction of the Amateur Sports Capital of the World.

Mindful that they didn't want the city to be used as a pawn, Frick and Hudnut understood the importance of being professional but not overly generous in negotiations. An initial meeting between Frick and Chernoff was "fairly brief" because Frick's 10-year-old daughter, Amy, suffered a ruptured appendix and was rushed to the hospital.

"Michael outlined what the Colts were looking for, and I outlined what the city was looking for in terms of a relationship," Frick said. "And we agreed to get back together."

Amy pulled through. Eventually, so did Indianapolis. Both sides continued talks, once meeting in Hawaii during NFL owners meetings. The 100-page lease would become the biggest deal for both.

The Colts desired a long-term commitment. The city offered 20 years with two five-year options. If the team didn't sell enough seats, the city guaranteed $7 million in annual revenue. Rent would be $250,000 per year. The Colts and city shared suite license revenues, the team taking the first $500,000 and Indianapolis receiving the rest. They shared concessions, video board, and signage revenues. The city kept the parking money. Game-day operating expenses would be the city's responsibility.

Irsay had a loan with a bank headquartered in Baltimore, which meant it would be called as soon as he relocated. In a Chicago meeting on March 27, Merchants Bank made a $15 million loan to offset Irsay's impending obligation and the city would help subsidize Irsay's interest payment, Frick said.

"In comparison to what cities now offer NFL teams, it was a money maker for our city," Frick said. "We made through the various revenue streams $2 million a year off the Colts coming to town."

Maryland's senate passed legislation to authorize Baltimore to seize the Colts by eminent domain on March 27. Irsay would cite that political push for advising Chernoff "to do a deal" the next day with Indianapolis, where the lease was signed. The Mayflower moving vans were dispatched to the Colts' facilities in Owings Mills, Maryland.

"Under the cover of darkness was terribly unfair," Frick said of the popular perception about the timing of the move. "It made it sound like there was a strategy [to] moving out at night. There wasn't. The strategy was moving as quickly as we could. It just so happened that by the time we got everything done on finalizing the lease with Chernoff here in Indianapolis, Chernoff flew to Baltimore to supervise the move."

Michael Smith, president of Mayflower's non-moving operations, has had his share of discussions about the timing.

"I've reminded people it's not easy to sneak up on somebody in a 60' vehicle that's painted yellow, green, and red with a diesel engine," he said. "It's hard to imagine us sweeping in and sweeping out."

Hudnut and next-door neighbor Johnny B. Smith, Mayflower's chairman and CEO, were at Frick's home when the vans started rolling. They would laugh in the coming years about how nervous they were at the time. The moving plan, formulated weeks in advance, sent trucks in various directions from Baltimore.

Hudnut recalled Johnny B. Smith saying in the early morning hours, "You know, Bill, I feel just like Dwight D. Eisenhower on D-Day. I know my troops are out there. I just don't know where they are."

Michael Smith (no relation to Johnny B.) had arrived in Florida on vacation when his 7-year-old daughter, Sarah, looked at a television and cried, "Daddy! Daddy! Those are your trucks!"

"It was really fun to be associated with Johnny B. and Bill Hudnut and to see the city just light up," Michael Smith said. "I have goose bumps now just talking about this, what it has meant to the city."

The City of Baltimore sued Johnny B. Smith, Hudnut, and Frick in Baltimore City Court.

"My life savings are at risk," Frick said. "We had to hire lawyers and pay a lot of money before the lawsuit was settled. It was settled because we got it into Federal Court, where you stand a better chance of having a fair outcome. The outcome would not have been fair in Baltimore City Court."

The Colts agreed to return Johnny Unitas memorabilia and other items as part of the settlement on December 10, 1985.

"What they were really trying to do was get the Colts to move back," Frick said.

That wasn't going to happen.

"I don't know that we really fully understood the implications from our actions," Frick said of Indianapolis landing the Colts. "But it was a dream realized."

31 Follow Colts on Twitter

If you're an Indianapolis Colts fan who isn't living the tweet life in the social-media Internet world of Twitter, you're missing out—even Colts owner Jim Irsay communicates with fans there on a regular basis. His Twitter followers numbered nearly 213,000 and counting as last spring approached.

Irsay doesn't hesitate to tweet team updates, be it weekly practice reports or the re-signing of players. He also spreads his wealth through an endless series of contests, offering money, Colts tickets, or other prizes to the first person to correctly answer whatever he's asking. The question could pertain to a song lyric, a tidbit of team history, or even just something that applies to the news of that particular day. He offered $500 to the follower who predicted the winner of a PGA Tour event in March 2013.

When Irsay fired vice chairman Bill Polian and vice president/general manager Chris Polian on January 2, 2012, the owner tweeted that he had heard the fans.

"Hearing our fans, whether it is season ticket holders calling in, on Twitter, on blogs, and all the ways they communicate, listen, you're always listening to your fans," Irsay said when asked about the tweet at the press conference. "They're your shareholders, and they're a part of this thing in such a big way."

He later added that wasn't why the Polians were fired, "But it's important to not block that out, just to take [fan feedback] in and also make the decisions that you know you need to make."

Fun-loving punter Pat McAfee lives up to his No. 1 jersey as the undisputed locker room Twitter leader among the players. And he's proud of that. His *Pat McAfee Show* account had about 105,000 followers by mid-March 2013. That's grown from about 18,600 just 20 months earlier. Talk about a growing army.

A 2011 exchange with fans showed how much of a kick he gets out of it. A Tuesday trip to the Bureau of Motor Vehicles in Brownsburg, Indiana, would have been a recipe for boredom if not for social media.

This is Twitter time, he thought when advised of a 58-minute wait.

"Let's talk about life," he tweeted from the BMV.

A follower asked, "U going for the [Nick] Nolte, [Gary] Busey, or Carrot Top look for ur drivers license pic 2day?"

The long-haired one responded, "Haha. Definitely Nolte."

Then McAfee tweeted, "I'm about to order food to this place. Do I ask other folks here if they want something or no? Would that be rude?"

Followers tweeted food suggestions as well as alternate BMV sites.

About 20 minutes later, the punter with personality punched his cell phone digits with, "Dude snoring next to me in here."

While some of the stars don't tweet—most noticeably quarterback Andrew Luck and wide receiver Reggie Wayne—a majority

Tweet, Tweet

Confirmed Colts accounts on Twitter:

Owner Jim Irsay—@JimIrsay
P Pat McAfee—@PatMcAfeeShow
OLB Robert Mathis—@RobertMathis98
CB Vontae Davis—@VontaeDavis23
K Adam Vinatieri—@adamvinatieri
LT Anthony Castonzo—@AnthonyCastonzo
S Antoine Bethea—@Tweez41
QB Chandler Harnish—@CHarnish8
LS Matt Overton—@MattOverton_LS
C Samson Satele—@satele66
TE Dwayne Allen—@Dallen83
TE Coby Fleener—@CobyFleener
DE Cory Redding—@CRedd90
LG Joe Reitz—@JoeReitz76
RB Delone Carter—@DeloneCarter
WR LaVon Brazill—@BrazillLaVon
WR T.Y. Hilton—@TyHilton13
CB Cassius Vaughn—@CassiusVaughn
RB Vick Ballard—@VickBallard
S Joe Lefeged—@JLefeged35
ILB Jerrell Freeman—@JerrellFreeman
OG Mike McGlynn—@Greezy_75
NT Josh Chapman—@The_Boss61
OT Ben Ijalana—@TheBiggerBen
NT Brandon McKinney—@BMcKinney96

of them do. Outside linebacker Robert Mathis takes the time to interact. Defensive tackle Cory Redding and safety Antoine Bethea tweet, too.

McAfee became so popular so fast, he was asked to speak at a Likeable You summit in New York City two years ago. "It's nice to actually have a voice," he said. "I can be myself. I don't have to worry about the Colts finding me or the media or bloggers putting words in my mouth. I can just show people I'm a regular person. I think a lot of things are funny. And I like to share. I tweet often and everything I tweet, in my mind when I read it, I think it's funny."

One word of warning, though. Hateful fans get three strikes, after which they are blocked forever with no exceptions. Not enough time in the day to deal with too much negativity when socializing.

On any given day, you have no idea what might show up on Twitter from anyone associated with the Colts.

When former Cleveland Cavaliers star LeBron James and his Miami Heat lost to Dallas in the NBA Finals, Mathis tweeted, "hah-hahhaaa wow people are congratulating the city of #Cleveland!!! Are...You...Kidding...Me??!?!?!!"

"Feel like lettin' my freak flag fly," Irsay tweeted one time. Good luck figuring out what the off-the-wall owner meant by that one.

Mike Chappell, beat writer for *The Indianapolis Star*, described the owner in a 2011 point-counterpoint analysis of Twitter as, "Different, that's a good description for Irsay. He's a stream of consciousness with a pulse, lots of money and a desire to reach out to his followers."

Irsay has used his account to stir the pot several times. As speculation swirled about quarterback Peyton Manning being sidelined for the start of 2011, the owner had many fans thinking Brett Favre could be signed with this tweet: "Brad, I'm in Hattiesburg...is it right or left at the Firechief?" That's Favre's Mississippi hometown.

Bus Cook, Favre's agent, played along via email when asked if he had heard from the Colts or Irsay, "Last I heard he was on Brett's tractor mowing the back 40!"

Signing up for Twitter is easy. Even if you're not inclined to share your thoughts, imagine the ones you will read by following the Colts.

McAfee tweeted when his BMV mission was accomplished, "06/14/2011 at 3:24 PM Pat McAfee became an Indiana Resident. Phone's still 412 but excited to be a legit Hoosier…(don't know what that is)."

32 Check Out Peyton's *SNL*, Commercials

Hilarious commercials were the beginning. Colts quarterback Peyton Manning expanded his comedic range when he hosted NBC's *Saturday Night Live* on March 24, 2007.

The laughs began with the opening monologue as Manning said, "It's been a fun year for me, as I have accomplished *two* of my life goals. One, I've appeared in over *half* of America's television commercials. And two, my team, the Colts, won the Super Bowl."

His smooth self-deprecating delivery kept getting laughs. He set up a joke in mentioning a visit to a Boston veteran's hospital to talk to 85-year-old patient Joe O'Malley. "Peyton, what do Tom Brady and the circus have in common?" Manning said O'Malley asked, referring to the New England quarterback. Manning replied, "I said, 'What's that Joe?' He said, 'They both have two more rings than you do.'"

Immediate applause quickly died down and some people actually booed.

"Joe, I just kind of want to say, 'Thanks,'" the quarterback said, "because of that comment, I'm gonna go back and work hard to be sure and kick y'all's ass *next* year!"

He introduced his family in the audience—father Archie, who played 13 NFL seasons and brother, Eli, the New York Giants' quarterback. Then Manning brought up his mother, Olivia, and said, "She didn't make it to the NFL, uh—she didn't have what it took. She got cut by the Dolphins, she tried in Canada for a bit, uh—she's a real disappointment to all of us, uh, you know—she's still a great lady, and we love her."

While many of the skits were entertaining, the best without question was a spoof of an NFL/United Way advertisement. Manning is shown playing football with a group of kids. After checking out of a play in his normal pre-snap routine, he rifles a pass that drills an unaware kid in the butt and knocks down the boy.

"Get your head out of your ass! Suck!" Manning yells, feigning disgust. Then he orders the dejected receiver to "go sit in a Port-o-let for 20 minutes." When the kid peeks out later, Manning screams, "Why is the door open?! Close the door!"

His extreme expectations of another youngster prompt the criticism, "Okay, I'm sorry—do you want to lose? I throw, you catch. It's not that hard, okay? Get the [bleep] out of here."

He shows the group how to break into a car when a siren sends everybody scurrying away with Manning yelling, "Cops! Cops!" When a boy is wincing through the pain of getting a Manning tattoo, the passer enviously says, "It's going to be there forever."

The narrator's summation: "Spend time with your kids, so Peyton Manning doesn't."

Manning's monologue joke about commercials was worth a laugh considering his status as the NFL's No. 1 endorsement machine with an extra $13 million paid to be a pitch man. The MasterCard "Priceless" ads were probably the funniest.

The star turns the tables on normal people when he cheers their work. "Say it with me! Say it with me! Here we go! Let's go, insurance adjusters, let's go! Let's go, insurance adjusters, let's go!" There's the infamous deli chant while watching a sandwich being made: "Cut that meat! Cut that meat!" The 30-second ad ends with Manning standing above people leaving work. "You're my favorite accountant! Tommy, please!" he said, holding his hand down to be slapped. "Johnny, please, you're on my fantasy team! You're my favorite worker!" When Johnny gives him a slap of the left hand, Manning screams, "Yes! Woo-hoo!" He looks and then shows that left hand. "Yeah, yeah, right here. Never going to wash that hand. Look at this right here."

"He just nailed his lines," said Brian Connors, MasterCard's director of brand development who attended the shooting. "He's great because he's every man's quarterback. But he's also a regular guy. I was so impressed with the way he carried himself, how cool he was, and what a gentleman he is. It's no wonder people like him."

In a Sprint NFL Mobile ad where he's wearing a fake black wig and moustache, Manning gushes about a video of himself on a phone by saying, "That guy is pretty good, if you like 6'5", 230-lb. quarterbacks, laser rocket arm."

A tip of the helmet to the folks in New England who run the Patriots' Gillette Stadium. During an early television timeout with Manning and the Colts offense on the field, the players looked up at the video board to see Manning in that Sprint NFL Mobile commercial. Patriots fans reacted as expected with a loud chorus of boos while those on the field laughed.

Peyton and Eli teamed up for an amusing sibling spat in an ESPN promo that had the brothers engaging in horseplay while on a tour of the Bristol, Connecticut, headquarters. Peyton finishes with a reverse leg kick to Eli's backside. Manning has also pitched Gatorade, Wheaties, and worked with Eli again in an Oreo-eating contest as well as a DirecTV spoof "Football Cops," where the crime-fighting duo busts a shady crime ring by throwing footballs at suspects.

Manning's body of work can be found in YouTube clips all over the Internet.

Perhaps his funniest commercial was for MasterCard, when he visited a hotel. Each interaction is intended to be an insult that an unassuming Manning takes as helpful advice.

On an elevator, the attendant assures, "You're going down, Manning." He responds, "That's right, I am. Fourth floor, getting a massage today. I'm excited."

An employee brings a fruit basket to his room and mutters, "Don't choke on it." Manning smiles and says, "Good call. I'll just cut it up and put it into a fruit salad or something."

On the balcony, he offers a "Morning" to a cleaning lady who snickers, "Take a hike." He expresses his appreciation with, "You know, I'm going to do that. The weather here is swe-e-et. Nice!"

33 "The House That Peyton Built"

Indiana native Forrest Lucas paid $121.5 million for two decades of naming rights on Lucas Oil Stadium in 2006, two years before the Indianapolis Colts' spacious $725 million home with a retractable roof and window opened.

The entrepreneur made his money as co-founder of Lucas Oil Products, a world leader in high-performance lubricants and problem-solving additives, and has expanded his brand through the ownership of more than 700 racing teams and the sanctions of various racing series and events.

First and foremost, Lucas has Colts quarterback Peyton Manning to thank for the exposure received from this NFL stadium. It's fitting that Manning was on hand for the groundbreaking ceremony.

Lucas Oil Stadium is called "The House That Peyton Built," because without the NFL's only four-time MVP leading the franchise to a league-record 115 wins in a decade through 2009, where might the city's football fortunes be?

"I think that's probably fair," said stadium director Mike Fox, when asked about the building's nickname.

"There's no two ways about it," said Colts radio voice Bob Lamey.

Unprecedented success attracted fans nationally and around the globe.

The facility, designed by HKS Inc., has been honored by *Stadium Journey* magazine as the best stadium out of 1,225 venues worldwide the past two years. Magazine editor Paul Swaney wrote in the January 2013 edition, "To be tops on our list, you've got to have it all: great fans, game day atmosphere, food and drink selection inside the stadium, set in an interesting and vibrant neighborhood, with a good return on investment." He concludes with, "Sports fans owe it to themselves to see the best that sports has to offer, and a trip to Indianapolis certainly qualifies as such."

The House That Peyton Built fits each criteria, and then some.

"It's the most beautiful venue I've ever been to," said longtime Blue Crew Fan Club member Dan Cole of Madison, Indiana. "Check out the race cars."

Two can't-miss Lucas Oil dragsters are angled into the air as spectators proceed through the front lobby for that first gaze inside.

"You feel it when you walk in the door," Cole said. "People are genuinely excited about their football team."

What's nothing short of astonishing is how the stadium has played host to a series of incredibly important events in just four years. The Colts have played three playoff games in their new home, including an AFC Championship Game in 2010.

The NFL was convinced enough to award Indianapolis with Super Bowl XLVI on February 5, 2012, when the New York Giants defeated the New England Patriots 21–17. The event was a rousing success for the city, which transformed the stadium's surrounding area into a one-week party atmosphere. The NFL, distinguished guests, and media praised Indianapolis for its hospitality and how everything was so closely connected.

"We're just nice people," Fox said of Hoosier hospitality. "Everybody that comes through the door, be it a guest, a client, a participant, we just try to treat them like they want to be treated. The NFL folks were just blown away with that. I still get emails from them.

"They still tell us, 'You guys were just so nice.' And I go, 'I hate to tell you this. You want me to say, 'NFL, we treated you so much better than everybody else.' We didn't treat you any differently than anybody else who comes through the door. That's just how we are.'"

While a sports stage arguably can't be more grandiose than for a Super Bowl, perhaps the loudest roar in the stadium's brief history was when the local "Underdawgs" from Butler University advanced to the men's basketball NCAA Final Four in 2010. When the Bulldogs jogged out for their practice session a day before the semifinal games, they were greeted by a thunderous roar from 40,000 fans. Butler almost pulled it off, their inspired run coming down to a final shot from near half court, a Gordon Hayward desperation attempt that missed by inches and bounced off the rim. Duke exhaled, then celebrated.

"I was off the edge of the court, and I was right in line from where he shot it to the goal, out of dumb luck," Fox said. "When he let go of it, I went, 'Oh my God, it's in.' And, oh my God, it almost did go in. It was that close.

"I remember telling my buddies that work at the NCAA, 'You know, if that would have gone in, I'm not sure we could have saved the floor.' And I'm not so sure I would have wanted to. That could have gone down as the most exciting moment in the history of college sports.'"

The event was a testament to the genius of the city's Capital Improvement Board, which wanted a multi-purpose facility that

Lucas Oil Stadium is lit for a preseason NFL game between the Minnesota Vikings and the Indianapolis Colts in Indianapolis on Friday, August 14, 2009. (AP Photo/Tom Strickland)

could be used for more than Colts games. The men's Final Four returns in April 2015.

"It truly is still multi-purpose," Fox said. "Everything moves. The roof moves. The window moves. The seats move. We've got curtains to reduce the size of the building. That's the biggest problem stadiums have. We can do 65,000 people in our sleep. That's what we do. To try to make it 35,000 or 40,000, that's harder for us to do, but we have tools in place to where we can make that transition in a couple of hours. That's a big deal for us. Our first year, we played basketball on a Saturday night and then we had a 1:00 Colts game on a Sunday. Not many places can do that. That showed me the capabilities that this place had."

Because his job requires checking on so many people, ensuring everything goes off without a hitch, Fox rarely takes any time to enjoy an event. He's been part of so many major attractions, dating back to his days of running the old Hoosier/RCA Dome, that his unflappable focus is on the job.

The Super Bowl provided an unexpected revelation.

"I was fortunately or unfortunately stuck in the press box and never got to see a play," he said. "Everything was going well. I had seen the halftime show rehearsal a dozen times. But I had never seen that halftime show when everybody had the glow sticks. So I snuck up to the window in the press box, they turn the lights out, they do the whole stage thing, Madonna comes out, and then all of a sudden the glow sticks break out.

"I turn to Frank Supovitz, who is the NFL's supervisor for the Super Bowl, and said, 'Frank, holy cow, our little town is hosting the Super Bowl.' It was halftime of the game when it hit me, when I just went, 'How did we do this?'"

34 Buy a Colts Jersey, Make Some Noise

Tim Millikan's earliest Indianapolis Colts games at the Hoosier Dome didn't include the atmosphere experienced today at Lucas Oil Stadium.

He often shared space with fans who showed up to see the other team. Those backing the Colts didn't make a lot of noise except in obvious moments. And most didn't dress accordingly.

"When we first started going to games, fans were wearing all kinds of different colors," said Millikan, one of the founding fathers of the team's Blue Crew Fan Club. "Many were wearing their Sunday best. You would look through the crowd and didn't see a lot of blue."

Millikan stood out. He wore his blue Colts jersey, and because the team struggled in those early years, Millikan had to be creative in sounding off.

"When the team was so bad, it was just a celebration to get a first down," he said of standing that first time to scream about something. "I would jump up and celebrate over-enthusiastically."

The next time the Colts moved the chains, fans near him in section 317 expected another reaction. He became known as "The First Down Guy," landing sponsorships that would enable him to pass out beads, bandannas, T-shirts, hats, and buttons.

"That was my claim to fame," he said.

Now 45 and living in Ingalls, Indiana, the demands of fatherhood have taken him away from Colts games. He misses it. But the home crowd has come a long way. Today's stands are a sea of blue.

"Everybody is wearing the same uniform," Millikan said. "They're wearing the same battle gear."

While authentic jerseys are expensive, outlets offer a wide variety of inexpensive replicas. To be a true blue Colts fan, one must own at least one jersey. That's when a fan truly testifies, "I'm committed."

"I have one closet full of nothing but Colts jerseys," said Blue Crew member Nathan Tilse, 53, of Clayton, Indiana. "Everybody should get a Colts jersey."

Some are autographed. Another is truly special a personalized jersey with his father's No. 36 and a "Tilse" nameplate. Fans scratch their heads trying to remember a Colts player named Tilse. His dad, Charlie, was a high school football star back in the day and actually tried out for the Baltimore Colts before deciding to return to Wauseon, Ohio, to run a landscaping business. Charlie died in 1988.

"I made it my own jersey," Nathan said. "I honor my father with it."

Now if he could just get his wife, Angie, on board with the jersey idea. "Angie is not about individualism," he said. She prefers a Colts T-shirt. But maybe some day.

Nathan offers advice to fans thinking about buying that first blue Colts jersey. "You know how the jerseys go," Nathan said. "Some are knockoffs, and after a while the names and numbers start to come off or fade. If you want a jersey, spend the money on a good one."

Some fans are adamant about jersey rules, that it's unacceptable to wear the jersey of a past player. "You don't wear 'em after they're gone," said SuEllyn Stevens, 27, of Westfield, Indiana. She retired her No. 18 for Peyton Manning, No. 88 of Marvin Harrison, and No. 4 of Jim Harbaugh. Her latest purchase is a No. 12 Andrew Luck.

"It was a good investment. He's going to be around for a while," Stevens said.

She took the back of her hand and smacked the other to emphasize, "You have to stay current on the jersey!"

Then don't just look the part at games. Scream your heart out.

"Free" 'n' "Rob"

The ocean breeze and beach view in Fort Lauderdale, Florida, created quite the cozy backdrop for a rare interview with Indianapolis Colts defensive line coach John Teerlinck the Thursday before Super Bowl XLIV in 2010.

While the team talked to reporters inside a hotel ballroom, the big guy who inspired his pass rushers to get after quarterbacks sat alone on a patio chair outside. His explanation for what mattered most when coaching pass rushers was simple, but he spelled it out uniquely: ack.

"It's dollar sign, a-c-k, and dollar sign," Teerlinck said. "Somebody is going to get paid. It might as well be us."

Dwight Freeney and Robert Mathis have made their share of money hounding quarterbacks. Freeney, who the Colts announced they would not re-sign in the 2013 off-season, departed with a franchise-record 107½ sacks. Mathis, his Pro Bowl partner, has 91½ sacks with two more years on his contract, which could mean breaking Freeney's record.

It's one thing for an opponent to be mindful of a special player. Colts foes had to game plan for both of them. In Freeney's prime, he drew triple teams. That helped Mathis, who proved over the years he could handle double-team blocks and still arrive at the desired destination.

Colts middle linebacker and defensive captain Gary Brackett said the scheme always started with those edge rushers, especially in key game situations.

"We know on third down, between him and Robert Mathis, we only have to cover for so long," Brackett said. "Cover for five seconds, then run to the ball."

Speed rushers come and go in the NFL. Freeney and Mathis have displayed strength and perfected moves to go with amazingly quick feet. Freeney's spin move was so fast and unexpected, offensive tackles lost their balance. Teammates tried to perfect the spin move in practice, too.

"I always watched them, both of them, when they came in as young players," said Colts all-time leading rusher Edgerrin James. "I watched Robert turn into a consistent Pro Bowler and Freeney go out and do his thing.

"The thing that always amazed me with Freeney is he was the worst practice player ever, then he would go out there and ball like

Getting "Crunked"

The in-game 2000 party didn't last long, but during timeouts when an Eminem song reverberated around the RCA Dome with a video shown of Indianapolis Colts players getting jacked up, it was time to "get crunked."

Nobody on defense seemed to get more enthused than defensive end Robert Mathis, who jumped around as if he couldn't control himself. Other players swayed in unison to the music even before the kickoff team ran down the field. Fans eventually wore "Get Crunked" T-shirts.

The idea originated when a player suggested in an interview the team needed to get "crunked up" on the field, said Ray Compton, former Colts vice president of sales and marketing.

Problem is, "crunked" is a euphemism for getting crazed or messed up on marijuana or alcohol. The term came from Memphis music in the late 1990s. The Colts even snuck in the Bob Dylan song, "Rainy Day Women," with the lyric, "everybody must get stoned," before the NFL intervened and decided the short-lived pep rally was a no-no.

it was nothing. I was with him two weeks ago, and that subject came up. I said, 'I've never seen somebody around a golf cart that much in practice and then go out and ball.' I always joked with him that I didn't know what he was doing."

The golf cart was Teerlinck's.

"I call it 'the office,'" the coach said during that pre–Super Bowl interview. "Freeney gravitates more to it than anybody else. What do they say? Membership has its privileges. You'll all be treated fairly, but not equal."

James got a kick out of rooming with a young Freeney for road games.

"I would keep him up at night and frustrated, and it didn't matter. He still would ball," the running back said. "Oh man, I had the phone going, I would have everything going. I just liked to get under Freeney's skin. He used to put his pillow over his head. He would come in with his headphones on and go to sleep with his headphones on. I would turn the lights on. I did everything. I just liked messing with Freeney."

Teammates always said it was as if Freeney was sleeping when in the huddle. He rarely uttered a word. He just set an example. A first-round pick with the 11th overall selection in 2002, Freeney heard so-called experts suggest the pass rusher went too high. That would be motivation throughout this career.

"Just give me some more ammunition," he often said.

Freeney had a career-high 16 sacks in 2004 and seven double-digit sack seasons.

Mathis came to the Colts as a fifth-round pick out of Alabama A&M in 2003. He immediately made an impact, flying around on special teams. Described as undersized at 6'2" and 245—and it was always difficult keeping his weight from dropping into the 230s during the season—Mathis had 10½ sacks in his second season. He's hit his career-high of 11½ sacks twice, in 2005 and 2008.

Freeney has the more flamboyant personality. Mathis typically keeps his conversations short but sweet. They have two different styles, but Mathis can make succinct work for him.

After registering a key sack in a rare defensive win in 2007, Mathis said, "You're just trying to get to 'em, any way possible, it don't even matter what time, just trying to get to 'em."

Yeah, they never forget the job description starts with ack.

Freeney has earned seven Pro Bowl honors, Mathis four.

"I almost feel naked out there without him," Mathis said of Freeney after the 2012 season opener, in which Freeney took a cheap shot to the back of the leg and was sidelined after eight plays.

Mathis still had two sacks in the game. But after the Colts lost 41–21 at Chicago, he showed his leadership qualities with a stern assessment.

"We've got to get hot, stay hot, keep it hot, point blank period," he said. "We're not going to make excuses. We've got to go to work and be men about it."

Longtime beat writer Phil Richards of *The Indianapolis Star* considers Mathis among his favorite players.

"Why, if I were a Colts fan with season tickets, would I buy jersey No. 98 to wear to games?" Richards said. "Because Robert Mathis is who and what he is.

"He's the runt of a family abandoned by his father and the last of six. He was the 195-lb. guard no one recruited. No one. Not a single letter. Alabama A&M gave him its final scholarship. Someone had to get it. The Colts took him in the fifth round of the 2003 draft. They thought they were getting a special teams player. That was 10 years, 91½ sacks, and five Pro Bowls ago. Mathis became a lethal pass rusher by making himself a lethal pass rusher. He worked. He outworked everyone. His teammates' recognition of that fact is implicit in Mathis' team captaincy. No Colt commands greater respect."

Richards mentions how Mathis declined to play in the 2012 Pro Bowl. "He stayed home to be with his infant twins, Robert Nathan and Nathan Robert," the writer said. "Yep, No. 98 is a great dad, too."

Colts radio voice Bob Lamey always marveled at how Freeney and Mathis complemented each other. "Unbelievable. I mean, what they did individually, how they did it, games changed because of what they did," Lamey said. "Freeney had incredible speed. Robert had incredible strength. Those two guys are going to be synonymous in Colts history with the word 'sack.'"

Lamey sounds like a proud grandfather when he commends Mathis for going back to college to get his degree. "Just to see him mature as a man with two sons and everything else," Lamey said, "I couldn't be prouder of any Colt we've ever had than Robert."

Before his final season with the Colts, Freeney acknowledged the obvious in preseason that it was a contract year. "If this is it, you want to cherish every moment you still have in this building and in this city," Freeney said.

By late December, he was even more astute.

"I've had a great run if this is it," he said.

36 What Happened in '59?

After finally reaching the pinnacle of their profession, the Baltimore Colts did it again in 1959. Nobody uttered the word "repeat." Because of what happened the year before, with the magnitude of "The Greatest Game Ever Played," the second time around hasn't been recounted with much detail.

"The '58 game was so off the board," said Colts Hall of Fame wide receiver Raymond Berry. "It had so many facets that you never would have put together at one time."

Berry admits he doesn't think much about the next year. Neither does Colts Hall of Fame halfback/flanker Lenny Moore. "Do you know what? This is true. Nobody talks about '59. In fact, I haven't even thought about '59," Moore said. "It was almost like '59 didn't exist."

Johnny Unitas threw Moore a 60-yard touchdown pass in the first quarter.

"I don't know. I have no idea," Moore said, laughing. "You know better than me."

The Colts were 9–3, just like the year before. The New York Giants (10–2) awaited in the NFL Championship Game, just like in 1958. This time, the title game was played at Baltimore's Memorial Stadium.

The Giants' Pat Summerall kicked field goals in each of the first three quarters to provide the visitors a 9–7 lead.

"The game was close for a good part of it," Berry said.

"We were down 9–7?" Moore asked.

In the final quarter, the Colts took apart the Giants' No. 1-ranked defense with 24 fourth-quarter points for a 31–16 conquest.

"Well, I'll be," Moore said, his memory still not kicking in details.

Unitas started it with a four-yard TD run, then threw a 12-yard scoring pass to Jerry Richardson. It was a highlight in Richardson's brief two-year playing career. (Richardson eventually founded the Carolina Panthers in 1993.) Defensive back Johnny Sample returned an interception 42 yards for another touchdown to make it 28–9.

"That really put it away," Berry recalled.

"I remember that," Moore said.

It wasn't until after a Colts field goal that the Giants scored their only touchdown. The game was well in hand. Unitas finished 18-of-29 passing for 264 yards and two scores. He was MVP for a second consecutive year.

That was the year Unitas won the first of three league MVP awards. He threw a record 32 touchdown passes. Nobody had topped 30 before, and nobody ever did in the 12-game regular season era. Unitas didn't even come close, his next-highest total was 25 TD passes in 1960.

Years later, *The Baltimore Sun* proclaimed the '59 finale, "The Game That Time Forgot."

"It's kind of a funny thing," Berry said.

"I don't remember," Moore said, still laughing.

37 Jeff Saturday, Epitome of Class

The culmination of a 2011 training camp practice at Anderson University provided an opportunity to give Indianapolis Colts center Jeff Saturday a golf-cart ride from the practice field to the locker room.

Chris Williams, AU's director of communications/community relations, did the driving. Approaching the Kardatzke Wellness Center, a half dozen fans saw Saturday and came running. Saturday spotted them, too, and asked Williams to "Pull over here." Autographs all around from the fan favorite.

"The people then came out of the woodwork," Williams said. "Like a dozen more came over, and he signed for every one of them."

Afterward, the inquisitive university administrator reminded Saturday that he didn't have to stop. Saturday enlightened him.

"The fans are everything," Saturday said.

Williams was impressed.

"That endeared Jeff to me," he said.

Saturday's rise to greatness explains how he stayed humble. The undrafted, undersized center out of North Carolina signed with Baltimore but was cut 46 days later in 1998. That sent him back to Raleigh to work in an electrical supply store.

A year later, he received a tryout with the Colts and made the team. He would start later that season—at left guard. The next year, Saturday became entrenched at center. He didn't miss a start for 85 consecutive games until 2004. He was selected for six Pro Bowls, five with the Colts, and started 188-of-197 games while with Indianapolis. His O-line was continually among the best in fewest sacks allowed—quarterback Peyton Manning took just 10 in 2009.

Former Colts tight end Ken Dilger said of Saturday, "He just worked his butt off to become a great center." And Saturday possessed one other special ability. "He knew how to give it back to Peyton Manning when Peyton was wrong, which wasn't often," Dilger said.

Manning and Saturday set an NFL record for most starts by a quarterback-center combination with 170.

When asked once at training camp about Manning, the NFL's only four-time MVP, having his hands on the center's butt all those years, Saturday joked, "There's nothing magical about those golden hands."

Popular radio host Bob Kevoian of *The Bob & Tom Show* marveled at how Saturday handled himself behind a microphone.

"Jeff was a real special guest," Kevoian said. "He just knew exactly what to say and how to say it."

Saturday and New England owner Robert Kraft were credited as key influences in resolving NFL and NFLPA differences for a new collective bargaining agreement that saved the 2011 season. A picture of Saturday hugging Kraft, whose dying wife had encouraged him to get the dispute resolved, was dubbed, "The hug felt around the league." It was a most unexpected visual, considering the bitter Colts-Patriots rivalry.

"His wife, Myra, who was sick the entire time, with him having to balance and juggle his time going back and forth, and she would push him to come to the meetings," Saturday said. "I have a ton of respect for what she did, even in her weakest moment, and for what he did and the sacrifice he made—I really do have a lot of respect for that situation and that family and how they handle their business. I think each and every one of us understood what he was going through, and I can't imagine it. I wouldn't wish that on anybody."

Myra Kraft died from cancer one day before the owners voted to ratify the labor deal.

Peyton Manning walks off the field with center Jeff Saturday (63) during the first half of the game against the Bills in Orchard Park, New York, on January 3, 2010. (AP Photo/ David Duprey, File)

Teammates started calling him "Governor Saturday" after the 4½-month lockout's resolution.

"We used to get on him and talk about political aspirations," said offensive guard Ryan Lilja, an expert at good-natured needling. "My hope is Jeff can springboard from his NFL career and his player representative career and succeed Mitch [Daniels] as [Indiana] governor."

"Jeff is somebody everybody should admire and follow," said former Colts strength and conditioning coach Jon Torine.

Colts radio voice Bob Lamey doesn't hesitate when asked what comes to mind about No. 63. "Class. Class. Class," he said. "He was and is one of the nicest guys I've ever met. He never backed away, if we got our butts kicked or won a game, he was always a stand-up guy. And what he did for the league in the strike [talks], it has to go down as one of the best jobs a player has ever done in those circumstances. When you've got the owners backing him as well as the players, you've done something right."

After a final season in Green Bay in 2012, the 37-year-old Saturday came home to sign a one-day contract and retire as a Colt on March 7, 2013. He graciously thanked everyone in a 20-minute press conference: owner Jim Irsay, management, coaches, trainers and equipment staff, players, his family—wife Karen and children Jeffrey, Savannah, and Joshua sat behind him—as well as fans.

Before the guest of honor took to the lectern, Irsay gushed. He mentioned his favorite play, when Saturday recovered a fumble for a touchdown in the AFC Championship Game victory over Kraft's Patriots in January 2007. That score cost Kevoian and Tom Griswold a bet. They thought they were safe in wagering Saturday would never score. Instead, the dynamic radio duo coughed up $10,000 to charity.

"Here's a man who came into the league, no one thought he was going to do much," Irsay said. "[He] wasn't a first-round draft pick and it's an individual who literally took this town and this state over with his integrity, with his love for the community, with this performance on the field, just an absolutely incredible individual. Going through the lockout, how he played a huge role in getting that settled, it was just absolutely incredible how Jeff has made his mark in this league and for the franchise."

Irsay announced Saturday would one day be in the Colts' Ring of Honor, a given, and that the center had accepted a front-office position in community relations, an obvious transition to franchise ambassador.

Personality Hall of Famers

Here are a few of the Indianapolis Colts' all-time good guys, never to be forgotten for their approachable demeanors with fans and media.

1. Running back **Edgerrin James**—Nobody enjoyed life more than Edge. It was if each day was his opportunity to remind everyone around him to have a good time. Interviews were always unfiltered, and the man's infectious smile left everyone else grinning after time well spent.

2. Tight end **Marcus Pollard**—His self-effacing nature and warm smile made you think he was just a normal guy, not a former basketball player who didn't play football in college but was able to convert his talents to the NFL. Pollard, at times, could rival Edge on the laugh-meter.

3. Defensive tackle **Tony Siragusa**—"Goose" was a classic when the Colts didn't have many outgoing players. The 340-lb. life of the party always kept his teammates loose and could drive equipment manager Jon Scott "crazy." If a rookie failed to bring donuts to work when it was his turn, that player found all of his locker items dumped in the team's hot tub. Scott would see the items floating around and shake his head. Siragusa strikes again.

4. Punter **Pat McAfee**—He developed a cult following long before an ill-advised morning swim in the Broad Ripple canal after a night of partying. His legion of admirers continues to grow from his opinionated tweets on Twitter. When fans meet players at public his functions, it's nothing short of amazing that they come away buzzing about the fun they had with the punter.

5. Center **Jeff Saturday**—The leader of the O-line, Saturday interacted with everyone the same—he was humble, appreciative of the conversation, and considerate. His tremendous heart was revealed again when, after two-time Indianapolis 500 winner Dan Wheldon was killed in a racing crash in 2011, Saturday stopped and asked a reporter, "Did he have family?" When told that Wheldon was married with two sons, a saddened Saturday expressed his sympathy for the family and for a man he had never met.

"Back in blue," Saturday opened, as if they were words he couldn't wait to say.

"I'm excited to retire as a Colt. I mean, this is my home. This is what we've supported for so many years. I was known, no matter what team I was playing for, as a Colt. So it's good to put that horseshoe on and go out that way.

"The community here, you're my wife and I's heart. That's the reason we're back in Indianapolis, we love living here. We love being a part of it."

He listed his own personal Colts Hall of Fame, the guys he had played with the most over the years: Marvin Harrison, Tarik Glenn, Manning, Hunter Smith, Reggie Wayne, Justin Snow, Ryan Diem, Dwight Freeney, Raheem Brock, Dallas Clark, Robert Mathis, Bob Sanders, Lilja, and Jim Sorgi.

Saturday said the record he shared with Manning is his favorite.

"It's a combination of how many things we had to go through, how many things we had to stay healthy and battle through injuries to keep going. It is a tremendous honor to hold that distinction with him of the greatest or the longest tenure of a quarterback-center," he said. "So very special."

38 The White House

A Super Bowl XLI victory meant the traditional trip to the White House in Washington, D.C. The Indianapolis Colts met President George W. Bush on April 23, 2007.

"That was special to me," said the Colts' Tony Dungy, the first black head coach to win a Super Bowl. "You obviously know that's always a part of it. I was definitely looking forward to that. It became more special to me. My dad, Wilbur, who I thought a lot about, his first teaching job was in Alexandria, Virginia, in 1951. He had come out of the war and gone back to school and got his teaching certificate, and he taught high school.

"Even though he had fought in World War II, it was still segregated schools, so he had to teach at an all-black high school. We got off the plane and got on the bus, and I'm in the first seat on the bus and we're riding to the White House, and we're riding through Alexandria. I thought, *Man, this is unbelievable. My dad a generation ago couldn't even teach at a white school, and now here I am leading a team to the White House to see the president.* Man, it was emotional for me."

He remembered his father's wisdom, about how anger and bitterness wouldn't have accomplished anything. How could his father make the situation better? He did his part by instilling knowledge in students so they would know as much as their counterparts at white schools.

"I thought about that," Dungy said. "His generation really did. They made it better. And now here's his son going to the White House, and what am I doing to make it one step better for the next generation? In my own little way, I think I did.

"I felt like I was representing a lot of other guys. I thought about what my dad had said. I couldn't do a lot to change things. I couldn't do anything to help the guys who should have got a chance before that. But if I did what I could do and we won, it would help other people get that opportunity later on."

Colts director of media content Craig Kelley wrote a President's Day blog on Colts.com in February to commemorate the White House visit. The team arrived at 1:00 PM on "a beautiful day" and toured the building prior to a South Lawn ceremony.

"Joseph Addai chided Peyton Manning that he had been there before," Kelley wrote. "Addai had been part of the LSU football contingent that visited after winning the 2003 national championship. Manning kept asking Joe to knock it off since it was his first time visiting on such an occasion. I think Joe enjoyed applying the needle."

The team presented the president from Texas with a Colts jersey and a special wooden Stetson with a horseshoe on the front. Afterward, a Colts contingent of Dungy, Manning, Dwight Freeney, Jeff Saturday, Gary Brackett, Adam Vinatieri, president Bill Polian, and Kelley were walking past the Rose Garden to speak with reporters when they heard a whistle. President Bush was standing in the doorway of the Oval Office and Kelley recalled him say, "Hey, where are you boys going?" The reporters could wait.

"Having home turf advantage to the extreme, President Bush spent 25 minutes telling us stories about the room and moments related to him and the other presidents," Kelley wrote. "He talked about the artwork, how each president chooses the color scheme, and he spent time explaining decorations that adorned his office. He spoke about his desk, which went back through many presidencies."

A photographer took their picture. They took turns shaking hands with their generous host.

"The President was great," Dungy said. "He talked about how he enjoyed the way our team played and the way we carried ourselves. He was getting a lot of criticism at the time. We kind of talked about that, how you have to do what you do, stick to your guns, and fight your way through things even through disappointments. It was a pretty special time."

39 Manning vs. Vanderjagt

The quarterback's words still stick to the kicker. Ask any Indianapolis Colts fan about Mike Vanderjagt.

"Idiot kicker." "Liquored up."

That's how Vanderjagt is remembered, for the agitated words uttered by quarterback Peyton Manning, and it's unfair. Well, at the very least, the second statement was false. Vanderjagt always insisted he was sober when, after a 41–0 road playoff loss to the New York Jets, he went on a Toronto, Canada, television show on January 29, 2003, and questioned the intensity of Manning and head coach Tony Dungy.

"Some guys have it," Vanderjagt said of Manning, "and some guys don't.

"All week before the Jets game, I'm like, '[No.] 18, we're going to handle it, me and you, we're going to win this game.' And he's like, 'Yeah, yeah, okay.' And I'm like, 'Peyton, show some enthusiasm, you're the quarterback and we need to win this game.' I just don't see it from him."

The kicker also offered an ominous perspective on the team's future. "I'm not a real big Colts fan right now, unfortunately," Vanderjagt said. "I just don't see us getting better.

"Coach Dungy, he's just a mild-mannered guy. He doesn't get too excited, he doesn't get too down, and I don't think that works, either.... I think you need a motivator, I think you need a guy who is going to get in somebody's face when they're not performing well enough."

Vanderjagt apologized, but four days later Manning fired back in a sideline interview at Hawaii's Pro Bowl.

"Here we are, I'm out at my third Pro Bowl, I'm about to go in and throw a touchdown to Jerry Rice, we're honoring the Hall of Fame, and we're talking about our idiot kicker who got liquored up and ran his mouth off," Manning told ABC-TV's Lynn Swann. "What has the sports world come to? We are talking about idiot kickers. He has ruined kickers for life. Sad thing is, he's a good kicker. He's a good kicker. But he's an idiot."

The public ate it up.

"I was watching the Pro Bowl, which tells you I need to get a life," said *The Indianapolis Star* columnist Bob Kravitz. "I heard Peyton say that, and I nearly fell out of my chair."

Vanderjagt was always known as the cocky and candid kicker from Canada who usually backed it up on the field.

"He was always honest," Kravitz said. "He was a little too honest for the organization."

Some were convinced Vanderjagt had a point. The Colts won an NFL-record 115 regular season games from 2000 to 2009, the most in a decade, but celebrated only one Super Bowl victory.

"They should have won more Super Bowls," Kravitz said.

Vanderjagt took offense to Manning's reaction, especially the "liquored up" allegation. Eight years later in an interview with Yahoo!Sports The PostGame, Vanderjagt divulged he had a three-page legal document in his Ontario, Canada, home signed by Manning, that testified "liquored up" was not truthful.

"People need to know," he told the reporter, making eye contact and keeping it, "first and foremost, I don't drink. I was 198 percent sober the night I went on TV."

After the controversy had lasted 10 days, Manning and Vanderjagt apologized to each other in a series of phone calls.

"Mike and I have settled this, and we both want to move on," Manning told *The Star* while vacationing in Hawaii. "We both know we screwed up."

Vanderjagt said he and Manning "talked as friends, both of us with our tails between our legs, I guess. We both said things we shouldn't have said and certainly in the forum we shouldn't have said them in. The minute we get on the phone, we had nothing bad to say about the other. We realized the last week and a half of both our lives has sucked."

In what was to be expected, Vanderjagt said Colts president Bill Polian "ripped me a new one...and rightly so."

Vanderjagt left the Colts as a free agent after 2005 and was out of the NFL less than a season later. He should be remembered as one of the league's best kickers—his career 86.5 percent success rate on field goals still ranks No. 1 for players with more than two seasons of experience.

But nobody talks about that.

Two years ago, Vanderjagt was a part-time resident of Marco Island, Florida, when he told naplesnews.com, "It happened between him and me. It was like two brothers having an argument, but it became a national argument."

40 Bill Tobin vs. Mel Kiper Jr.

Who in the hell is Mel Kiper Jr.?

Bill Tobin ensured the NFL nation wouldn't forget when the Indianapolis Colts' director of football operations angrily questioned the analyst's credentials on April 24, 1994.

Nineteen years later, Kiper is grateful. "There's no question it was huge," said Kiper, now 52. "I owe a lot to Bill Tobin."

Asked if he put Kiper on the map, Tobin said with a chuckle, "Well, I kind of did, looking back on the whole situation."

Kiper, who has written an NFL draft report for 35 years and been an ESPN draft analyst since 1984, became a household name after Tobin took him to task on the first day of the 1994 draft. The Colts had selected running back Marshall Faulk with the second overall pick but surprised Kiper by using the fifth overall choice on linebacker Trev Alberts. Tobin didn't concern himself with choosing a quarterback because he had signed free-agent Jim Harbaugh, originally a Tobin first-round pick in Chicago.

"I think it's a typical Colts move," Kiper said of the Alberts pick. "To pass up on [quarterback] Trent Dilfer when all you have is Jim Harbaugh, give me a break. That's why the Colts are picking second every year in the draft, not battling for the Super Bowl like other clubs in the National Football League."

When Tobin entered the Colts' locker room to address the media, he started off by saying, "What do you want to talk about first? Our players or that jerk in Baltimore?"

Tobin's most memorable sound bite is still getting Internet video clicks.

"Who in the hell is Mel Kiper, anyway?" he said. "I mean, here's a guy who criticizes everybody, whoever they take. In my knowledge of him, he's never even put on a jockstrap, he's never been a player, he's never been a coach, he's never been a scout, he's never even been an administrator, and all of a sudden, he's an expert. Mel Kiper has no more credentials to do what he's doing than my neighbor, and my neighbor's a postman and he doesn't even have season tickets to the NFL."

Tobin had earned NFL distinction as a general manager in Chicago before he was hired in Indianapolis in 1994. He understood the Colts' national perception.

"Indianapolis had moved there 10 years earlier, and Jim [Irsay] had been the general manager," Tobin said. "They hadn't really done anything. They were still on first base. They hadn't accomplished much. They were kind of the doormat of the national media, making fun of who the Colts selected. I'm not saying they were a joke, but they were made fun of because of their decision-making.

"I had a lot of confidence in what I was doing and what my intentions were in Indianapolis. I wanted to change the attitude there. I stood up and said, 'No more. We know what we're doing, and there's a new sheriff in town.'"

Kiper was unaware of Tobin's rant. An ESPN producer advised they were coming back to the analyst for a reaction.

"Respond to what?" Kiper asked.

"He's ripping you," the producer said.

"I didn't know anything else, what he said or anything," Kiper said. "The draft kept going, and the last thing I'm thinking about is what Bill Tobin is thinking in Indianapolis."

Kiper fired off another zinger when asked about Tobin's criticism.

"I have a right to my opinion, and he has a right to his," Kiper said. "You can't go for Jim Harbaugh and pass up Trent Dilfer. Forget it. That's why the Colts are the laughingstock in the league year in and year out."

Tobin said other NFL executives, including Pittsburgh's Tom Donohoe, phoned to congratulate him on calling out Kiper. "What I said there, probably 300 personnel people in the league would have liked to have said it," Tobin said.

As it turned out, Harbaugh played his finest football for the Colts. He had a career- and league-best 100.7 passer rating in 1995 and took the team to the AFC Championship Game. Harbaugh received AFC and Comeback Player of the Year honors, a Pro Bowl selection, and is in the Colts' Ring of Honor.

"My instincts were much better than his," Tobin said of Kiper.

Dilfer played 13 seasons for five teams and won a Super Bowl ring with Baltimore but largely because the Ravens set league records for defense. Dilfer made one Pro Bowl but didn't turn out to be a franchise quarterback. Alberts didn't pan out as injuries reduced his disappointing career to just three seasons.

"I had zero issue with Bill Tobin saying what he did," Kiper said. "In fact, I'd defend him. He has a right to defend his pick. I can understand him taking exception to what I said."

But the analyst had already learned this much about broadcasting, "You have to have a strong opinion. If you don't, you shouldn't be on TV."

Kiper still hears Tobin's voice every week. The intro to his Saturday morning ESPN Radio show *Dari and Mel* with Dari Nowkhah includes some of Tobin's rant.

"We laugh every time," Kiper said. "Was it a great thing for me? Absolutely. People still talk about it with me to this day. I think most fans look back at it as a one-for-the-books moment at the draft. It's probably the most memorable moment in ESPN's NFL Draft day history."

41 NFL Old School vs. Hollywood Funny Man

A 41–6 embarrassment at Miami on *Monday Night Football* extended a slide to five games before the Indianapolis Colts' lost 2001 took a nasty turn for the worse on a radio show.

The Colts had several injury issues, including two-time NFL rushing champion Edgerrin James who hurt his left knee at Kansas City in what was reported as a sprain. James practiced on the sore knee on November 2. The next day, it was swollen and stiff. On November 21 the team announced James had torn his anterior cruciate ligament and was placed on injured reserve.

Fast forward to December 12, when Colts president Bill Polian agreed to appear on *Mark Patrick on Sports*, a daily Indianapolis afternoon radio show on WNDE 1260 AM. Patrick also lined up

Jay Mohr, a former stand-up comic who appeared part-time for two years on *Saturday Night Live* then dabbled in acting, most notably his portrayal of rival sports agent Bob Sugar opposite Tom Cruise in the 1996 movie *Jerry Maguire*. By 2001, Mohr had added Fox Sports analyst to his list of titles.

They didn't play nice, to say the least, talking over each other so often that portions were inaudible. Here are transcript excerpts from 17 minutes of radio that would not soon be forgotten.

Mark Patrick: "Jay, did you just hear the…(interrupted)"

Jay Mohr: "Yeah, I did. And I'd like to preface everything by saying this isn't a good story for anybody. And certainly, my message to Mr. Polian would be don't shoot the messenger. I don't make the news. And as far as Mr. Polian saying there's not a shred of truth to it, there is a lot of shred of truth. There is a lot of truth to it. On October 25, Edgerrin James tore his ACL. Fact."

Bill Polian: "I know all of that. I've heard you recite that. I want you to respond to the following statement, please…(interrupted)"

JM: "Well, it gets really dull when you keep interrupting…(interrupted)"

BP: "I'm not interested in your programming here (talking over Mohr). I'm interested in the truth."

JM: "Yeah, I am, too."

BP: "I want you to respond to the statement, No. 1, that Drew Rosenhaus is Edgerrin James' agent."

JM: "That was false. That was false. That was absolutely false."

BP: "You told a lie. That was a falsehood, am I correct?"

JM: "That was a falsehood, correct. Drew Rosenhaus does not represent Edgerrin James and I think that…(interrupted)"

BP: "Am I correct in that assumption?"

JM: "I've already answered you, Mr. Polian. And that's pretty much…(interrupted)"

BP: "No, you have not answered me. I'm…(interrupted)"

JM: "No, I said yes, that's untrue, and that's pretty much the only concession you're going to get out of me because I'm going to stand by the rest of my story. I don't make the news."

BP: "Let me ask you this then. Where is your evidence? Please produce it. X-rays, MRI reports, doctors' reports, ah, 'They made him practice, put him in a state of denial, the Colts, tore two more ligaments in his knee while practicing with a classic torn ACL.' Please produce the evidence for that."

JM: "Mr. Polian, did Edgerrin James tear his ACL?"

BP: "Please produce the evidence for the statement as follows. And I presume you're going to have to do this somewhere down the line for the lawyers."

Mohr continued to ask if he could speak.

JM: "Maybe we should do this separately if it's not going to be an open conversation."

MP: "All right, Mr. Polian, please."

BP: "I'm not interested in having a conversation with you, sir. I'm interested…(interrupted)"

JM: "Apparently not, because I haven't said anything, Mr. Polian."

BP: "I have no interest in having a conversation with you!"

JM: "Then why are we on the radio right now? Why are you so angry if you're not interested in having a…(interrupted)"

Mohr tells Polian to hang up if he doesn't want to have a conversation. Mohr decides to ignore the interruptions.

JM: "I'm going to keep talking and hopefully there's a cough button.…The Associated Press reported on November 18 that Dr. [John] Uribe gave the diagnosis. According to *The Indianapolis Star*, your home newspaper that covers your team, that he had a classic torn ACL. And on November 18, three weeks after October 25, quote, 'The Colts have refused to address that diagnosis' end quote."

BP: "Who?"

JM: "Excuse me, I haven't made my point yet. That, sir... (interrupted)...please."

BP: "Who's that from?"

JM: "*The Indianapolis Star*."

BP: "You are, you are accusing us of gross negligence. You are accusing...(interrupted)"

JM: "I *am* accusing you of gross negligence. That's absolutely ... (interrupted)"

BP: "... 'tore two more ligaments in Indy while practicing with a classic torn ACL.' But, you're accusing us of gross negligence... (interrupted)"

JM: "Yes I am."

BP: "... based on a report from a *newspaper reporter*?"

Mohr continues to ask for a chance to speak without interruption.

JM: "You are a madman. This is nuts."

BP: "People's reputations are at stake here."

JM: "Yeah, and your reputation should be very soured on the fact that you let a guy practice with a torn ACL."

BP: "Uh, sir, I'm very happy to deal with that when you deal... (interrupted)"

JM: "Whoa, whoa, whoa. You're happy to deal with what? You're happy to deal with what? You're happy to deal with what? The fact that you let Edgerrin James practice with a torn ACL for three weeks?"

BP: "You have not made.... You lied about Drew Rosenhaus. You will not answer me so I'm going to take it that you're lying. (interrupted, inaudible)"

JM: "You're crazy. You're insane. No wonder the Colts are doing so poorly. You are an absolute madman. And everyone listening to the radio knows the general manager of their favorite team is a madman (talking over inaudible Polian)."

Mohr and Polian eventually agree on something—that they're both not getting anywhere with the other.

JM: "Look, we can sing together. We can't talk together. This is going nowhere. You are an absolute madman in the middle of a pre-rehearsed diatribe."

Patrick tries to be a calming influence, but to no avail.

MP: "All right, I'm going to call this a truce right now because…(interrupted)"

BP: "Oh, there is no truce, sir! There is no truce!…(interrupted)"

JM: "Mr. Polian, you are a madman."

The heated exchange finally ends.

BP: "You're the Drudge Report of sports."

JM: "I'm the Drudge Report? Well, you know what? We'll see. I don't think my credibility took a nose dive on this one. I think it was yours, Mr. Polian."

BP: "Well, sir, we can respectfully disagree on that point."

JM: "That we can."

A day later, Colts owner Jim Irsay defended Polian's position but acknowledged to *The Indianapolis Star*, "Bill could have been a little bit more controlled to get his points across because they were very clear. But his emotion is natural because it has been a long season, a tough season. When someone starts talking loosely…says those sorts of things…it's very hurtful."

Polian agreed.

"I was passionately defending the horseshoe, this franchise, the people who work here…," he said. "It's like a family. When someone in your family is unjustly attacked, you respond and you respond passionately. I did. I wish my delivery had been more measured. I might have made a better presentation. Certainly if there were some that were offended by my passion, I'm sorry for that. But I was attempting to make very clear that the allegations that had been made were completely and totally unfounded."

The Colts finished the season 6–10.

42 "Monday Night Miracle"

The calendar is fast approaching the 10-year anniversary of arguably the most unforgettable game in *Monday Night Football* history.

Did you miss the end? Some viewers turned it off, and who could blame them? Many in a sellout crowd of 65,647 had already headed to the exits, convinced of the outcome. The Tampa Bay Buccaneers led the unbeaten Indianapolis Colts 35–14 on October 6, 2003. The clock at Raymond James Stadium indicated there was less than four minutes remaining.

Not the best 48th birthday present for Colts head coach Tony Dungy. Nor was it the homecoming he had envisioned in his first game back in Tampa, Florida, where he had been fired after the 2001 season.

"I remember thinking in the first half, we couldn't play worse if we tried to play worse," Dungy said almost a decade later in a telephone call from his home in Tampa.

The Buccaneers' No. 1 ranked, Tampa-2 defense designed by Dungy, had allowed just 22 points in three previous games. And it padded the lead to 21 on cornerback Ronde Barber's 29-yard interception return for a touchdown with 5:09 remaining.

"When you're down 35–14, yeah, I figured we'd need a miracle," said kicker Mike Vanderjagt.

"You're thinking it's going to be an awful plane trip home," center Jeff Saturday said.

Then an amazing thing happened as many at home went to bed and some hasty Tampa Bay fans drove off with the stadium in their rear-view mirrors. Buccaneers coach Jon Gruden described it as his "worst nightmare."

After Barber's score, rookie Brad Pyatt returned the ensuing kickoff 90 yards to the Buccaneers' 12-yard line. Dungy was thinking about pulling Manning when Pyatt provided the longest return in his short career. On fourth down, James Mungro scored on a three-yard run with 3:37 remaining.

The Colts' Idrees Bashir recovered the onside kick. Manning converted another fourth down on a 28-yard TD pass to Marvin Harrison with 2:29 remaining. When the Colts got the ball back, Manning and Harrison clicked again for a 52-yard pass play to the Bucs' 6. Ricky Williams scored on a one-yard run with 35 seconds remaining to force overtime.

The overtime lasted a while. The Colts drove into field-goal range. Vanderjagt barely missed a 40-yard field goal wide right. The most accurate kicker in NFL history couldn't believe it. But he got a second chance. The Buccaneers' Simeon Rice was called for unsportsmanlike conduct, an obscure transgression known as "leaping," when a player jumps to block a kick and lands on his teammates.

Vanderjagt's second chance would be from 29 yards out—a chip shot yet still dramatic. The kick started right, deflected off the fingers of Bucs defensive end Ellis Wyms at the line, then banked off the inside of the right upright and through with 3:47 remaining to give the Colts a most improbable 38–35 victory.

"I called tip bank," Vanderjagt said.

He later added, "Nobody and their grandmother picks us to win this game."

It was the first time in NFL history a team has ever come back from a 21-point deficit with four minutes remaining to win a game. And it was the Colts' first 21-point, fourth-quarter comeback in franchise history.

In the fourth quarter and overtime, Manning completed 18-of-26 passes for 235 yards with one TD and one interception.

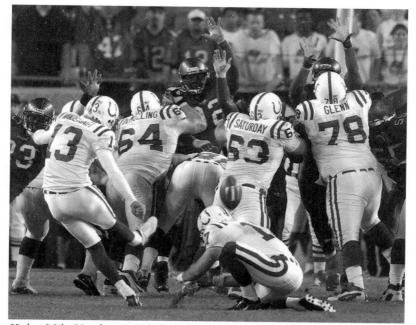

Kicker Mike Vanderjagt (13) kicks the game-winning field goal from the hold by Hunter Smith (17) in overtime to beat the Tampa Bay Buccaneers 38–35 early Tuesday morning on October 7, 2003, in Tampa, Florida.
(AP Photo/Chris O'Meara)

"That damn Peyton Manning," Gruden bemoaned, "he really irritated me today."

"It was very, very special, just the fact that our guys didn't give up," Dungy said. "More than anything, that kind of showed us what we could do and was a precursor to the AFC Championship Game [in January 2007] when were down three scores, that we could come back and win it. It showed me it didn't matter what the score was, that we could still come back and win the game."

Count *MNF* analyst and former Super Bowl–winning coach John Madden among the stunned. "It was totally beyond belief," he said. "I've never seen or taken part in a comeback like that in my life."

It turned out to be quite a Dungy homecoming and a birthday worth remembering.

"I'd have to say that was the most memorable, no question," he said.

43 At Home in the Dome

Mike Fox started as an intern at the new Hoosier Dome in 1984. From a stadium perspective, the timing for Indianapolis landing an NFL team was perfect. The $77.5 million, 19-story-high dome with an inflated roof—81 sections of Teflon-coated fiberglass held together by steel cables—had its grand opening May 3, 1984, about two months after the Colts arrived.

Fox had been a men's basketball student manager at Indiana University, where his responsibilities included being a referee at Hoosiers scrimmages for Coach Bob Knight. So it was with personal interest that the dome's first major event brought Knight and the U.S. Olympic men's basketball team to face a group of NBA All-Stars on July 9, 1984. As it turned out, the dome's first major event drew the largest crowd, 67,596, in the stadium's 24-year history.

"The NBA All-Stars had a very big Hoosier flavor," said Fox, now 51 and Lucas Oil Stadium director. "Larry Bird, Quinn Buckner, Isiah Thomas, Jerry Sichting. Short of one of the playoff games the Colts held toward the end of the life of the dome, I still say when Larry Bird was introduced in that stadium on that night, that was the loudest I ever heard it. It was the place to be."

The dome did more than just alter the city's skyline and become the Colts' home. It hosted five NCAA Final Fours, high school state championships, the 1985 NBA All-Star Game, and the 1987 Pan American Games closing ceremonies.

Fox became stadium director in 1988. Before hosting the first NCAA Final Four at the dome in 1991, he was determined to ensure everything went according to plan. A hotel room was reserved for Fox in the adjoining Convention Center, and he stayed there for 13 days.

"I never went home," he said. "I was young, and I knew this was a very important period for Indianapolis. If it was going to screw up, it wasn't going to screw up because of me and because of effort. I moved in on a Thursday night before the high school state finals and didn't leave until the Tuesday after the NCAA Final Four was done. That was back in the day of courtesy cars. I put just 11 miles on mine."

The Hoosier Dome was renamed the RCA Dome in 1994 when $10 million over the course of a decade made for a lucrative naming rights deal. What visitors might remember about the place was being hit by a gust of air upon entering.

"It was like you were walking into a balloon," Fox said. "That's what it was. A giant balloon. It was very hot technology in the stadium world for about 18 months. That's when we built our stadium. It was Minnesota, Syracuse, and maybe there were a couple others. And then the next technology is what Atlanta has with the Georgia Dome, same type of roof but it wasn't air-inflated."

The dome's capacity of 56,000 and change made it the NFL's smallest stadium, but there wasn't a bad seat. Fans sensed they were on top of the field. Bench seating in the upper deck deviated from the individual seats in today's massive stadiums. When the games weren't sellouts, fans could spread out. When the joint was jumping, few venues could rival the decibel levels. The building would shake. Spectators say they never sensed this moving sensation more than when the Colts rallied to defeat New England 38–34 in the AFC Championship Game on January 21, 2007.

Mike Fox's Favorite Dome Memory

When asked about his favorite Hoosier/RCA Dome memory, it's tough to top when Mike Fox's alma mater, Richmond High School, won the boys state basketball title in 1992.

But earlier that year, there was a more important day.

"I proposed to my wife in there," the stadium director said of making an honest woman of longtime girlfriend Rhonda Schipp. "Right in the middle of the field. It was Valentine's Day. Truth be told, I'm pretty sure she knew it was coming. I had been given several ultimatum dates, and this was just about the last one. We had dated four years. I was running out of time.

"I got some guys on the staff involved. I'm going to get her over here for some reason. I want the lights on, but when I get my radio on and say, 'Now,' turn out the lights and turn on the scoreboard, 'Rhonda, will you marry me?' on the scoreboard, and hit our favorite song, Don Henley's 'Last Worthless Evening.'"

They got hitched that July. The proud parents of two sons still joke about their magical dome moment, when almost everything played out perfectly.

"You've got 60,000 empty seats staring at you, you've got music playing and the scoreboard going," Fox said. "Instead of just saying, 'Yes,' she said, 'Are you going to get down on one knee?' Are you kidding me?

"I did. And I got the right answer."

"It was designed to shake," Fox said. "They all are. Every building. Even the skyscrapers, they're designed that way because of earthquakes and codes. If it was shaking, that was okay. I would notice it most when everybody stood up for the *National Anthem* and sat down because they were all moving at the same time."

What few knew about that title game, and several other times, is the dome roof leaked.

"We patched it all the time," he said. "Any structure that big, I don't care what it is, it has leaks. They all leak in some form or fashion. During the AFC Championship Game, there was a leak right in the middle of the roof. We had snow on the roof, and it was melting. We just kept watching it. It never got to be where anyone noticed. As the guy who runs the place, I noticed more things than most other people."

Fox recalled how accessible the dome was to downtown in that it was connected to the Convention Center and had skywalks to the Circle Centre Mall and hotels.

"You honestly think it's going to last forever," he said. "When we said we were going to build the new one, I'm going, 'Can't we just fix this one up a little bit? Some paint and some new carpet and stuff?' But then you go see the other ones around the league and it's like, 'Okay, I get it now.'

"That period from 1984 to 2008, I'm not a big historian on the city of Indianapolis but I would argue that was the biggest 25 years worth of growth this city has ever had. That building and the people who came into it and the events we were able to attract I think were a big part of that growth. I'm proud of that."

The Colts played their final season at the dome in 2007. The last game was a playoff disappointment as San Diego rallied for a 28–24 AFC Divisional round victory on January 13, 2008. The Colts finished with a 111–88 record, counting the postseason, at the Hoosier/RCA Dome.

As $725 million Lucas Oil Stadium neared the end of construction, it dwarfed the old dome. The city's skyline had changed once again. The dome was deflated September 24, 2008. A quarter century of memories came flooding back as the roof collapsed in about 45 minutes.

"I was okay with it until the actual deflation day," Fox said. "That was a hard day. That was a really hard day. It all kind of hit me. All they did was turn the air off, and it slowly came down."

The physical structure was imploded December 20, 2008. It took 875 explosive charges. The dome came crumbling down in a cloud of smoke in less than 30 seconds.

"When they demolished it, I was sitting up high in Lucas Oil Stadium right up near that North window, and I didn't have any emotion at all that day," Fox said. "You kind of look behind you and say, 'Yeah, this is better.'"

44 End of Unitas Era

The Baltimore Colts' 16–13 Super Bowl V win over Dallas probably meant the most to the guys still on the roster from a Super Bowl III loss to the New York Jets. What nobody knew then was the Colts wouldn't celebrate another Super Bowl championship for 36 years. And that victory came in another city—Indianapolis.

In 1971, a 10–4 season ended with a 21–0 AFC Championship Game loss at Miami. The head coach on the other sideline was former Colts mentor Don Shula. He was building something with the Dolphins, who would lose Super Bowl VI to the Cowboys but return the next two postseasons to celebrate back-to-back Super Bowl titles, including the NFL's only perfect season of 17–0 in 1972.

The Colts were headed in the other direction. The team had a new owner in July 1972 in Robert Irsay, who bought the Los Angeles Rams and swapped them with Carroll Rosenbloom for the Colts. The winds of change were about to blow with the impulsive Irsay in charge and strong-minded Joe Thomas as his general manager.

Despite the fact head coach Don McCafferty had won a Super Bowl as a rookie coach two postseasons before, he was fired after a 1–4 start in '72 and replaced by John Sandusky. Colts players released a joint statement: "Don McCafferty has unjustly been made to bear the burden of our poor performance this year. He has prepared us well, as he has done for 14 years."

McCafferty, who had been with the organization since 1959, coached one year at Detroit, going 6–7–1. Sadly, he suffered a heart attack and died on July 28, 1974, at the age of 53.

His '72 dismissal precipitated sweeping changes for the Colts. It quickly became apparent that Sandusky was expected to carry out his new front office's mandates, regardless of the player. A 39-year-old John Unitas was the first casualty, immediately benched and replaced in the lineup by Marty Domres. Unitas was outraged by the most publicized of many roster-shuffling edicts Thomas demanded of Sandusky, who was fired at season's end anyway.

Unitas vowed he wouldn't play another year for the Colts and demanded a trade to a winning team. He got half his wish. After the 5–9 season ended, the Colts dealt their legendary star to San Diego for a future consideration. The Chargers were 4–9–1 the previous year. The trade date was January 22, 1973. Baltimore fans were numb with shock about their hero. Unitas wasn't the same, and he never panned out wearing the lighting bolts in San Diego. He played in just five games, was benched for rookie Dan Fouts, and retired after a 2–11–1 season.

Life didn't get any better back in Baltimore. Head coach Howard Schnellenberger, a Shula assistant for the '72 Dolphins' perfect season, couldn't reverse the losing trend. The Colts went 4–10 in 1973, then Schnellenberger was ousted after starting the next season with three losses.

On Schnellenberger's website, he said his firing was the result of an argument with Irsay about whether to play Domres or Bert Jones at quarterback. Irsay had insisted Schnellenberger play Jones, but the head coach refused. The website states, "In an interview years later, Schnellenberger said he planned to put

Jones in but changed his mind after Irsay demanded Jones enter the [third] game."

Thomas took over team turmoil, and the Colts floundered to 2–12.

45 Remember George Taliaferro, Too

As the NFL has soared in popularity, several names have become synonymous with the Colts franchise: Manning, Unitas, Marchetti, Harrison, and Irsay, among others.

Most don't remember George Taliaferro, but they should. As the first black player ever drafted by the NFL in 1949, he helped turn the tide of diversity toward what it is today.

"That is the ultimate compliment to a life well-lived," said Taliaferro, now 86 and living with his wife, Viola, in Bloomington, Indiana.

He was one of the Baltimore Colts' best players on those first two teams in 1953 and 1954. That was four years after the Chicago Bears had selected the three-time All-American halfback/quarterback from Indiana University in the 13th round with the 129th overall selection.

Much like Jackie Robinson breaking the Major League Baseball color barrier in 1947, Taliaferro faced racial discrimination in high school, college, and the NFL. The league had banned blacks from 1933 until 1946, when the Los Angeles Rams signed Kenny Washington as a free agent and later added Woody Strode.

Taliaferro commends his wife, as he did Rachel Robinson in helping Jackie, for not letting bitterness overcome him. "Jackie Robinson in my judgment is the only African American who could have integrated sports," he said. "None of the other African American athletes would have put up with the bullshit that Jackie Robinson did."

Character came from the home. Taliaferro was two months old when his family moved from Gates, Tennessee, to Gary, Indiana. His father, Robert, and mother, Virnater, reaffirmed two certainties for as long Taliaferro could remember.

"Mother and I love you, and you must be educated," Taliaferro said, repeating his father's words. Robert and Virnater had fourth- and sixth-grade educations and wanted a better life for their children.

Growing up so close to the Windy City, Taliaferro followed the Bears. "I knew everybody who ever played for them," he said. "As a kid, I bragged to everyone how I was going to be a great football player for the Bears."

An early childhood lesson would eventually prevent him from realizing that dream. He was supposed to dig up some land so his father could plant the spring garden. Taliaferro put it off to go swimming with friends. He didn't return in time to do as he was asked, which coming from Robert meant it wasn't a request but a command. Robert saw the land wasn't dug up, raised his right index finger and said, "A man is no more or no worse than his word."

Taliaferro started digging up the land at 4:30 that afternoon. He finished—with the assistance of a lantern—at 5:00 AM. And he never forgot Robert's words. "My father died before that incident was ever repeated," he said.

Robert wasn't alive when the Bears drafted George in 1949. Taliaferro had signed a contract with the Los Angeles Dons of the All-America Football Conference but could get out of it by paying back $4,000. Virnater reminded him of Robert's words. Taliaferro honored his Dons commitment. He played for the New York Yanks in 1950–51, then the Dallas Texans in 1952. The Texans became the Colts the next year. Taliaferro hated how blacks were treated as "three-fifth humans" in public. His wife had to sit in a specified stadium section.

"I was one angry football player, and I played the very best I could possibly play," he said. "It was the one opportunity I had to beat up white boys and be applauded for it."

That first year in Baltimore was his last of three consecutive Pro Bowl selections. He gave it everything he had, then his body wore out after a final season with Philadelphia in 1955. Hall of Famer George Halas called the next year. Taliaferro had one final chance to fulfill his childhood dream to play for the Bears. But once again, he turned it down.

"George Halas asked me to try out, but I told him I was no longer the football player of yesteryear," he said.

Still, the call was the kindest of compliments at the end of his career.

"Isn't that something? Just incredible," Taliaferro said.

He had a bachelor's degree in health and physical education but was reduced to selling cars and substitute teaching at a Baltimore elementary school for black students. He eventually returned to his college alma mater where he taught for 17 years. His wife is a retired juvenile court judge. They have four daughters, who have given them five grandchildren and one great-grandchild.

"My legacy ought to be that I had the opportunity built on the backs of slaves and I took advantage of it," Taliaferro said. "I wanted everybody to remember I was somebody."

He beams with pride at the sight of that Colts horseshoe helmet.

"Oh, absolutely," he said, "because I know from whence it came and I had a small role."

46 Greatest NFL Turnaround

Peyton Manning's rookie year had proven to be an exercise in humility as the Indianapolis Colts finished 3–13 in 1998. But throughout his celebrated NFL career, the quarterback said playing right away sped up his learning curve. While the team had the same record before his arrival, which made drafting him possible, there was some reason to think the Colts would be better in 1999.

Perhaps not as good as they became, but at least a modest improvement. To the surprise of many, the Colts went 13–3, a 10-win improvement that was the best turnaround in NFL history.

"That was a great team," Coach Jim Mora said. "We got on a run there."

Before the draft, the Colts traded running back Marshall Faulk to St. Louis for two draft picks. That meant the Colts were in the market for a running back, and Colts president Bill Polian struck gold with his fourth-overall selection of Edgerrin James, who as a rookie won the NFL rushing title with 1,553 yards. Other key parts were already in place. Wide receiver Marvin Harrison was one of the game's fastest deep threats, and he caught 115 passes for 1,663 yards and 12 TDs. The Colts had solid tight ends in Ken Dilger and Marcus Pollard. Offensive left tackle Tarik Glenn was entrenched at perhaps the most important position on the line, defending Manning's blind side. Right tackle Adam Meadows and left guard Steve McKinney were solid.

Perhaps the more looming question pertained to the defense, which welcomed pass-rushing defensive end Chad Bratzke via free agency. The former New York Giant had 12 sacks. Outside linebackers Cornelius Bennett and Mike Peterson were the top two tacklers and combined for eight sacks, as well. The defense, which was ranked 17th, allowed the league average 333 points.

The season started off so-so as the Colts dispatched Buffalo 31–14 at home, but blew a 28–7 lead in a 31–28 loss at New England on Adam Vinatieri's 26-yard field goal with 35 seconds remaining. After a 27–19 win at San Diego, the Colts stumbled again in a 34–31 home loss to Miami. The Colts blew a 17–9 lead in the third quarter and lost on Dan Marino's two-yard TD pass to tight end Oronde Gadsden with 27 seconds remaining.

The Colts had every reason to think they should have been 4–0 instead of 2–2. They started making amends for failing to finish. After falling behind 13–0, they rallied for a 16–13 road victory over the New York Jets on a Mike Vanderjagt field goal in the final seconds. It was the start of an unforgettable run. Three consecutive home wins opened eyebrows, particularly a 34–24 triumph over the Dallas Cowboys. Back-to-back road wins over the New York Giants and Philadelphia Eagles stretched the win streak to six games. The Colts, at 8–2, were bona fide AFC Eastern Division contenders. Manning appeared on the November 22 *Sports Illustrated* cover with the headline, "So Good, So Soon."

They kept winning. After a 13–6 defensive victory over the Jets at home, Manning and Marino engaged in another shootout, this time in Miami and with a different result as the Colts prevailed 37–34. Vanderjagt drilled a 53-yard field goal on the final play to decide it. Manning enjoyed his first-ever victory over New England in a 20–15 home win, then the Colts edged Washington 24–21 at the RCA Dome. The victory locked up a home playoff game for the first time in the city's history.

"It's been a fast turnaround," Manning said. "It's definitely come faster than we expected. We knew we'd be a better football team this year, but we didn't know that we'd be this good."

Down 28–19 in the fourth quarter at Cleveland, James ran for a touchdown and Vanderjagt delivered a 21-yard field goal with four seconds remaining for a 29–28 victory that ran the win streak to 11 games and locked up the division title and a first-round playoff bye. The win streak tied a club record first set in 1964 and matched in 1975–76. It was the first time the Colts had won 13 games since the 1968 squad went 13–1 but was upset by the Jets in Super Bowl III.

A 31–6 loss at Buffalo to end the regular season snapped the string, but the Colts had earned the AFC's No. 2 playoff seed. The 2008 Dolphins have since duplicated the Colts' 10-win turnaround record, going 11–5 the year after finishing 1–15.

For a franchise that had celebrated just three postseason appearances since starting anew in Indianapolis 15 years earlier, the 1999 season would be forever mentioned as the year the Colts took another important step. "The Triplets"—Manning, Harrison, and James—were named to the Pro Bowl.

But the thrill ride abruptly ended with a 19–16 AFC Divisional playoff loss to Tennessee at the RCA Dome.

"We would like to remember we won 13 games this year and a division championship," Mora said a day later. "I think that was an outstanding accomplishment by this team and this organization."

47 Startling "Sit-Down" of 2009

It's been three years since the "sit-down." Fans haven't forgotten. Neither have the players.

The day before he retired as an Indianapolis Colt on March 7, 2013, center Jeff Saturday shared his one regret in 14 NFL seasons with *The Indianapolis Star* columnist Bob Kravitz.

Flash back with a shudder to December 27, 2009, when the Colts passed on pursuing perfection. Well, as Saturday reminded, it's not as if the entire organization signed off on the decision. The best bet is president Bill Polian gave the order to sit starters on a 14–0 team, and head coach Jim Caldwell did as he was directed.

"That's the only thing I wish we would have done differently," Saturday said. "I was in favor of [going for perfection], but obviously I got out-voted [by management]. When we pulled everybody and just let it go by the wayside and ended up losing—that was a great opportunity we had. As a player, perfection is the highest goal you can reach. And we were so close."

The timing made it downright infuriating.

"I don't think there's any question it was a Bill Polian decision," Kravitz said on the day Saturday retired. "I think Bill tried to prepare the city, but he didn't prepare the city well enough. He tried to say this might happen. The Cornelius Bennett injury in 1999 really freaked him out. Bennett played in a meaningless game and got hurt and wasn't able to play against the Tennessee Titans in the playoffs that year. His own personal history was part of that decision."

The Colts led the 7–7 New York Jets 15–10 in the third quarter at Lucas Oil Stadium. The Colts had the ball, but quarterback Peyton Manning, center Saturday, and the offensive starters were told to take a seat. Cameras fixed on their faces. They didn't look happy.

Fans were outraged. An unbeaten team, for at least another quarter or so, heard nothing but boos. Colts management played it safe to avoid possible serious injuries that could impact the postseason. Backup quarterback Curtis Painter entered, got drilled from behind, and fumbled. The Jets recovered the bouncing ball for a touchdown, and the rout was on. The Jets won 29–15.

"During a game, that's the most reaction I've ever seen," Kravitz said. "Social media went crazy. Polian thought the media set off the firestorm, but the truth is, he set off the firestorm."

Colts players bit their lips as best they could about how they surrendered an NFL-record regular season win streak of 23 games. It was easy to see in their faces what they wanted to say, and how they were upset by the way an unblemished run ended. They knew what was at stake. They had a chance to join the 17–0 Miami Dolphins of 1972, the only team to finish perfect.

Colts wide receiver Reggie Wayne was asked if he wanted to take that shot. "Who wouldn't?" he said. "I mean…who wouldn't? Doesn't everybody want to be a part of history? Not a season goes by that you don't hear about the '72 Dolphins."

Manning, arguably the most savvy athlete in handling the media, gave the textbook company line. "We are followers of our head coach and the people in the organization who lead us and give us direction," he said. "That's the way we've always done around here. Our job is to take instructions from our superiors and follow those instructions."

It sure seemed as if he left out "like it or not."

Former Colts head coach Tony Dungy, who retired after the previous season and took an analyst job on NBC's *Football Night in America*, offered his support of the sit-down by saying, "You have an obligation to win the Super Bowl, not to go undefeated."

Polian said the timing of the decision rested with Caldwell, although the president had made it clear before and after the sit-down that a perfect season wasn't the objective. "Jim was going to make that call whenever he felt it was appropriate," Polian said afterward.

Asked about the fan backlash, Polian said, "I understand that.… I can."

He would hear more of it the next day on his weekly radio show. No matter. Polian enraged fans even more when he defiantly called 16–0 "inconsequential."

Blue Crew Fan Club president Randy Collins didn't hide his disgust. "Betrayal," Collins said. "You play the game to win. We paid to see a good football game. This is a once-in-a-lifetime thing."

Kravitz tried to connect the dots of logic through his fingers on his laptop computer. But he couldn't. If the team was concerned about playing it safe, why did Manning play the entire game when the Colts were ahead 34–10 at Arizona in the final quarter? Why did Manning finish a rout of Seattle, ahead 31–3 with eight minutes left? And what was the explanation for why Manning didn't come out at Tennessee with a 31–9 lead and five minutes remaining?

"Why don't you protect the franchise then?" Kravitz wrote.

Three years later, the scribe spoke in negative absolutes. "It's one of the worst things I've seen in professional sports," Kravitz said. "The biggest shame of it is, take the fans out of the equation, the players wanted it desperately, and they could have had it. I remember middle linebacker Gary Brackett left immediately after the game. I've talked about it with him since. He left early because he didn't want to say anything he would regret."

Mike Lopresti of Gannett News Service wrote, "The boos from the stands might fade, but the ridicule won't. The Colts let history go with a whimper. For their legacy's sake, they'd better be steel in January."

They were. They beat Baltimore 20–3 and the Jets 30–17 to reach Super Bowl XLIV.

Then came February. They lost 31–17 to New Orleans at Miami.

48 What a Decade!

The large horizontal frame can't be overlooked when walking through a hallway in the Indianapolis Colts' Indiana Farm Bureau Football Center on West 56th Street.

Encased in glass are 10 hats and 11 folded T-shirts that represent six AFC South Division titles, two AFC championships, a Super Bowl XLI victory, reaching Super Bowl XLIV, and 115 Colts wins from 2000 to 2009, the winningest regular season decade in the NFL's 90-year history.

"It's a tapestry," owner Jim Irsay told *The Indianapolis Star*, "of amazement."

Led by quarterback Peyton Manning, wide receivers Marvin Harrison and Reggie Wayne, defensive ends Dwight Freeney and Robert Mathis, and for six seasons running back Edgerrin James, the Colts redefined the term "glory years." The Colts, Pittsburgh, Dallas, Denver, San Francisco, and the Oakland/Los Angeles Raiders were the only franchises to win 12 or more games as many as seven times in four decades since the 1970 AFL-NFL merger. The Colts did it in seven consecutive seasons from 2003 to 2009.

"I coached 21 years in this league before I got to Indianapolis," said Dungy, who won 85 regular season Colts games from 2002 to 2008. "I was with some good teams, playoff teams, division champions, and I'd never won 12 games in my life."

Dungy hit that mark every year with the Colts but one, when he won 10 in his first season. His 2005 team won its first 13 games by at least a touchdown, another league record. No team had ever won 23 consecutive regular season games until the Colts, ranging from the last nine contests in 2008 then the first 14 in 2009.

The Colts finished the decade 115–45 in the regular season. Head coach Jim Caldwell became the first rookie coach in league history to win his first nine games when the team started 14–0 in 2009. They reached the playoffs nine times, including eight consecutive years from 2002 to 2009. And that playoff streak extended one more year into the next decade in 2010.

The Pro Football Hall of Fame Selection Committee named Manning, Freeney, Harrison, James, kicker Adam Vinatieri (who also won three Super Bowl rings with New England), and head coach Tony Dungy to the NFL's All-Decade Team.

Irsay shelled out money for talent. Manning, Freeney, safety Bob Sanders, and tight end Dallas Clark received contracts that made them the highest-paid players at their positions in NFL history. The owner invested about $225 million in guaranteed bonuses to keep a critical core of a dozen players together.

"He made a commitment in the early years when we were among the lowest in league revenue," Polian said. "This was Jim Irsay's vision."

Another key was coaching continuity. Assistants with the Colts for eight seasons or more included offensive coordinator Tom Moore, offensive line coach Howard Mudd, wide receivers coach Clyde Christensen, running backs coach Mike Murphy, and defensive line coach John Teerlinck.

But as Moore always reminded in every interview, "It's about the players."

No player stood out more than Manning, who drove the team to seven fourth-quarter comebacks in 2009, the most in a single season since the 1970 merger. Five times in the decade, Manning engineered regular season comebacks after trailing by at least 17 points, another NFL record.

49 See a Colts Home Game

If you've purchased a Colts jersey, the next goal should be to experience a home game at Lucas Oil Stadium.

"At least one time in your life, you have to come down and see a game. I love our new stadium. It's great," said Blue Crew Fan Club member Nathan Tilse.

"It's not just to see 'The Luke,' that in itself is a beautiful facility, but it's the atmosphere," said longtime season ticketholder Eric Griffin, 45, of Greenwood, Indiana. "The Colts made it a point that it would be a fan-friendly place. It's electric in that place. It's an emotional experience even for me after all these years."

The Colts started playing at $725 million Lucas Oil Stadium in 2008. That first view of the field won't be forgotten. Everything is seemingly in immaculate condition, the FieldTurf practically glistening. The concourses are spacious, bathrooms are plentiful, and fans have a greater choice of concessions than in the old RCA Dome.

A walk around those concourses is like surveying the sights of a museum with so many attention-grabbing pictures and banners. Allow at least one extra hour on that first visit to take it all in.

"I've been going to games for so long, since I was 7, I just love it," SuEllyn Stevens said. "We sit right by where the opposing team runs out. Everybody is classy, except for when the New England Patriots come out of there. You really get the sense you're part of it."

The venue is massive—you could fit more than two RCA Domes inside. While the altitude in the top sections is significantly higher than the dome, the sightlines are excellent.

"There are more than 20,000 seats in that place that are higher than the last row of the RCA Dome," said stadium director Mike Fox. "We have had very, very few complaints as far as the sightlines are concerned. Sure, it's a hike to get up there, but it's not like it's a bad seat. I have a lot of friends who have seats in the first five or 10 rows of the terrace level and they say, 'We love it. We can see the play develop.' The seats are wide enough, and you have enough leg room. It's built for everybody."

When the window and retractable roof are open, fans enjoy a nice breeze. Two gigantic high-definition video screens—97' wide and 53' high—add to the in-game experience. Colts fans

Touchdown Monkey

Remember that blue stuffed animal that became so popular at Indianapolis Colts games in 2001? The Touchdown Monkey was born after the Colts worked with the Roman Brand Group agency on a series of TV commercials in conjunction with the "Believe" campaign that would eventually be renamed, "Believe in Blue."

One commercial showed a male Colts fan who believed his little blue monkey could bring good luck to the team. He worshipped the God monkey. Bob Lamey's radio voice could be heard calling a touchdown pass to Ken Dilger, and the fan was shown celebrating with his Touchdown Monkey. At the end of the commercial, the fan has an Extra Point Monkey.

A Sack Monkey was later introduced as part of a four-year run in which 25,000 of these furry blue keepsakes were sold. Some can be found for sale on the Internet, with an asking price as much as $50.

have learned what's expected of them. Holler "First down!" when prompted. When the defense is on the field, make as much noise as humanly possible. When the offense is at work, keep quiet. The "Touchdown Song" is an invitation for bedlam.

"It's totally different when the window and the roof are open," said Eric Van Wagner, 50, of Greenwood, Indiana. "Maybe because it's a nicer day, but it seems like the games are bigger."

Van Wagner suggests the fans still have a ways to go to provide the sound and fury the team heard at the indoor RCA Dome. He's not the only one who remembers the old place fondly.

"You could hear the percussion in your chest," Tilse said of the dome.

"The atmosphere isn't yet where it needs to be, but once we get a stronger defense, we'll get a different breed of hard-core fans," Van Wagner said. "I think we'll come around."

So consider yourself invited, fans. The Colts are 30–13 at Lucas Oil Stadium, counting the playoffs.

50 Dean Biasucci Is No Matt Dillon

Years before he had solidified himself as an NFL placekicker, before someone called into an ESPN show hosted by Chris Berman with the contest-winning nickname of Dean "Fish don't want to be a sushi," Dean Biasucci was also an aspiring actor.

He majored in drama at Western Carolina. Even when he kicked, he yearned to make something out of his "other" career. Biasucci joined the Indianapolis Colts in 1984, chosen in a five-kicker tryout to replace the injured Raul Allegre after the season opener. While kept for the remainder of the season after Allegre returned because of his lengthy kickoffs, Biasucci was among the final cuts in the 1985 camp.

The Colts phoned periodically to suggest they were thinking about bringing him back. An offer didn't come until after that season when head coach Rod Dowhower sold Biasucci on giving the Colts a second chance instead of trying out for another team. He beat out Allegre this time and stayed with the Colts from 1986 through 1994. They were mostly lean years for the franchise. The team's combined record in the Biasucci years was 62–87.

But in three of his first four off-seasons, Biasucci stayed in Indianapolis and worked on his acting at the Indiana Repertory Theatre. He was Mark Antony in *Julius Caesar*, and the title role was played by Michael Gross of *Family Ties* TV fame.

In the 1989 off-season, he ventured to New York City and took acting classes at Carnegie Hall and the Lee Strasberg Institute. For three off-seasons, he rented a place in Manhattan. Strasberg's third wife, Anna, was one of Biasucci's acting teachers.

One January day in 1990, Biasucci joined Strasberg's sons, Adam and David, for a six-on-six touch football game in a park next to actor Al Pacino's house in Nyack, New York. Pacino, who would earn eight Academy Award nominations and win once for best actor as Frank Slade in 1992's *Scent of a Woman*, was on the opposite team.

"There was snow on the ground," Biasucci said. "I was playing quarterback, and Al was rushing. I roll out to the right on one play, and Al is rushing, he falls as I throw a touchdown pass to one of the Strasbergs. Al gets up, looks at me and says, 'Nice pass.'"

Afterward, everybody headed to Pacino's place. "Al's family was there. We all watched TV and ate," Biasucci said. "Al was very nice. Nobody else had a clue who I was. They thought I was just one of Al's friends. So I told them who I was. 'You're the kicker?'"

He often ate at Elaine's, a popular Manhattan bar/restaurant. Biasucci recalled dining with Pacino one time, Woody Allen on another occasion, former New York Mets first baseman Keith Hernandez, and even former TV newscaster Walter Cronkite. When a new club opened with wall-to-wall celebrities including NBA Hall of Famer Michael Jordan, Biasucci was rescued from a long line around the corner by Hernandez. The kicker got to move to the front and enter with his baseball buddy.

"We're at this place where everybody is somebody. It was incredible," Biasucci said. "So we're about to leave later and we're at the coat check. Two New Yorkers walk up and one says, 'You're somebody.'

"I tell him, 'No. I'm not.'

"He persists, 'No. You're somebody.'

"No, really, I'm nobody."

The inquisitors finally thought they had figured it out.

"You're Matt Dillon," one guesses, an understandable case of mistaken identity considering Biasucci was a good-looking, 27-year-old man with brown hair.

"Actually, no, I'm Dean Biasucci, kicker for the Indianapolis Colts," he informed them.

"You're Dean Biasucci?" the man replied with skepticism.

"Yes, I am."

"Yeah, right. And I'm Lawrence Taylor," the man sneered. "Come on, you're Matt Dillon."

"I couldn't convince them," Biasucci said. "And I actually used to get that a lot. People would say, 'Did anybody ever tell you that you look like Matt Dillon?'"

The proverbial shoe would sometimes be on the kicker's other foot. Biasucci recalled eating at Elaine's next to Hockey Hall of Famer Mark Messier and asking, "So, Mark, what do you do?"

"I play hockey," Messier said.

"Oh, really? Who do you play for?"

"I play for the Rangers."

Biasucci really didn't know. And it would happen again. He was hanging out with actor D.B. Sweeney another time when they ran into another NHL great, Chris Chelios.

"So, Chris, what do you do?" the kicker asked.

Biasucci recalled Sweeney interjecting, "Hey, dumbass, don't you know who that is?'"

"Gosh, man, I felt like an idiot," Biasucci said.

That made him more understanding and sympathetic when Colts fans didn't recognize him in Indianapolis.

"They would feel bad that they didn't know me," he said. "I'd tell them, 'That's okay. You don't have to feel bad about that.' But they would apologize. And I would say, 'You're not supposed to know me. I don't have my jersey on, and we're at an Olive Garden.' I would start to feel worse than they did."

He almost boosted his profile with the 1996 movie *Jerry Maguire*. Biasucci was at a Los Angeles party with agent Leigh Steinberg, who introduced the retired kicker to movie director Cameron Crowe. The chit-chat led to a cameo appearance. Biasucci is one of many men at a bachelor party thrown for the title character, played by Tom Cruise. Just before cameras started rolling with Cruise entering the bachelor party, Crowe wanted Biasucci in front to the side.

"On the big screen, I saw myself right at the corner of the screen," he said. "But when the movie went to TV or video, it doesn't show up. I got cut out!"

While chatting with Crowe during a filming break, Biasucci asked rather boldly about getting a line in the movie. Crowe was a good sport and agreed. So when actors were called back a month later for "pick-ups," Crowe flew the kicker back to California. Biasucci is one of the clients Cruise's character tried to convince to stay with the agent after Jerry Maguire had been fired.

"I was one of his phone calls, and I had more than one line," Biasucci said. "But it never made the movie."

Biasucci is now 51, the divorced father of three children, and he lives in Charlotte, North Carolina. He and a business partner build apartment communities.

He never was Matt Dillon. But he had his fun, on and off the field.

"Living in New York City, it was probably one of the best times of my life," he said. "The only thing that would have made life better was if we won more football games."

51 A Lady and Her Coaches

Cathy Catellier saw the Mayflower vans roll into Fall Creek Elementary School in 1984. She couldn't miss them. The backyard to her parents' home was adjacent to the school.

"That was like my playground growing up," she said.

Betty Miles, Catellier's mother, was walking around that school with Jayne Boyd, Catellier's sister, a few days later. Front-office executive Bob Terpening and head coach Frank Kush tapped on a window and exchanged pleasantries. Miles invited the men to join her family for dinner at an establishment known then as the Irish Pub. Catellier's husband, Steve, met her at the pub. A short time later, Kush and Terpening arrived.

"The guys in the bar went wild," she said. "'Oh my gosh, it's Frank Kush!' It was like everybody stood up."

Catellier had been thinking about returning to work after staying at home to tend to two children who were now in school. After three hours of "just talking," she asked if the Colts needed any help. Kush advised her to stop by the next Monday. She did, resume in hand, but Pete Ward was the only one in the office to accept it. Everybody else was at a Hoosier Dome ceremony to welcome the team.

"By the time I actually got home, I got a phone call from Pete, who said, 'Frank Kush wants you to come and work,'" she said.

She started the next day, April 3. Her office was the old first-grade classroom. She remembers trying to avoid leaks from the ceiling when typing game plans. And there were those tiny toilets.

"I thought I might work, oh, maybe five years," Catellier said. "But it gets in your blood."

For 18 years, she was an executive assistant to the Colts' head coaches, from Kush to Jim Mora. She counted 95 assistants over the years, too. The men taught her football. That education began on her second day when Kush asked her to diagram a play designed for the tight end.

"I didn't tell you I knew anything about football," Catellier recalled telling a surprised Kush. "I didn't know where the tight end went."

Catellier gets credit for helping Tom Zupancic land a job as strength and conditioning coach. After finishing the U.S. Olympic

Trials as an alternate in wrestling, Zupancic sent a resume to the team then followed up with a phone call. And he kept calling. At one point, he phoned eight days in a row. Finally, Catellier said something to Kush, basically telling him to do something about Zupancic's job inquiry so she wouldn't have to keep taking the phone calls. Kush called Zupancic and hired him.

While grateful to Kush for her employment opportunity, she soon realized he could be unpredictable. "Frank was like Dr. Jekyll and Mr. Hyde," she said. "You never knew what you were going to get from him."

One day in early December 1984, he caught her off guard again.

"He came to me and said, 'I've got to leave, and if anybody asks where I am, tell them I'm duck hunting,'" she recalled.

She shook her head, thinking, *What was up with that?*

Sure enough, Terpening came around later and inquired about Kush.

"He's duck hunting," she said.

Terpening didn't know what to make of it, either.

"He just sort of rolled his eyes and walked away," Catellier said.

As it turns out, Kush had flown to Arizona to see about a new job. Her first head coach quit the Colts on December 13 with one game remaining in a 4–12 season to coach the United States Football League's Arizona Outlaws. Zupancic recalled when Kush drove out of the school parking lot for the final time.

"It was pouring down rain, just pouring," Zupancic said. "He rolled his window down about 2" and said, 'You're a hard worker. You'll be alright.'"

Catellier's next head coach was Rod Dowhower. He didn't last two seasons. Call it a woman's intuition, but she sensed the man knew he was going to be fired before the pink slip came after 13 losses in 1986. Well, it was woman's intuition *and* the fact she kept seeing fewer books on Dowhower's office shelf. He had started taking stuff home long before the day came to say farewell.

Head Coach History

1953: Keith Molesworth 3–9 regular season
1954–62: Weeb Ewbank 59–52–1, (2–2 postseason, two NFL titles)
1963–69: Don Shula 71–23–4 (2–3 postseason, one NFL title)
1970–72: Don McCafferty 22–10–1, (4–1 postseason, Super Bowl V win)
1972: John Sandusky 4–5
1973–74: Howard Schnellenberger 4–13
1974: Joe Thomas 2–9
1975–79: Ted Marchibroda 41–33 (0–3 postseason)
1980–81: Mike McCormack 9–23
1982–84: Frank Kush 11–28–1
1984: Hal Hunter 0–1
1985–86: Rod Dowhower 5–24
1986–91: Ron Meyer 36–35 (0–1 postseason)
1991: Rick Venturi 1–10
1992–95: Ted Marchibroda 30–34 (2–1 postseason)
1996–97: Lindy Infante 12–20 (0–1 postseason)
1998–2001: Jim Mora 32–32 (0–2 postseason)
2002–2008: Tony Dungy 85–27 (7–6 postseason, Super Bowl XLI win)
2009–2011: Jim Caldwell 26–22 (2–2 postseason)
2012: Chuck Pagano 11–5* (0–1 postseason)

* While Pagano was being treated for leukemia, offensive coordinator Bruce Arians served as interim coach with a 9–3 record. But as a matter of NFL statistical record, all games count toward Pagano's mark.

"He felt his job was on the line," she said. "I think he felt it was coming."

She remembered his considerate nature, how he would always ask her, "Are you okay?"

One of the most difficult aspects of the job was seeing her bosses come and go. She couldn't help but get attached.

"I would bawl," she said. "You worked so many hours together. And we had such a small coaching staff. You would spend more time with them than with your own family."

When Ron Meyer was hired, he gave Catellier the okay to hire some help. She remembered how owner Robert Irsay wanted a coach who wore a suit and tie. Meyer did that when he showed up for work. "Ron and I got along great," she said. "He was just a classy guy."

Ted Marchibroda returned in '92. Each coach seemed to be wired differently. Marchibroda got rid of the couch Meyer had in the office and added a table used mostly to study film. A treadmill was also brought in so Marchibroda could study film while pacing through a workout. Either in his office or across the hall, she would hear that familiar sound of "clickety-click-click-click" from the film projector. The coaching staff spent so much time in that room. Inevitably, the assistants' language would be profane, especially after the ugly losses. Those guys would get so worked up, they forgot about Catellier being within earshot.

"They would come out of there and apologize," she said, chuckling. "I told them it was okay. I tuned it out."

When Marchibroda wasn't re-signed after the '95 team's thrilling run to an AFC title game, she took that hard. Asked which coach's departure affected her the most emotionally, she said, "Losing Ted. Ted was just a remarkable man."

Then there was Mora. Nobody was more intense. Catellier recalled former strength and conditioning coach Jon Torine saying he never saw another man, including players, work out as hard as Mora. It beat duck hunting.

"She was awesome," Mora said of Catellier. "She was not only a good person from being an executive assistant, she was a great friend. She was outstanding. I loved Cathy."

Mora is retired in California. He and Catellier, 62, still exchange Christmas cards each year.

"I loved him, too," she said. "When I think of all these guys, I have a grin on my face. That's what made the job so wonderful, the different personalities for each man. They were all great in their own ways. It has been a privilege."

When Mora was fired after 2001, Catellier agreed to become owner Jim Irsay's executive assistant. "I loved the coaching end of it. I was like, 'Can I think about it for a minute?'" she said. "But how do you turn an owner down?"

She smiles and laughs at the thought of how—many years before that transition—she was the inspiration for an oft-repeated joke. "Robert Irsay used to say to Jim, 'Why do you have to go through an agency to hire people?'" she recalled. "'Why don't you just go to a bar and pick them up like you did Cathy?'"

Ring of Honor

Wide receiver Bill Brooks was understandably grateful to be the first player inducted into the Indianapolis Colts' Ring of Honor in 1998.

Regarded by the team and fans as one of the all-time good guys in the locker room and with the public, Brooks referred to playing for the Colts from 1986 to 1992 as "a very special time in my life." His best season for receiving yards was 1,131 as a rookie. He had a career-high 72 receptions in 1991.

Brooks, 49, still lives in Indianapolis with his wife, Holly, and daughter, Brianna. When he attends a game at Lucas Oil Stadium, the humble man says he tries not to look up at his name on the façade, unless someone points it out to him. "I feel uncomfortable about the attention," he said, "but it is an honor to have your name in the Ring of Honor, and I am very thankful to [owner] Mr. Jim

Irsay. You look back on it and you think about your teammates and the bonds you had with them, the struggles you went through, the games where you fought through the adversity."

He played 11 seasons for three NFL teams and finished with 583 catches for 8,001 yards and 46 touchdowns. But more than the numbers, Brooks is remembered for his respectful nature. There are Hall of Famers who played for the Colts—Marshall Faulk and Eric Dickerson—who aren't in the Ring of Honor, presumably because they weren't always on good terms when they played in Indianapolis. Nobody utters an unkind word about Brooks.

"As a young child growing up, I'd have to give credit to my parents for how they raised me," Brooks said. "They taught me to respect people and be polite to everyone. Most importantly, in my Christian belief, Jesus Christ is the driving force behind me and who I am. I love God, and His demonstration of love for me teaches me how to love others, as well."

The first person to be inducted was late owner Robert Irsay, father of the current Colts owner, in 1996. Retired head coach Ted Marchibroda, beloved by players in two stints with the team—1975 to 1979 with Baltimore and 1992 to 1995 with Indianapolis—was added in 2000.

"That's the greatest honor I've ever received," Marchibroda said.

Seven-time Pro Bowl offensive lineman Chris Hinton, who played for the Colts from 1983 to 1989, joined the Ring of Honor in 2001. Four years later, on the 10-year anniversary of the 1995 AFC Championship Game team, "Captain Comeback" quarterback Jim Harbaugh was included, too.

"People ask me why Jim Harbaugh is up there in the Ring of Honor," Colts longtime radio voice Bob Lamey said of Harbaugh, who was with the team from 1994 to 1997. "We had two 21-point comebacks that year. We got to the playoffs. He put the Colts on the map with what he did."

Jim Irsay saluted the fans by honoring the 12ᵗʰ Man in 2007. Then came head coach Tony Dungy, the Super Bowl XLI champion and the winningest coach in franchise history with a record of 85–27.

The past two seasons have celebrated the great careers of wide receiver Marvin Harrison (2011) and running back Edgerrin James (2012), who each rewrote the franchise record books in receiving and rushing categories, respectively.

"It was an honor [that] I played for the Colts, and I want to tell everyone thank you," James said during the halftime ceremony on September 23, 2012.

The Colts' all-time leading rusher was particularly pleased the ceremony included a series of highlights from his playing days on the stadium's large video screens.

"Oh man, it's good [for my kids]," James said. "They get to see that I know what I'm talking about. I wish I could still move like that."

Eden, James' 8-year-old son, was impressed.

"He's a playa! He's a playa!" the boy shouted.

53 Peyton Manning's Homecoming

Peyton Manning was perfect in the "Big Easy."

Unless, of course, you asked him. "Well, I overthrew Dallas Clark on that one," the Indianapolis Colts quarterback said after throwing six touchdown passes in a 55–21 primetime rout of the Saints in New Orleans, Manning's hometown, on September 28, 2003.

One TD pass shy of tying an NFL single-game record, Manning overshot Clark on an incomplete third-quarter pass to the

Wide receiver Marvin Harrison (88) catches a touchdown pass from quarterback Peyton Manning in the first half against the New Orleans Saints on Sunday, September 28, 2003, in New Orleans. Behind Harrison is Saints safety Tebucky Jones. (AP Photo/Alex Brandon)

end zone. There was also another near-miss just beyond the reach of wide receiver Marvin Harrison.

Ho-hum. Manning had to settle for a perfect passer rating, completing 20-of-25 passes for 314 yards and calling it a night with four seconds remaining in the third quarter after throwing an 11-yard TD pass to Clark for a 48–13 lead. The touchdown was Clark's first in the NFL, not that many remembered.

"Your first touchdown, you want it to be meaningful, you want it to be something that changes a game or a game-winning touchdown, but mine was one of the six he threw at New Orleans down in the Superdome," Clark said years later. "Mine, I think, was the sixth one. You almost kind of felt bad for 'em, like shouldn't we just run it out?

"I caught my first NFL touchdown and there's probably 10 people in the stands, and the networks should have switched the game to some reality show so nobody would see it. My family would have to go on the Internet to find out, like it wasn't on TV anymore."

The Colts set a record for points scored on the road. And they did it without running back Edgerrin James, who sat out with a back injury.

"Peyton was ballin', man," James said the next day.

The former Isidore Newman High School star slung it around like he was taking apart some prep team back in the day. Half of Harrison's six catches were for scores as he finished with 158 yards receiving. Before the Saints could blink, Manning hit running back Ricky Williams on a 17-yard TD pass in a 93-second scoring drive then found Harrison on touchdown throws covering 14 and 79 yards for a 21–0 lead.

"Once we got the momentum," Colts coach Tony Dungy said, "it was like a shark in the water."

And that big fish sure was hungry.

Manning's last three touchdown passes came in his final quarter of work. Running back Dominic Rhodes caught a 12-yarder and Harrison reached the end zone from 32 yards out before Clark capped the visitors' 24-point third quarter. Defensive end Dwight Freeney scooped up a fumble and ran 19 yards for the Colts' final score early in the fourth.

"Everything worked," said Colts offensive coordinator Tom Moore. "I can't explain it."

Manning's early exit snapped a string of 1,633 consecutive snaps. The perfect quarterback rating of 158.3 was the NFL-record third of his 84-game, regular season career. He added a fourth in 2008 and still owns that league mark.

"Every now and then, you're going to have a night that belongs to one team," Manning understated.

54 Buy *The Jersey Effect*

That's right, you're reading a book and being advised to buy another. If you're a Colts fan or a sports enthusiast who has children, Hunter Smith's work is well worth it.

The retired Indianapolis Colts punter, known for his insightful interviews and big-picture perspective as a player, set out with co-author Darrin Gray and teammates from the Super Bowl XLI championship team to make a difference in sports culture with 2011's *The Jersey Effect: Beyond the World Championship*. It's not just a compilation of guys reliving their glory days. These are life lessons from 11 men who want to help athletes, coaches, and parents keep sports in proper perspective. The book is in its fourth printing.

"It has done exceptionally well," said Smith, 36, a father of four who retired in 2010 and lives in the Indianapolis suburb of Zionsville. "The response has been fabulous and continues to grow. I feel like, from people reading it, it's impacting sports culture. That's why we wrote it. It's because we've lost a proper perspective on sports in our culture, and we need to regain that if we're going to raise young men and women of character."

The book's tribute to John Outlaw, a coaching mentor when Smith was growing up in Sherman, Texas, sums it up. Months before his death, Outlaw told Smith, "They ain't gonna put any of them wins in your casket."

The book includes chapters written by former Colts players Justin Snow, Tarik Glenn, Jeff Saturday, Ben Utecht, Matt Giordano, Dylan Gandy, and Reggie Hodges, as well as former head coaches Tony Dungy and Jim Caldwell. The only chapter from someone still connected to the Colts is by quarterbacks coach Clyde Christensen. Dungy, who coached the Super Bowl XLI team and is a best-selling author, wrote the foreword.

"We've taken a different aspect of life from each of their lives, a different aspect of their career, a different thing they struggled with and pursued it in each chapter," Smith said. "I'm the narrator and reflect on each chapter, then I have my chapter."

While it's a faith-based endeavor, the authors advise it's not just about preaching Christianity. Smith and Gray wanted to delve into more of the psychology of how the popularity of sports can mislead people into straying from what is important.

"It only takes two years for 78 percent of NFL football players to be divorced and/or bankrupt," Smith said of a *USA Today* 2006 report. "It doesn't just affect professional athletes. It affects everyone. If you're a coach, parent, or player at any stage, this book will make you more well-rounded, more well-adjusted in your approach to sports. As a result, preemptively we're going to reach into the lives of people and see a big chunk taken out of this crisis because I believe it starts much earlier."

They see the sports craze doing damage when youngsters are starting out, then it manifests. "What this book does is give a four-dimensional approach to being a great student athlete," said Gray, referring to academics, athletics, social, and spiritual aspects.

Gray, 45, of Fishers, Indiana, worked for six years with Dungy on All Pro Dads, a national fatherhood program. "If football really builds character, then the longer you play and the higher up the football ladder you go, the more it should benefit you," Dungy wrote in the foreword. "It would make sense, then, that players who make it to the NFL level and have a long professional career would reap the most benefits from the sport and have the most successful lives after football.

"But that's not the story the facts tell. When you look behind the scenes, it appears that the higher up you go in the game, the more problems you have."

Smith says his faith and encouragement from parents Reggie and Sherilyn to pursue a variety of interests helped him avoid the trap of placing too much of an emphasis on sports. His mother took him to Dallas at a young age to buy that first guitar. Smith is still playing today with The Hunter Smith Band, which was working on a second album during the winter and planned a grassroots tour across the Hoosier State in the summer of 2013.

Smith's brother, Reggie, became an attorney. His sister, Allison, is a teacher.

"I thought it was a great concept, a great idea for a guy like Hunter who is so talented in so many ways, a husband, a father, a friend, an athlete, musician, and a writer," said Snow, 36. "The guy is brilliant."

"It puts some meaning and deeper values into our lives other than just football," said Christensen, 57. "I think people will enjoy the read and enjoy Hunter's insight into it."

Smith shares Utecht's story about when the tight end ran onto the field for Super Bowl XLI and heard someone yelling. It was Utecht's father. For a moment, Utecht got caught up in the spotlight telling his father, "Not now, not now." Then he realized his mistake. He ran over to the stands. Both father and son were in tears as the Colt said, "It all started with you, dad."

"Returning to what really matters is what the book is all about," Smith said. "I cry every time I tell that story."

55 Ryan Lilja Rocks His Helmet

The Super Bowl XLI celebration lasted through the night in Fort Lauderdale, Florida, then the exhausted Indianapolis Colts boarded busses in the morning. There sat offensive guard Ryan Lilja, instant comic relief as usual, in a suit, sporting sunglasses—and still wearing his helmet.

"It was hilarious," said right offensive tackle Ryan Diem. "Just classic Lilja. Lilja being Lilja."

Colts punter Hunter Smith said, "It was one of the funniest things I've ever seen," then added, "Talk about not wanting to let the moment go."

Symbolism for some, but Lilja confesses his enduring visual at the end of a memorable ride was a bit more complicated than that. It wasn't until three years later, when the Colts had returned to Miami for Super Bowl XLIV, that Lilja had a good laugh and shared the previously untold saga of how his helmet went missing but ended up where it belonged, with him on that bus.

The Vince Lombardi Trophy presentation had just begun as the Colts celebrated Super Bowl XLI on the field after defeating Chicago 29–17 at Dolphin Stadium.

"[Center] Jeff Saturday has got his son down there, his wife was pregnant at the time I believe, and his little daughter, Savannah, she's trying to see," Lilja said of the 4-year-old girl. "I put her on my shoulders. Jeff's friend, Chad Henderson, took my helmet for me and had my Super Bowl hat and the shirt they give you on the field. So he's got it, and in the midst of all the chaos, I go into the locker room and I forgot about the helmet."

The team returned to its Fort Lauderdale hotel for the all-night party.

"We all had a great time celebrating afterward," Diem said. "We all had a late night. I'm not really sure if Lilja ever changed out of his suit."

Time to leave, and Lilja had yet to think about his helmet.

"Coming out the next morning to go to the busses, I get in the elevator and Chad is in there," he said. "To be honest with you, I completely forgot that I gave him the helmet to hold.

"I said, 'Hey, what the heck are you doing, man? That's [No.] six-five, that's my helmet.' What are the odds? He's coming down from the 16th floor or whatever, I'm on seven and getting in, and I see my helmet and am thinking, *What the heck?*"

Respectfully returned to its rightful owner, Lilja proceeded. "I've got my helmet in tow, and I'm walking out to the bus," he said. "What am I going to do with it? You're going to put it on your head. So that was the image that some of these guys have shared with me and had fun with it."

Lilja, of course, had to sell the move as perfectly natural. "It felt good," he said. "There was still confetti in the helmet and some sand in there. You want to live it up. I've never worn a helmet with a suit and sunglasses before. I wanted to see how that felt."

But encourage a comedian with laughter, as teammates did when boarding the bus, and he's going to milk it. So Lilja didn't take it off.

"I rocked it, man," he said. "I had it on the plane that way, too."

56 Attend Training Camp

If there is ever an opportunity to have personal interaction with the Indianapolis Colts, it's during training camp at Anderson University.

Aside from the players walking over to the ropes to sign autographs and mingle after every practice, fans are as close to the field as possible to watch the team work out. About a 40-minute drive North on Interstate 69 from Indianapolis can make this happen.

"For any hard-core Colts fan, coming up to training camp to see the people you see on TV is a must-do," said Chris Williams, Anderson University director of communications and community relations. "If your house is painted blue or you have a horseshoe on your car if you're one of those kinds of fans, you need to be at training camp."

Oh, and the only cost is for parking. Practices are free.

The Colts and AU post the camp schedule in advance. There can be changes, so it helps to check before making the trip. Sometimes, the afternoon workouts will be moved inside if there's inclement weather. Fans typically get shut out on those. But there's about three weeks of practices, enough of a window to see such stars as quarterback Andrew Luck, wide receiver Reggie Wayne, and outside linebacker Robert Mathis, to name a few.

"It's a grassroots opportunity," said Williams, whose private Christian university with an enrollment of 2,600 students welcomed the Colts back to town in 2010 after the team spent 11 years training at Rose-Hulman Institute of Technology in Terre Haute, Indiana. "For many fans who can't afford to see them at a game, it's a great experience getting to know players and coaches. They are very good about autographs. They take a lot of time. That's a level of appreciation they have for their fans."

The Colts' return in 2010 drew about 85,000 fans, which contributed an estimated $6.5 million boost to the economy, Williams said.

A few tips might make the day more enjoyable. While volunteers distribute maps, a layout of camp and parking is online at www.Anderson.edu/Colts. The team either practices in Macholtz Stadium or two fields next to where the college Ravens play their games. Lawn chairs are permitted, but the fields have bleachers.

In case out-of-town fans don't check the state map, Interstate 69 has billboards on both sides before Exit 26. Take Indiana 9/Scatterfield Road to Fifth Street or University Boulevard. Some campus streets are closed, so stick to the main path.

It can get hot, so fans are encouraged to hydrate beforehand. Water and drinks are available at a concession stand. Water fountains are located under the stadium near the information booth at the entrance. First-aid stations can provide health care to fans overcome by the elements or other issues. Scope out these stations upon arrival.

Be prepared to walk 5 to 10 minutes to get to the practice fields from the parking lot. The only shuttle service is a golf-cart ride for fans parking in handicapped areas with mobility challenges. Wheelchair users need to collapse the wheelchair and transport it on a golf-cart seat.

Parents and/or family members must keep children 12-and-under with them at all times. Parking fees are per session, and the lot should be entered from Fifth Street. If you leave to have lunch, you'll have to pay to return for a second practice on two-a-days. The money goes to the university to offset expenses.

Fans can't use video cameras, flash photography, or laptops during practices. Personal coolers are not permitted in the stadium area. The university is an alcohol- and smoke-free campus.

Service pets are allowed, but no other animals are permitted. No bicycles are allowed at camp. Bicycle racks are available along University Boulevard.

Colts City offers interactive fun with inflatables, sponsor booths, giveaways, and register-to-win chances as well as the Colts-In-Motion traveling museum, cheerleader autograph sessions, and visits from the mascot Blue among other attractions. But it's not set up every day, so check the schedule.

57 Golf Cart Camp Capers

The body of water referred to as Lake Rose-Hulman became the unlikeliest of parking places for Indianapolis Colts golf carts—somehow stuck on a dock in the middle of the pond.

The prank became an annual occurrence when the team visited Terre Haute, Indiana, for training camp from 1999 to 2009 at Rose-Hulman Institute of Technology. Off-the-record whispers suggested quarterback Peyton Manning was the mastermind, but nothing was ever proven. If anybody snitched, they would risk being an obvious target for another elaborate prank. And reporters didn't dare cross that line with Manning. He was too important of an interview.

One season removed from his days with the Colts, Manning acknowledged what many already knew when contacted by equipment manager Jon Scott.

Yep, it was No. 18 all along.

Accomplices remain unknown, although there's no doubt he had help in pulling the dock to the bank and loading a golf cart of the next victim. President Bill Polian's cart ended up out there.

Defensive end John Chick (97) and defensive back Antoine Bethea (41) get a ride on a golf cart during Colts training camp in Anderson, Indiana, on Tuesday, August 10, 2010. (AP Photo/Darron Cummings)

Strength and conditioning coach Jon Torine and director of broadcast services Jeffrey Gorman suffered the same surprise.

The carts were used as a means of transportation because the Colts' practice fields were about 400 yards away from the locker room. The cafeteria where the Colts ate had large windows with a picturesque lake view. Waking up to see your golf cart on the dock wasn't exactly the most enjoyable way to start a day.

"I think mine was in 2000," said Torine, 39, now living in Fair Haven, New Jersey. "I can't find my golf cart. I come up to eat breakfast and I look out there and see the golf cart and laugh, 'Look at that.'"

Torine eventually put two and two together and realized that was his ride. Head coach Jim Mora approached. Torine feared the worst from the no-nonsense coach.

"Now I'm worried about Jim," he said.

"Is that your golf cart?" Mora asked.

"Yes, coach, I think it is," Torine said, somewhat sheepishly.

"That's hilarious," Mora said, laughing. "How did they get that out there?"

A relieved Torine remembers thinking, "Thank God he's not pissed."

Another time, Torine couldn't open the door to leave his dorm room.

"I cracked it, and the damn golf cart is in the middle of the hall," he said.

He remembers Manning's predictable smirk when confronted about being behind such practical jokes.

"Peyton always had his pat answer, 'I'm really flattered you would think it was me because I know it's good stuff, but it wasn't me,'" Torine said. "Don't kid yourself. He's proud of this stuff. There's nothing that he puts a finger on that he doesn't try to do 'A' work, including the golf cart prank."

Tight end Ken Dilger, a Manning teammate from 1998 to 2001, remembers the golf cart gags and many others. "I saw some of the golf cart shenanigans," Dilger said. "Nobody was off limits to Peyton's pranks. He could definitely dish it out, but he couldn't take it."

Gorman didn't take it so well, either. That meant he would be a repeat target. "I went to where my golf cart was parked, and it was gone," he said. "I thought maybe possibly an intern had grabbed it for an emergency, they needed it. I checked two other places, and it wasn't there. Then somebody said, 'Hey, there's a golf cart on Lake

Classic Quotes

A few Colts quotes to remember:

"For everybody in this locker room and organization, the ultimate goal is the Super Bowl. That's plan A. I really want this to be 99.9 percent plan A, and .1 percent plan B [Pro Bowl in Hawaii]. If plan B is the option, it's not a bad thing to have. Sit back and Mai Tais on me."
—Wide receiver Reggie Wayne in 2010 on preferring to play in the Super Bowl rather than a week earlier in the Pro Bowl.

"I always thought that if I didn't feel it, the other person was hurting more. But I've realized over time that if I hit somebody and it hurts me, it hurts them even more. It depends on the way I feel."
—Safety Bob Sanders, on what makes a big hit.

"Everybody has got their day coming, man."
—Sanders, self-explanatory.

"The more you talk, the more you show your ignorance."
—Defensive end Robert Mathis, known for succinct statements.

"I never thought 'Sodapop Curtis' would announce my retirement. I always thought I would be the one to announce it. I'm a huge fan of the movie, but that caught me way off guard. I can't explain it. I know he is a friend of [owner] Jim's [Irsay], and Jim sounded surprised."
—Peyton Manning, referring to actor Rob Lowe's character in the 1983 movie *The Outsiders* after Lowe tweeted the quarterback would retire due to a neck injury. Manning refuted the tweet in an exclusive interview on January 23, 2012.

Rose-Hulman.' I looked, and sure enough. On top of that, I had to pay one of the custodians at Rose-Hulman 20 bucks to get my golf cart back. It ended up costing me money. Geez."

Gorman, 44, didn't hesitate to confront Manning. "I was so mad, and I knew exactly who it was that I went to Peyton's dorm room and I complained," Gorman said. "Peyton said, 'I don't know nothing about what you're talking about. Nothing.' He straight-faced me."

In retrospect, it's not a good idea to even mention it.

Later on, Manning asked to check out an unsuspecting Gorman's dorm room.

"So he walked around, and on the back door to where I was staying there was a second entrance way through the door," Gorman said. "What he had done was come in and unlock that door. While I was sleeping, he or one of his henchman came in and grabbed my truck keys. They stole my truck the next morning. I couldn't find it. I called campus police. I thought, *Oh, my truck's been stolen. Unbelievable.*

"Then one of the players said to me, 'Hey, I think I found your truck. Check down about 300 yards from the dorm.' I called campus police and said, 'It's on property, 300 yards down.' The guy called me back and said, 'We found your truck.' It was on the 50-yard line of the practice field covered in Saran wrap."

Torine had ventured out for his 5:00 AM run on a trail near the woods when he spotted Gorman's truck. "That was beautiful," Torine said. "I saw that, and I almost couldn't finish my run, I was laughing so hard."

Gorman laughs about it now and calls Manning "the master prankster." But he still isn't buying the notion that being a prank victim meant Manning liked him. "Some other people said that, including [owner] Jim Irsay, 'They wouldn't mess with you if they didn't like you,'" he said. "But I was still pissed off. I was spitting hornets, I was so mad."

Gorman got his truck keys back at the end of that day. He was never permitted to get Manning back.

Torine suggests that wouldn't have been a smart move. "Don't try to beat somebody with time, resources, and intellect," Torine said. "You're never going to win."

58 Program Practical Joke

While the Colts carved out a new identity in Indianapolis, a quest that commenced with a lot of losses, general manager Jim Irsay and director of operations Pete Ward tried to maintain a healthy sense of humor.

"In '85, Craig Kelley was in his first year," Ward said of the assistant director of public relations. "Craig was a newcomer and kind of cocky. So for the last home game of the year, Jim and I had 25 bogus programs printed up. Frank Hancock, he works in sports graphics, helped us with it. He put Craig Kelley's picture on Bob Irsay's picture in the owner bio."

The plan to hatch these bogus programs was contingent upon the Colts having their season finale locked up late in the fourth quarter against Houston. The team entered 4–11, so it wasn't a given. But the Colts did their part.

"Late in the fourth quarter, the clock is ticking down and the game is wrapped up," Ward said of the 34–16 victory at the Hoosier Dome. "As part of the plan, Jim called and said, 'You and Craig come up here and bring as many programs as you can.' So I had the box of bogus programs and took them up to Jim's box."

Ward paused and laughed as he remembered what happened next.

"Jim says, 'What the [expletive] is going on, Craig?!' He shows Craig the bogus program. Craig doesn't know what to say. 'See if it's the same in every program!' I'm going through the box and saying, 'Oh, God, it's in every program.' Craig is speechless."

Irsay let Kelley sweat. Kelley was convinced he was out of a job.

Irsay eventually delivered the punchline. Ward recalled how Irsay looked at Kelley and finally said, "Well, all I've got to say, Craig, is…Merry Christmas."

Kelley hasn't forgotten it to this day.

"It was a function of working for a great guy like Jim Irsay," Kelley said. "Thankfully from their end, we were winning the game. We were all in our late twenties, we've all grown up together in this organization. We've all seen each other go from single guys, helping each other move to different places around town, married now, and that kind of stuff.

"It was a fantastic practical joke. I have to tip my cap to the shrewd planning of Pete Ward."

Kelley suspects he became the target because of a previous misunderstanding involving the employee use of team cars as part of a local dealership agreement.

"I had borrowed the keys of Bob Eller, who was my boss," Kelley said. "I borrowed Bob's car to pick up somebody at the airport. I went out, I clicked the unlock button, and Pete's car unlocked and I drove Pete's car completely by mistake. Pete had thought I had done it on purpose. So when he went out to get his car, it was gone. But it was in total innocence, so that kind of precipitated the joke."

Ward first got him back by snatching Kelley's LSU football helmet and putting it on the roof of the Colts complex. Kelley laughs about that and then again about the program practical joke.

"To this day, Pete doesn't think I was innocent," Kelley said. "But I was. Who knew that the car keys operated multiple cars at that point. It was all out of innocence, but hey, it was a great joke. It was an outstanding joke. All's well that ends well. We still laugh about it now. And I still have one of those programs."

59 Faint and a "Full Moon"

Losses took such a toll, that the mind and body relented for Indianapolis Colts head coach Rod Dowhower midway through the 1986 season. After enduring a 5–11 season in '85, the next year became overwhelming.

The Colts had traded for quarterback Gary Hogeboom during the off-season in an exchange of second-round '86 picks, but he separated his shoulder in the second game. The team nose-dived to 0–7, and most of the games weren't close.

After a 24–13 loss at Buffalo, the winless Colts returned home to face Miami on October 26 in a rematch of a Week 2 drubbing. This time, the game was winnable. It came down to the final minutes.

Then disaster struck.

"We're behind by four, but we're driving down the field," recalled the Colts' Pete Ward, then the team's director of operations. "It's fourth down. [Quarterback Jack] Trudeau does a little dink over the middle to running back Owen Gill. There's no one in front of him. He could have gone for a touchdown, and we would have won."

"Fourth-and-10," recalled Craig Kelley, then-assistant director of public relations. "It was a screen pass, and it probably had a little bit too much air under it. By the time Gill caught it, he had an open field to the end zone. The Dolphin player made a shoestring tackle. Otherwise, we walk in for a score, and the losing streak is over."

The game-saving stop in a 17–13 loss leveled Dowhower, then 43.

"Rod Dowhower faints on the sideline," Ward said. "Radio voice Bob Lamey is going nuts. 'Rod Dowhower is down on the ground!' Trainers and doctors are hovering over him, 'Get him up.' He's woozy and trying to walk."

Kelley was on his way to the field from the press box during the fateful play. "I remember Bob Lamey's radio call, which was typically emotional," Kelley said. "You didn't know what could have happened. It could have been a horrible situation with all the emotions of competition, but this was certainly more benign. He just hyperventilated and passed out."

As Dowhower tried to collect himself on the sideline, something was amiss. "Rod's pants are ripped, and it was R-rated," Ward said. "Jon Scott, the equipment manager, and offensive line coach Tom Lavot were walking behind Rod with a towel over his butt."

Scott remembers it well. "When he was down, we thought Rod had suffered a heart attack. I thought, *Oh my gosh,*" Scott said. "Prior to that game, he had gained a little bit of weight, so we made his pants a little bit bigger. For whatever reason, he came to us to get a jockstrap instead of some regular underwear. When the pants split, there was no underwear there. It was just a full moon.

"We were all scrambling to get something. We were trying to catch up to him. He had no idea. He was walking over to get to Dolphins coach Don Shula. It was kind of a team effort, stuffing the towel down the back of his pants. Here he is, going over to shake hands with Shula with a towel draped out of his pants."

Dowhower was fired after the Colts slid to 0–13. While he would work for five other NFL teams and was a head coach in college at Vanderbilt, he would never again be an NFL head coach. He finished his brief NFL head coaching career with a 5–24 record.

"But Rod was a great guy," Ward said.

"He was," Kelley said. "Like everything else in this business, it plays out in public. This is the ultimate reality-show business. I did feel bad for him. You feel bad for anybody who suffers a humiliating moment."

60 No. 1 Fan Not Forgotten

Upon relocation to Indianapolis in 1984, the Colts began training camp workouts at Anderson University, a private Christian college that is about a 40-minute drive north of the Hoosier State's capital city.

Danny Hulse was there to greet them when they arrived.

He was the 12-year-old fan with one left leg who was confined to a wheelchair but always sporting a smile when his team hit the practice field. His affinity for the Colts provided a respite from the harsh reality of a failing body. Hulse was just two years old when diagnosed with neurofibromatosis, a genetic disorder of the nervous system that causes tumors to grow on nerves. He broke his right leg at five—it wouldn't heal and was amputated.

"Every year we came out," linebacker Barry Krauss said, "it seemed Danny had a different type of cancer."

The Colts bonded with the kid. His parents, Nancy and John, saw the immediate connection. The Hulse family made it to practice as much as possible, even two-a-day camp workouts in sweltering heat.

"I still hear from people occasionally who were there when Danny was," said Nancy, 69, who lost her husband, John, in 2012. "I believe God put the Colts in Anderson for Danny. And I believe God put Danny there for the Colts. John and I believed the Colts gave Danny more time."

She recalled the extra attention shown to her son, especially by Krauss, tight end Pat Beach, and Jim Irsay, then vice president and general manager.

"Jimmy Irsay was a good friend to Danny," Nancy said.

Krauss, strength and conditioning coach Tom Zupancic, and equipment manager Jon Scott did something special for Danny. At practice, the players opened a path for the boy to be wheeled onto the field where he was presented a No. 1 Colts Fan jersey.

"Danny felt so special that he had those guys," Nancy said.

In the later stages of his illness, Danny required oxygen. He could be stubborn about taking it. Nancy knew how to solve that problem.

"I could call Barry any time, any place, and say I needed help, and he would do it," Nancy said. "He'd call in about 10 minutes."

Krauss cleverly reminded Danny how the boy would see the linebacker getting oxygen during games. Then he asked if Danny was getting his oxygen. That ended the squabbling.

The Colts didn't win much in those early years. They went 4–12 that first season in Indianapolis, 5–11 the next year, and 3–13 in 1986. It didn't matter to Danny. The team gave him tickets to attend games in a handicap-accessible area. Inevitably, another fan would criticize his team. That didn't fly.

"Danny was a sweet, positive kid, but you didn't bad-mouth his Colts," Nancy said. "He always said, 'Those guys are winners. I don't care what the scoreboard says.'"

By 1986, Danny's condition worsened as cancer spread to the skull. Treatment was aggressive, Nancy recalled, with about 70 chemotherapy treatments. The teenager endured 17 surgeries in his 12 years of sickness. By May, Danny suspected the inevitable and asked his mother, "Am I going to die?"

"I never lied to that child a day in his life," Nancy said. "I told him his body had not responded to the treatments. 'It doesn't look good.'"

The decision on whether or not these exhausting treatments should be continued ultimately rested with Danny. He was afraid to disappoint doctors by discontinuing chemotherapy. Nancy stressed the decision was his. He decided it would come down to what the latest X-rays revealed. The tumors were larger, the cancer had continued to spread. Danny decided enough was enough.

"He decided then, 'Whatever time I have left is mine,'" Nancy said.

By September, Danny was gravely ill and hospitalized. Krauss rushed to see him. The linebacker was always upbeat and positive. Danny pulled through.

"Barry has a beautiful smile," Nancy said. "And Barry would bring his daughter, Ashley, to the hospital at times. And he wouldn't break down in front of Danny. That's another one of the things Danny said, 'The guys aren't afraid of the cancer. They will hug me.'"

The Colts were 0–13 and about to embark on a road trip to Atlanta. They wanted to fly Danny with them, but he was too sick to travel. They ended their winless skid with a 28–23 victory over the Falcons on December 7, 1986, then brought the game ball back to give to Danny.

"He had more than one," Nancy said proudly. "They gave that kid everything."

Danny knew he didn't have much time in the end. He gave players, including Krauss, a special keychain. On the back were the words, "Love, Danny."

That 1986 season was challenging for Krauss, who blew out his right knee. He needed three surgeries because of an infection.

"They basically said my career was over, but Danny inspired me to come back and I played another five years," Krauss said. "When I was rehabbing, I'd look at him and think, 'Really? And I'm always worried about my pain?' Danny was always smiling."

Danny Hulse died December 28, 1986, one month shy of his 15th birthday. Krauss phoned the family to express his sympathy and ask about funeral arrangements.

"You don't have to come," Nancy recalled saying. "You were there when he needed you most."

Krauss, now 56, was taking a sales trip to Alabama when recounting Danny's story in a lengthy phone call. The tone of his voice cracked when he recalled Nancy's words after Danny was gone.

"There was nothing more he could do," Nancy said. "He did it all. He did it when it counted."

When the Colts reported for camp the next summer, a training tent was renamed with a sign in Hulse's honor. About a decade later, Krauss phoned Nancy and John to do a documentary on their son. He asked if she could bring the No. 1 Colts jersey. Danny had worn that jersey in his casket, but Nancy had it removed before burial. She wanted to keep it as a special memory of her son and the Colts.

"'Danny wanted to be buried in your jersey,'" Krauss recalled Nancy saying, his voice uneven with emotion, 26 years since Danny departed. "That still touches me."

61 Unloading at Indy

The Mayflower moving vans split up after rolling out of the Baltimore Colts complex to give the impression they were headed in different directions. They all ended up in the same place in 1984—abandoned Fall Creek Elementary School in the 4900 block of Kessler Boulevard East Drive in Indianapolis. It was the most unlikely of headquarters for about 16 months until the team moved into their current complex at West 56th Street.

"It leaked like crazy," recalled Colts chief operating officer Pete Ward, who had been promoted to director of operations shortly after the relocation. "The linoleum hallways created large puddles when it rained from the leaky roof. The hallways were painted with yellow, green, and brown farm animals. It took me back to kindergarten."

Sue Kelly, a stay-at-home mother of three who lived a couple of blocks away, visited two days after the trucks unloaded and volunteered to help. That's what she did a lot of back then. She volunteered at school functions and church. But this offer would change her life.

"It's been a blessing for me," said Kelly, who is still with the Colts today.

Going back to school, at first, meant learning not to take a wrong step. "There were certain tiles you didn't walk on," she said. "We knew where to walk or the water would seep up through the tiles and get your feet all wet. And the toilets in the bathrooms were the little kids' toilets."

The Colts quickly realized they needed to address a lengthy list of priorities. "We kind of had our first meeting here, me and Jimmy Irsay and Bob Terpening and [head coach] Frank Kush, and we didn't even know what our address was," Ward said.

Irsay, son of owner Robert Irsay, was promoted to general manager on April 26. Terpening was named assistant general manager.

"Jim's office was the school library," Ward said. "He had the biggest office in the history of the NFL.

"It was like starting from scratch. We didn't have stationery. We didn't know our address. We didn't have a phone or a switchboard, a receptionist, stationery and envelopes, a copier or a fax machine, which was critical back then."

The receptionist job was important because civic and business leaders as well as fans were constant visitors. The Colts had yet to hire someone to handle tickets or hire a public relations contact to field media requests. The locker room was in the cafeteria. The weight room was in the gym/auditorium. The team had one AstroTurf field in place before summer, but that was the only practice field. Each coach had a classroom for an office.

"It was like, 'Okay, let's make a list and let's just go down one after another and get things done,'" Ward said. "We knew we needed to hire somebody to answer the phones pretty damn quick. Sue Kelly came over and asked if we needed any help. Cathy Catellier ran into Frank Kush at the Irish Pub and he said, 'Do you want a job?' She said, 'Sure.' So she was hired. And Sue and Cathy are still with us."

Catellier is owner Jim Irsay's executive assistant. Kelly is a receptionist.

"It's been a good ride," Kelly said. "I think the thing that impresses me the most is how much we've grown and how professional the people have been. Jim has hired some good people and surrounded himself with good people. It all really starts with Jim."

Even after the team's controversial relocation, Ward didn't give much thought to the uncertainty of the situation. "It was a tumultuous time," he said. "It was exciting but tumultuous. I was young and single so it probably didn't worry me as much as other people. It was hard work. I remember proofing stories for the game program at 2:00 in the morning. But I had a lot of energy back then. It was exciting."

Season tickets were offered on April 18. A clip-out advertisement was printed in *The Indianapolis Star*. In a 13-day period, the team received 30,000 applications for 143,000 season tickets. That was enough to fill the 60,127-seat Hoosier Dome more than twice.

Ticket manager Larry Hall was hired that May. He had been working for the Cincinnati Bengals. "I started two months to the day after the Mayflowers landed," said Hall, now 53 and still with the team.

Hall recalled how Robert Irsay borrowed an Illinois lottery machine to determine the order of handling ticket applications. Indiana didn't have a lottery machine. The Illinois machine spit out the number six, so every sixth request was submitted for a season ticket. Anybody who didn't get their request processed was placed on a waiting list, Hall said.

A new NFL market was eager to embrace the Colts, who were greeted at the Hoosier Dome for an introductory press conference by a crowd of about 20,000.

"Indianapolis fans were just so excited," linebacker Barry Krauss said. "So much excitement. To this day I feel bad for the true Baltimore Colts fans. They lost their franchise. But from a players' standpoint, it was an exciting time for us."

Krauss hopped in a limo with offensive tackle Chris Hinton for a ride around town. When they stopped, people inquired who they were. When advised these men were Colts, fans gushed.

Kelly said she never knew the Colts were coming to town. She read about it in the newspaper. She admits to not being much of a football fan. That changed.

"I was at the kids' school and everybody was talking about it," Kelly said. "It was wild. The funny thing is my brother was a top executive at Mayflower. He knew and didn't say a word. Small world, huh? They say the older you get, the smaller the world gets."

62 A Kush Cut in the Middle of Camp Practice

The franchise took a nosedive after the Colts' last playoff game in Baltimore in 1977. Head coach Ted Marchibroda exited after back-to-back 5–11 seasons. But things would get worse, spiraling downward to unthinkable depths of disarray and disappointment during the 1980s.

"In '81, we may have been the worst team in history," said Pete Ward, who started out as a public relations intern that year. "We had probably the worst defense in history. We broke 16 records for a lack of defense. We won two games, and they were both against the New England Patriots."

That was also the year the Colts drafted Holden Smith, a wide receiver out of California, in the 11th round with the 288th overall selection. While players come and go in the NFL each year, Smith is remembered not for what he did on the field but for how his brief career ended.

He didn't report to the Colts that first year, choosing instead to try out baseball. A year later, with Frank Kush now head coach, Smith made the team. He caught two passes for 36 yards that season. It would be his only year.

During 1983 training camp at Goucher College in Baltimore, Kush had seen enough of Smith and cut him. It's noteworthy because the coach sent the player packing in the middle of a camp practice!

"I was in my office," said Ward, in his second season as a full-time administrative assistant. "I was the guy who would process guys out. Holden came into my office and said, 'I need a flight home. I got cut.' I looked at him like, 'What? You didn't get cut. What are you talking about?' He said, 'No, Frank just cut me.' I said, 'Maybe you misunderstood. He's not going to cut you in the middle of practice.'

"Practice ended, and Holden was still sitting in my office. And all of these players came into my office and they're holding court in my office. 'Aw man, that was BS, Holden.' 'You shouldn't stand for that, Holden.'"

More players joined the protest. Smith became enraged.

"I'm kind of nervous, they're all getting Holden Smith fired up right in my office," Ward said. "I'm like, 'Guys, could you move it out to the lobby?'

"Holden says, 'I'll be right back,' and he goes upstairs to the cafeteria. The players and coaches were eating. He poured two root beers and went over behind Frank and dumped them on Frank in front of the team. There was some tussling going on."

A *Baltimore Sun* story reported Smith went after Kush for his teammates. "I did it for them," Smith was quoted as saying. "Everybody wants to pour something on him or hit him. Everybody feels good about it."

Kush accused Smith of "going through the motions" in practice. Smith contended he couldn't practice at full speed because of a pulled hamstring.

The dispute didn't end with soda. According to *The Sun*, Kush finished his meal in a drenched shirt, but was then showered with obscenities from Smith as the coach walked from his dorm room to team offices. When Kush returned to his dorm room, Smith took one more run at the coach.

"Holden followed Frank to his room and was kicking and pounding on his door," Ward said. "So we got Holden out of there and put him in a hotel. The kind of crazy part is that Frank went home that night, and Frank's apartment was literally right behind the motel that Holden Smith was staying at. I didn't realize that until later."

Smith never played in the NFL again.

"I figured I'd end up making a little scene," Smith told *The Sun* of his behavior. "I'm going to get to him somehow. I'm going to show him he ruined my life. I want him to remember for the rest of his life."

Kush, inducted into the College Football Hall of Fame in 1995 for his success at Arizona State, didn't last long in the NFL. The Colts were 0–8–1 in his first season, 7–9 the next year, and he quit with one game to go in a 4–12 season in '84, the Colts' debut in Indianapolis. The record was in stark contrast to his 176–54–1 mark with the Sun Devils, with whom he had only one losing season.

It's been said some Colts players celebrated when Kush quit. Somewhere, Smith undoubtedly did.

63 Ball Boy Beginning

As the 13-year-old son of Baltimore Colts owner Robert Irsay, Jimmy Irsay started out literally at the bottom as a ball boy in 1972.

Quarterback Bert Jones was drafted the next year. The rookie bonded with the ball boy. "He was the guy who picked up the dirty jocks and everything else in the locker room," Jones told *The Indianapolis Star* in 2009. "He'd spend most of his evenings in my room in training camp. He kind of matured. We matured as a team."

The younger Irsay went from grabbing dirty jocks to one day determining the men who would wear them. Jim Irsay was named vice president and general manager in 1984 at the tender age of 25. He became the Colts' owner in 1997 after his father's death. Jim Irsay will tell you, after all that he has achieved as an owner, the '75 Colts team has a special place in the man's heart.

He flew about three dozen members of that '75 team to Indianapolis to honor them before a Colts game on November 8, 2009, at Lucas Oil Stadium. The players who joined former head coach Ted Marchibroda on the field included Jones; running back Lydell Mitchell; wide receiver Roger Carr, offensive linemen George Kunz, Ken Mendenhall, and David Taylor; and defensive standouts Mike Curtis, Bruce Laird, John Dutton, and Fred Cook.

Some players attended the team's practice the day before. Everyone joined their host for dinner that evening at the Colts complex. It's not the first time Irsay has given former Colts the red-carpet treatment. He's hosted several Hall of Famers, including tight end John Mackey, wide receiver Raymond Berry, and head coach Don Shula.

"Y'all may not know the heart of Jimmy Irsay," Jones said. "He has a spectacular heart. Jimmy grew up with this 1975 team."

The '75 team stood in back of the south end zone while the current Colts warmed up. They posed for group pictures and hugged. At one point, quarterback Peyton Manning came over to talk to Jones.

"The Colts have a wonderful legacy in Baltimore, and Jimmy was a part of that legacy," Jones said. "But they've moved. They're in Indianapolis, and they're doing spectacularly here. They belong right here. It's a wonderful place, a wonderful time."

Former Baltimore Colts linebacker Stan White, who works in radio for Baltimore Ravens games, had nothing but positive things to say about his former ball boy. The trip to Indianapolis could have been awkward, considering Robert Irsay's controversial franchise move from Baltimore in 1984, but Jim Irsay made the weekend special.

"We always liked Jimmy Irsay a whole lot," White said, a few days before the Colts lost to the Ravens at Baltimore in an AFC Wild Card Playoff game on January 6, 2013. "We know he's done a great job there, and he's always reached out to the guys.

"He had the '75 team out there a couple of years ago and gave them rings from the AFC Eastern Division championship, rings that his father didn't give us. He's a class guy, and he's done a great job in Indianapolis. I'm really happy for him."

Thirty-eight years ago, the Colts improved by eight wins to finish 10–4. But the season turned out to mean more than wins and losses. The bonding experience for a ball boy and his team resonated on both sides.

"Because of that, we all had this sense of family," Jones said. "It was a signature time for this ballclub in the '70s and a signature time for Jimmy Irsay."

64 Kelvin Hayden's Super Bowl Ring

He grew up a Chicago Bears fan on the south side of Chicago, raised by his mother, Lynette. Against his former favorite team with his mother in the Dolphin Stadium stands, cornerback Kelvin Hayden ensured he would be remembered with a 56-yard interception return for a fourth-quarter touchdown that locked up the Indianapolis Colts' 29–17 Super Bowl XLI victory over the Bears on February 4, 2007, in Miami.

After the jubilant on-field celebration amid a steady rain, Hayden couldn't be found in the locker room with his teammates. He was still on the field, sharing the moment with his mother.

He would eventually share more than that with Lynette. After receiving his Super Bowl XLI ring, Hayden gave it to his mom. He never would have won it without her.

"Giving her my ring is my way of saying thank you," Hayden said during training camp the next season. "My agent wanted to see it, and my mom's work is not too far from my agent's firm. I went to go pick it up, and she brought it out early so her whole job was like, 'Oh wow! Can I take a picture of that?'

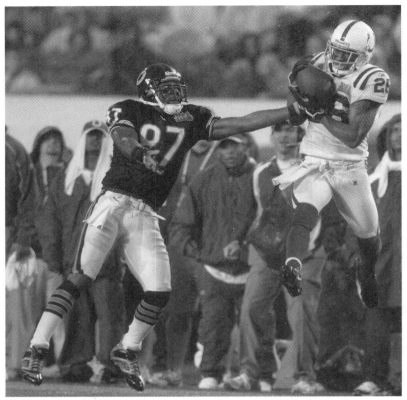

Colts cornerback Kelvin Hayden (26) intercepts a pass intended for Chicago Bears wide receiver Muhsin Muhammad (87) during the fourth quarter of Super Bowl XLI at Dolphin Stadium in Miami on Sunday, February 4, 2007. (AP Photo/Jeff Roberson)

"They said they were for the Colts all the way, but I don't believe that."

Hayden eventually returned home to play for the Bears in 2012.

"Everybody was saying, 'Oh, you just had to do it to us, didn't you?'" he told the *Chicago Tribune*. "And they said if anybody had to do it to the Bears, they were glad it was me."

That was his first career NFL interception. And it came against the man who converted Hayden from wide receiver to cornerback before his senior year at Illinois, Bears offensive coordinator Ron Turner.

A second-round draft selection in 2005, the always upbeat Hayden had to be patient about playing time. He didn't even start that Super Bowl—cornerback Nick Harper exited with an ankle injury late in the second quarter to set the stage for Hayden's glory.

After leaping high to snag the Rex Grossman pass along the sideline, he landed but an inch or two from being out of bounds. Hayden followed a caravan of Colts defenders to the end zone for the game's final score to secure the team's only Super Bowl title since the franchise moved to Indianapolis in 1984.

Asked outside the locker room if he realized what he had just done, he smiled and said, "Yeah, and against my hometown team."

Hayden hung on to that touchdown football as a keepsake. And that's not all.

"It's in my basement at home with everything I wore in that Super Bowl: the jersey, the gloves, the cleats," he said. "I put it all in a frame. The ball is in a case sitting right in front of it."

65 Bill Belichick Started as a Colt

The thought probably makes today's Colts fans cringe. But it's true. Before Bill Belichick became the no-nonsense head coach of the hated rival New England Patriots, he was a 23-year-old "sponge who absorbed everything" as a rookie assistant on Ted Marchibroda's 1975 Baltimore staff.

Marchibroda affectionately called him "Billy." Fresh out of Wesleyan University in Middletown, Connecticut, Belichick earned $25 per week and free lodging at Howard Johnson's. He was literally happy to be along for the ride—work days began with him driving Marchibroda and assistants Whitey Dovell and George Boutselis to Memorial Stadium. The Chrysler belonged to the head coach.

"I just know he was a hard-working guy," Marchibroda recalled. "You didn't see him again until the assignment was finished."

Belichick was responsible for charting defensive tendencies. He recorded downs and distances and how the defense lined up in formation and tackles.

In the years after leaving the Colts, Belichick blossomed into a defensive guru. He was Bill Parcells' defensive coordinator on two Giants Super Bowl winners. Belichick has added three more Super Bowl rings and has been named NFL Coach of the Year as many times since becoming Patriots head coach in 2000.

Anyone who has ever sat through a Belichick press conference knows the man can be as devoid of emotion as anyone. In the week leading up to the Patriots' trip to Indianapolis to face the Colts in an AFC Championship Game in January 2007, reporters were stunned at Belichick showing a different side when asked about his NFL origin.

The man gushed. Well, as close as he could come to gushing. He talked at length about his good old days with the Colts.

"I worked right outside of Earl Weaver's office," he said of the old Baltimore Orioles manager. "I wrote down all of the films. Every player was all on one card. Punch out the holes, put an ice pick in, drop the cards out, do the breakdowns, do probably 15 to 20 for [assistant coach] Maxie Baughan and the defensive coaches in the old Baltimore Memorial Stadium.

"I remember that. I learned probably more football in that room—it was a cinderblock closet, really—but I probably learned more football in that room than any place else I've ever been. It was like a graduate course in football."

Colts fans probably laugh when informed this rival coach, a man who guided the Patriots past the Colts twice in the playoffs including one AFC Championship Game, grew up a Baltimore fan. He admired Coach Don Shula and he started listing off the names: Johnny Unitas, Raymond Berry, Lenny Moore, Gino Marchetti, Ordell Braase, "Big Daddy" Gene Lipscomb, and Art Donovan.

"I can give you the whole team if you want," Belichick said.

His father, Steve, coached 33 years at the Naval Academy in Annapolis, Maryland. Dad taught son how to do defensive breakdowns. They attended Colts games.

Marchibroda remembered Belichick didn't say much on the job.

"That's because I didn't know anything," Belichick advised.

The memories kept coming back. At one point, the Colts couldn't use the stadium because the Orioles were in the World Series.

"We were practicing across the street at Eastern High School, pushing that 'Don't Walk' button and all of that, going across the street like an eighth-grade team would do," Belichick said with a smile.

The workdays could last as long as 18 hours. He ate it up.

"It was great just being able to ride in the car and sit and listen to Ted and Whitey and George talk about the different aspects of the game, of the team, of all of the things that they were dealing with, and to be able to absorb all of that from dawn to dusk...but it was a lot longer than that," he said. "It was tremendous."

Marchibroda pleaded to get approval on a $4,000 salary for Belichick, but general manager Joe Thomas refused. Belichick called the Detroit Lions, for whom his father had played fullback in 1941. His second job paid $10,000 and came with a car, a 1976 Ford Thunderbird.

But Billy would have stayed in Baltimore for $4,000.

"I'm deeply indebted to Ted for giving me that opportunity," he said. "There was no financial reward to it, but there was a personal and professional reward that I could never repay him for."

66 Dickerson Deal Pays Dividends

Desperate to turn around the team, general manager Jim Irsay pulled off a blockbuster 1987 trade for future Hall of Fame running back Eric Dickerson.

"He was their first legitimate big-time name player," said Mike Chappell, Colts beat writer for *The Indianapolis Star* since the team arrived in 1984. "It sort of put them on the map."

"He had won. He had broke records," strength and conditioning coach Tom Zupancic said. "When he walked into the locker room, the bar was raised. It raised the bar in the locker room 3'."

The Colts gave up running back Owen Gill, first- and second-round picks in 1988, and a second-round '89 pick to the Rams and sent unsigned rookie linebacker Cornelius Bennett to Buffalo. The Bills dealt first-round picks in '88 and '89 as well as a second-round '89 selection to the Rams.

"We finally had a marquee offensive player. Wow!" linebacker Barry Krauss said. "We actually had more than just three-and-outs. He was a great, great football player. He took us places. It was awesome to watch him. He gave the defense a breath."

In an interview with Chappell, Irsay acknowledged a sense that something needed to be done to bolster the franchise.

"From the Colts' standpoint, that was something big for us, that was something that took us out of not being on *Monday Night*

Running back Eric Dickerson (29) looks for running room during the AFC Divisional playoff game between the Indianapolis Colts and the Cleveland Browns on January 9, 1988, in Cleveland, Ohio. The Browns won the game 38–21. (AP Photo/Paul Spinelli)

Football for 10 years, not winning, not doing anything for virtually a decade," Irsay said.

Colts director of operations Pete Ward picked up Dickerson at the airport. "We were driving down the freeway and had the radio on," Ward said. "WIBC was saying, 'This is undoubtedly the biggest sports news in the history of Indianapolis.' We were chuckling about that. There was an aura about Eric. You knew you had maybe the best of all time, and he was riding in the car with me."

There wasn't much time for Dickerson to prepare for his Colts debut. Back to the airport he went to join the team for a road game against the Jets.

"I remember they were walking through plays in a hotel ballroom that night with Eric," Ward said. "He came in during the middle of the first quarter and the Jets coaches were scrambling, giving signals, making adjustments. I think his first play was a run around right end for like 13 yards. It was like a man among children."

The Colts defeated the Jets 19–14 to improve to 4–3. Dickerson played in nine games and ran for 1,011 yards and five TDs. The Colts finished 9–6 and qualified for the playoffs, an Indianapolis first. But they lost 38–21 at Cleveland.

"In '87 we went to the playoffs, in '88 we should have gone to the playoffs, and in '89 we should have gone to the playoffs. It wasn't Eric's fault," Ward said.

The Colts were 9–7 in '88 with Dickerson running for 1,659 yards and 14 TDs. One game in particular brought credibility to the franchise. The Colts made their *Monday Night Football* Indianapolis debut on October 31, 1988, a 55–23 "Halloween Massacre" of Denver at the Hoosier Dome. Dickerson ran for four touchdowns before the Broncos scored. The Colts led 45–10 at halftime. Colts fans were ecstatic about the drubbing of quarterback John Elway, who had refused to play for the Colts after being drafted with the No. 1 overall pick in '83. Elway, who was traded to

Denver shortly after that draft, was replaced by Gary Kubiak after the game got more out of hand.

"That was the first time we got an all-around boost of excitement from a national perspective," Zupancic said.

The Colts finished 8–8 in '89 when Dickerson ran for 1,311 yards and seven TDs. He set an NFL record with seven consecutive 1,000-yard rushing seasons.

Despite being the NFL's highest-paid player, contract disputes and injuries as well as his outspoken criticism of the franchise soured the end of Dickerson's Indianapolis experience. When contract-extension talks were stopped by owner Robert Irsay, Dickerson lashed out at Jim Irsay, saying he "deserves to be a general manager as much as Daffy Duck does" and that the team "couldn't beat some of the worst Canadian league teams."

"He will never be in the Colts' Ring of Honor," Chappell said of Dickerson, referring to the Daffy Duck wisecrack.

When the runner said he couldn't play because he was hurt, the team thought he was dogging it. The Colts placed Dickerson on the inactive list for seven games after a contract holdout in 1990. Then came a disastrous '91. Trouble began in preseason after a game at Denver. Dickerson flew to California for a TV talk show, upon which Dickerson ripped the Colts. In September, he shoved *The Indianapolis News'* Tom Rietmann in the locker room and had to be restrained by defensive back Eugene Daniel.

"It was much ado about nothing," Rietmann says now. "He apologized. He's in the Hall of Fame and he deserves it."

They ran into each other after a game in Oakland years later when Dickerson was retired. "He greeted me like I was his best friend," said Rietmann, who covered the Colts from 1984 to 1991.

The Colts imploded to a forgettable 1–15 in '91. As he walked off the field after a season-ending 17–3 loss at Tampa Bay, Dickerson made it clear that would be his last game with the team. He was traded in early '92, fetching fourth- and eighth-round picks from the Los Angeles Raiders, but he was never a standout player again. He retired after two more seasons as the NFL's second-leading rusher with 13,259 career yards. Dickerson was inducted into the Pro Football Hall of Fame in 1999.

Irsay didn't hold a grudge. He invited Dickerson to return to Indianapolis and be honored that year.

"Of course there were bumps in the road," Irsay said, "but time goes by and you have to move on. When I think of Eric, I remember the good times and laugh at some of the others."

67 Playoff Heartache at Home

What fans likely remember, other than there were too many boisterous Tennessee Titans backers in the RCA Dome on January 16, 2000, is running back Eddie George breaking a tackle and sprinting into the clear.

What fans might forget is a pivotal moment early in the fourth quarter when Titans kicker Al Del Greco saw Colts punt returner Terrence Wilkins step out of bounds on an 87-yard runback to the Colts' 3 with the home team behind by a touchdown. So close to a game-changing play, and then it came back.

The Colts' first-ever playoff game in Indianapolis was supposed to end differently. Although both the Titans and Colts finished the regular season 13–3, the Colts were AFC East champions and the home team. But the Titans dominated the second half and celebrated a 19–16 victory.

Down 9–6, George broke the big run just three plays into the second half. Colts inside linebackers Mike Peterson and Mike Barber blitzed. The Titans called a trap.

"The perfect play," strong-side linebacker Bertrand Berry told *The Indianapolis Star*. "They caught us."

Barber got swept to the left. Peterson tried to spin back but was pushed away to the right. George ran 68 yards for the touchdown. While the visitors led just 13–9, the score dramatically shifted momentum. The Colts had bottled up George and the Titans' run game for much of the game. Twenty-two runs gained six yards or less. Tennessee had two carries for 11 and 15 yards. But the biggie went for 68.

"I feel pretty darn good about how our defense played," Colts coach Jim Mora said afterward, "other than the one long run by George."

Del Greco's foot and his eyes were vital the rest of the way. The kicker had made three of his four field goals, and the Titans were leading 16–9 when Wilkins caught the punt and appeared to give the Colts the spark they so desperately needed. Standing at the Colts' 34, Del Greco saw Wilkins' right foot step out of bounds. Instead of first-and-goal at the 3, instant replay confirmed a 63-yard turnaround. The ball came back to the Colts' 34.

"I was standing there and pointing," Del Greco said. "[Coach] Jeff [Fisher] came over and asked me if I was sure. I told him I was 100 percent sure he stepped out. I couldn't see any way they could find that he didn't. His whole foot was out of bounds."

The replay showed the outside of Wilkins' shoe touched the sideline on consecutive steps.

"I didn't know I stepped out," Wilkins said. "If I knew I stepped out, I would've quit running. I guess I did, though. That hurts, man."

How big was that play? Fisher didn't have his challenge flag, it had been forgotten by an assistant equipment manager. The head coach called a timeout to ensure the play would be reviewed. When he returned home, someone sent a framed picture box containing a red challenge flag and a hammer, the tool to be used in the event of another challenge emergency. Fisher liked it so much, he hung that framed red challenge flag in his office.

Del Greco kicked his fourth field goal for a 19–9 lead. The Titans limited the Colts' fourth-ranked offense to just 305 total yards. The only touchdown, on a Peyton Manning 15-yard run, came with 1:51 remaining. Running back Edgerrin James, the NFL rushing champ, managed a mere 56 yards on 20 carries.

"It was that kind of day," Manning said.

The Titans' Yancey Thigpen caught the subsequent onside kick, and the Colts' season was history.

"They outplayed us today," Mora said. "Not by a lot, but they outplayed us enough to win the game."

Defensive end Chad Bratzke suggested he would eventually feel better about the team's 10-win improvement, the best turnaround in NFL history, but it would take a few days. "This is it; no more football for us this year," he said. "Right now, that hits hard."

Mora was asked 13 years later what he remembered about the game. "I don't know if we were as good as Tennessee," he said of the Titans, who won at Jacksonville to advance to Super Bowl XXXIV, where they came up one yard shy on the final play of potentially tying the game in a 23–16 loss to the St. Louis Rams.

68 Another Playoff Heartbreaker

Expectations were understandably higher for the Colts in 2000 after the record 10-game turnaround a year earlier. The key pieces were still in place. The defending AFC Eastern Division champions thought they had learned from the previous year's accomplishments as well as a 19–16 AFC Divisional playoff loss to Tennessee at the RCA Dome.

"The Triplets" returned to form as quarterback Peyton Manning led the NFL with 4,413 passing yards, running back Edgerrin James won his second consecutive rushing crown with 1,709 yards, and wide receiver Marvin Harrison caught a league-best 102 passes.

But the follow-up season was more of a struggle. The Colts' defense was 25th in rushing defense at 120.9 yards allowed per game. In total defense, the unit ranked 21st at 334.8 total yards allowed per game. The lingering question from a year before was still the same—there's enough "O" but what about the "D?"

The Colts opened with a 27–14 win at Kansas City's Arrowhead Stadium. A 38–31 home loss to Oakland set them back, but then came two wins, 43–14 against Jacksonville and 18–16 at Buffalo. A 24–16 loss at New England dropped them to 3–2 but precipitated a three-game win streak: 37–24 at Seattle, 30–23 against the Patriots, and 30–18 over Detroit.

Just when it seemed the ship had been righted, the Colts dropped a 27–24 road game to Chicago at Soldier Field. It was an embarrassing loss. The Bears had entered the game 1–7 and would finish the year 5–11. After a 23–15 home win over the Jets, the Colts' playoff hopes were suddenly in jeopardy when they lost three in a row. The first two were close ones, 26–24 at Green Bay and 17–14 at home to Miami. A 27–17 loss at the Jets exposed the run defense as running back Curtis Martin went off for 203 yards in 30 carries, a game he said at the time was the best of his career. The Jets didn't win another game and ended up 9–7.

On the brink of playoff elimination, the Colts rebounded with three consecutive wins—44–20 over Buffalo, 20–13 at Miami, and 31–10 over Minnesota—to finish 10–6 and earn an AFC wild-card berth as the sixth seed. The Colts had split the regular season meetings with their first-round playoff foe, Miami. The road win in Week 16 reminded the Colts that they could travel to the Sunshine State and knock off the 11–5 AFC East champions.

On December 30, 2000, everything was looking up for the visitors again as the Colts led 14–0 at halftime. And they should have had a larger lead, considering Miami's Jay Fiedler had thrown three interceptions, Colts holder Hunter Smith had called for a fake field goal run but was stopped short of the first down, and Colts wide receiver Jerome Pathon dropped a sure touchdown pass, forcing the team to settle for a field goal try.

Back came the Dolphins in the second half. They opened with a 70-yard scoring drive as running back Lamar Smith punched it in from two yards out. Miami then kicked a field goal, but Mike Vanderjagt hit a 50-yarder to make it 17–10. The Dolphins put together a game-tying scoring drive of 80 yards with Fiedler throwing a nine-yard TD pass to tight end Jed Weaver with 34 seconds remaining to force overtime.

The Colts had a chance to win it in extra time after forcing the Dolphins to punt. But Vanderjagt caught some turf and was wide right on a 49-yard field goal attempt. "I let my teammates down, I let my organization down, I let the city of Indianapolis down," Vanderjagt said. "It's a pretty big burden to carry into the off-season."

Miami took advantage of the miss with a 61-yard drive. Smith capped the 23–17 win with a 17-yard TD run. He ran for a team playoff-record 209 yards on a playoff record 40 carries. Once again, the Colts' run defense had been exposed.

A day later, Mora said, "I know the expectations at the beginning of the year were very, very high for this football team, and that was based strictly on what our record was last year. I personally think they were too high."

In the Colts' 10 victories, they allowed just 82.6 yards rushing per game. In seven losses, that number jumped to a 154.8-yard average.

Colts president Bill Polian accepted blame for not building a better defense.

"The constant to go beyond that is to have, if not a dominating defense, at least a defense that's reliable at all times," he said. "And I don't think, from a personnel standpoint, that we had a reliable defense. That's my fault. We've got to get better in that personnel area. You look at the teams that advance, they'll be the ones with the most reliable defense."

Mora, 0–6 in NFL playoff games, became the only coach in league history to win at least 100 regular season games and not win in the playoffs. His six losses tied the league record for consecutive defeats in the postseason, a dubious distinction shared with Steve Owen who coached from 1939 to 1950.

"I don't feel snake-bit, fellas, believe me," Mora said after the game. "There's nothing to being snake-bit. You either get it done or you don't."

Twelve years removed from what would be his last playoff game, Mora summed up the Miami loss as, "A lot of games are winnable in the NFL that you don't win."

When his playoff record is broached with the suggestion that going 0–6 was unfair because he had proven he could win in the NFL, he set the record straight with a sharp rebuttal.

"It's not unfair," he said. "It is what it is. Look at George Allen's playoff record. Look at Chuck Knox's playoff record. I coached in the USFL, had a lot of good players, and we beat George Allen, we beat Marv Levy. We won seven USFL playoff games and lost only one."

Allen had a 2–7 record in the NFL playoffs. Knox's postseason mark was 7–11. Mora, who still owns the record for most regular season wins (125) without an NFL playoff victory, coached the USFL's Philadelphia/Baltimore Stars to three consecutive championship games and won the last two.

69 Mora Goes, Polian Stays, Dungy Arrives

When Indianapolis Colts president Bill Polian was asked in the 2001 preseason if head coach Jim Mora needed to win a playoff game, it set the executive off in an angry outburst that ended a rather brief interview.

Mora had lost playoff games the previous two years, so it was a fair question. What's ironic is by season's end, after the Colts slid to 6–10, Mora and Polian didn't see eye to eye and owner Jim Irsay had to decide between the two.

"Had not Bill Polian wanted to fire Vic Fangio, who is one of the best defensive coordinators in the league, as well as special teams coach Kevin Spencer, I wouldn't have lost my job," Mora said in February 2013.

Irsay liked Mora but eventually sided with Polian.

"He didn't want me to go," Mora said of Irsay. "It was a tough decision. But it came down to me or Polian."

Polian said at the time of the firing, "My feeling was that we needed a change in defensive approach. Not because Vic isn't a good coach. He is. Not because his system is not good. It is. I just think with the young players we have, we need a different approach."

The Colts had started off the season with a couple of wins, 45–24 at the New York Jets and 42–26 against Buffalo at home. But then the season took a decidedly wrong turn. In what would be remembered as Tom Brady's first NFL start at quarterback, New England thrashed the visiting Colts 44–13, a resounding beating that included two interceptions returned for touchdowns. The lopsided loss prompted one reporter to ask Mora the next week if offensive players should practice tackling.

The NFL had already delayed the season one week after the 9/11 attacks, then the Colts had an early bye week. What should have been a well-rested team returned home and lost a maddeningly frustrating 23–18 game to Oakland. While Peyton Manning threw two touchdown passes to Marvin Harrison and running back Edgerrin James ran for 116 yards, the Colts played catchup all game, especially after yet another interception return for a touchdown gave the Raiders a 13–3 lead in the second quarter. The Colts' last gasp ended with another interception at the Raiders' 44 in the final minute.

Another home game didn't reverse the trend as the Patriots' David Patten single-handedly demoralized the Colts defense by contributing on four scoring plays. He opened a 38–17 rout with a 29-yard TD run in the first quarter, then he went the distance on a 91-yard pass play and threw a 60-yard TD pass to Troy Brown in the second quarter. New England led 28–6 at halftime. Brown finished the scoring with a six-yard TD catch in the final quarter.

The Colts were in desperate need of a win and they got one, but it came at too high a cost. James, the NFL rushing champion in 1999 and 2000, tore his left anterior cruciate ligament in a 35–28 victory at Kansas City. While James assured everyone he was okay, he wasn't. Speculation swirled about the severity of the injury into late November before the Colts finally announced their workhorse back was out for the season and needed surgery.

While the Colts won their first game without him, 30–14 at Buffalo, a 4–4 record would be the final high point.

In the next game, Manning took a vicious shot that left him bloodied and with a broken jaw. He missed only one play, but the Colts lost 27–24 to Miami. That began a five-game losing streak. Manning pressed to make plays because the defense was surrendering points at an alarming rate. During the skid, opponents scored an average of 36.2 points per game. Mora cracked after a 40–21 home loss to San Francisco and went off on his infamous "Playoffs?!" tirade.

Another injury had an impact as linebacker Mike Peterson, who made 104 solo tackles the year before, suffered a torn knee ligament and was lost for seven of the last eight games. The Colts allowed a combined 107 points in the next three games, two of those losses. Before their 10th loss, 42–17 at St. Louis, some in the media had questioned if the intense Mora had lost his fire. Rams coach Dick Vermeil wasn't buying that and responded on a conference call, "Some people don't know what they don't know, and they never will."

The Colts closed out Mora's coaching career with a 29–10 home win over Denver. The defense finished the season with 486 points allowed, the most since 1981's hapless 2–14 team gave up 533. Mora sounded like a man who knew the pink slip was coming.

"I will not quit. I want to coach here," Mora said, tears trickling from angry eyes. "I should be the coach here. I'll just tell you that right now. I should be."

Two days later, he was fired.

Two weeks later, Tony Dungy was hired. He had been fired just eight days earlier by Tampa Bay. Irsay initially phoned Tampa to tell Dungy he was the owner's only choice. Carolina had also interviewed the coach, but contrary to reports, there wasn't much of a bidding war. Irsay made it clear he would pay whatever it took.

"We weren't going to be outbid for Tony Dungy," Irsay said. "He was going to be a Colt for sure."

Dungy's reputation as a defensive guru grew with the Buccaneers, but they couldn't score points. Now he was joining a team that had an explosive offense but couldn't stop anybody.

Polian tried to address as many defensive needs as possible in the 2002 draft, using seven of eight selections on that side of the ball. While four of his picks didn't provide much in the way of help, two most certainly did. The first-round pick, defensive end Dwight Freeney, became a pass-rushing cornerstone and the team's all-time sack leader. Linebacker David Thornton, taken in the fourth round, was a solid contributor with a team-high 145 tackles in his second season.

70 Building the First Winner

The Baltimore Colts were just 3–9 in 1954, but important steps were taken the next year with the arrival of running back Alan Ameche, the third overall pick in the NFL draft. Wide receiver Raymond Berry, chosen in the 20th round a year before, also came on board. The team finished 5–6–1 in its second season under head coach Weeb Ewbank.

Ameche, the Heisman Trophy winner out of Wisconsin, ran for 961 yards and nine touchdowns, earning the honor of NFL Rookie of the Year. "The Iron Horse" was also rewarded with the first of four consecutive Pro Bowl selections.

Berry's Hall of Fame career began quietly with just 13 catches for 205 yards as a rookie in 1955. The only time Berry would ever catch fewer passes was his final season, when he had 11 in seven games in 1967. But he had no idea his career would blossom and couldn't be accused of having an over-inflated opinion of where he stood with the team.

"I almost got cut," Berry said of his rookie preseason camp, "and John [Unitas] did get cut."

Pittsburgh never gave rookie quarterback John Unitas a chance. The future Hall of Famer didn't get so much as a single snap in preseason games before being released. Unitas was a Pittsburgh native drafted in the ninth round by the Steelers. It's been said the Steelers' ill-fated decision to send Unitas packing incurred "The Curse of Unitas." Pittsburgh made the same mistake twice by trading future Hall of Fame quarterback Len Dawson to Cleveland after the 1959 season. From 1955 through 1971, the Steelers didn't reach the playoffs a single time and had just four winning seasons.

Among those making the Steelers roster instead of Unitas was Ted Marchibroda, whose NFL playing career was uneventful but he later distinguished himself as an endearing head coach in two stints with the Colts, in Baltimore and in Indianapolis. The retired coach has been asked many times over the years what stood out about the rookie Unitas. There wasn't much to recollect.

"They never gave Johnny an opportunity to show what he could do," Marchibroda said. "I don't remember anything about him as a player or anything in training camp."

Marchibroda's playing career ended in 1957. He passed for 2,169 yards with 16 touchdowns and 29 interceptions. Unitas ended up with 40,239 passing yards, 290 touchdowns, and 253 interceptions. Marchibroda and Unitas had played against each other once in college, when Marchibroda was at St. Bonaventure and Unitas was at Louisville. Marchibroda chuckles about winning that game.

"We took 'em there, so maybe I was better," Marchibroda said jokingly.

A few friends, including former longtime Buffalo Bills coach Marv Levy, tease him about landing a job instead of a legend. Unitas told *Sports Illustrated* in a 1957 interview, "I passed for three or four touchdowns in scrimmage and I got away on a couple of 30-yard runs, but they never let me play in exhibitions."

Several reports cited Coach Walt Kiesling's ill-fated belief that Unitas wasn't smart enough. The Steelers went 4–8 that season. Unitas played semi-pro ball for the Bloomfield Rams, making $3 per game the rest of that year.

Receiver Raymond Berry (82) makes a catch against the Minnesota Vikings on December 9, 1963. (AP Photo)

While the 1956 Colts ledger suggests an uneventful 5–7 record, the franchise unknowingly added its greatest cornerstone in Unitas. "That's when the genius of Weeb Ewbank started asserting itself," Berry said.

Berry recollects a Louisville coach called Ewbank on behalf of Unitas, asking the Colts coach to give the quarterback a look. The next preseason, Unitas hopped a ride to Baltimore with another player for a Colts tryout and was signed to be a backup. When quarterback George Shaw broke his leg in the fourth game, Unitas entered in an inauspicious debut—his first pass was intercepted and returned for a touchdown. He also had a fumble.

Years later, when Marchibroda was back in Baltimore, he golfed with Unitas. The former Colts coach recalled mentioning the passer's reputation for having an unorthodox playing style. "He wasn't afraid to try things," Marchibroda said.

The coach recalled Unitas stating clearly, "I knew what I was doing."

Berry thought his NFL days were numbered when he showed up for '56 camp. "I was on the list to be cut and be replaced," Berry said.

But Ewbank saw something in both Berry and Unitas and kept them. Unitas completed a rookie-record 55.6 percent of his passes. His last touchdown pass for the season was thrown in the season finale and was the start of a record 47-game streak with at least one scoring pass.

Baltimore added another key building block in 1956, drafting future Hall of Fame halfback/flanker Lenny Moore with the ninth overall draft pick. Like Unitas, he redefined his position as a two-way threat, sometimes runner and other times receiver.

In 1957, the Colts improved to 7–5. It wasn't good enough to make the playoffs after the team finished with losses in their last two games on the West Coast, 17–13 at San Francisco and 37–21 to the Los Angeles Rams. Six Colts including Unitas, Ameche,

Gino Marchetti, and Art Donovan made the Pro Bowl. It was the first of 10 Pro Bowl selections for Unitas.

The team's Pro Bowl honorees didn't include Moore despite the fact that his 488 yards rushing were just five fewer than Ameche on 46 fewer carries. Another building block was added with the first-round selection of Ohio State offensive tackle Jim Parker with the eighth overall pick. Parker would become an anchor for the offensive line with eight Pro Bowl selections. He played tackle and guard.

After five years of building, the Colts were poised for a memorable 1958 when they won their first NFL championship.

71 Patriot Games, Playoff Growing Pains

Any Indianapolis Colts fan can tell you about the New England Patriots. Those guys from Foxborough, Massachusetts, always seem to get in the way.

As fate would have it, Patriots quarterback Tom Brady made his first NFL start against the Colts on September 30, 2001. But of course. Who else would have been more appropriate, considering the years to come, when the Patriots and Colts would engage in some epic confrontations? Brady won that first game 44–13 at home, and with Bill Belichick as his head coach he has a 10–4 record against the Colts since his debut. Brady won the first of three Super Bowls in his first season as a starter.

A November 30, 2003, game at the RCA Dome stands out. The matchup of 9–2 teams came down to the final moments. The Colts had a first-and-goal at the 2-yard line. Patriots linebacker

Willie McGinest had hobbled off with what many saw as a fake knee injury to stop the clock and give his reeling defense a chance to regroup. It worked. Two Edgerrin James rushes gained one yard. A third-down pass to the corner of the end zone sailed incomplete. Then James was stopped on fourth down for no gain by McGinest, Ted Washington, and Rodney Harrison. McGinest sprinted down the field in celebration. That knee looked just fine.

"It's easy for me to say he faked it," said Colts radio voice Bob Lamey. "It sure looked like it."

Those teams met again in the frigid cold at "The Razor," Foxborough's Gillette Stadium, for the AFC Championship Game on January 18, 2004. Colts quarterback Peyton Manning threw four interceptions. Colts receivers complained to no avail that they were held by Patriots defenders. Colts wide receiver Reggie Wayne took a shot to the head from safety Eugene Wilson and no penalty flag was thrown. The 24–14 Colts loss left more than a sour taste.

Colts president Bill Polian, a member of the NFL's Competition Committee, was asked outside the locker room for his opinion of the officiating and vowed, "I'll express it to the appropriate people at the appropriate time."

A day later, Colts head coach Tony Dungy weighed in. "The disappointing thing to me is there were some things that happened in the game that I just know in my heart in the regular season would be penalties," Dungy said. "Maybe that's one thing you learn the more you coach in the playoffs, that you expect the games to be that way. Maybe we've got to coach a little differently in the playoffs."

Entering the next season, the NFL announced one of its rules of emphasis would be to enforce defensive holding, a clear reaction to the previous Colts-Patriots game. The defending champion Patriots hosted the Colts in the primetime season opener on a

Thursday night. Manning threw an interception at the Patriots' 1-yard line. James fumbled twice inside the Patriots' 20-yard line, including one at the 1-yard line while stretching for the goal line. When Colts kicker Mike Vanderjagt missed a 48-yard field goal with 19 seconds remaining, the Patriots escaped with a 27–24 victory.

Once more the two teams would meet again in the postseason, this time in the AFC Divisional round, again at Foxborough. And it wasn't close. The Patriots prevailed 20–3 in another numbing result for the visitors.

"We had a great team, a great coach, a great owner; too many greats to be sitting here sad," Colts tight end Marcus Pollard said in the locker room.

The Colts would finally break through against their nemesis in the next two regular seasons, both times in New England, with 40–21 and 27–20 victories. But the most important Colts triumph was to come as Manning rallied his team from a 21–3 deficit to a 38–34 win over New England in a memorable AFC Championship Game on January 21, 2007, at the RCA Dome. Cornerback Marlin Jackson's interception of a Brady pass ended it. The Colts moved on to win Super Bowl XLI in two weeks.

Looking back six years later, the defensive coach in Dungy is proud of how his team endured after all those previous frustrations against the Patriots.

"Marlin's interception, there's plenty of interceptions and we've intercepted Tom Brady a few times, but to go to the Super Bowl and get that ball and know you're going to the Super Bowl, I can't remember a play like that in my career," Dungy said.

72 "It's a New Era"

In the end, it was about Irsay intuition.

Indianapolis Colts owner Jim Irsay didn't need much time to weigh the pros and cons of what to do with his franchise after a 2–14 collapse in 2011. A day after the last game, on January 2, 2012, Irsay began to clean house with the firing of vice chairman Bill Polian as well as Polian's son, Chris, vice president of football operations and general manager.

Irsay would say more than a year later it was a decision he had thought about for some time as the season was coming to an end. Bill Polian was a six-time NFL Executive of the Year and had provided his owner a Super Bowl XLI ring and a playoff team in 11-of-14 seasons. But it's no secret the man had a legendary temper and didn't always play nice with others. While his son had risen through the front-office ranks rather quickly, some decisions had been called into question. It's fair to surmise Irsay lacked confidence in Chris Polian running the franchise as the 69-year-old Bill Polian neared retirement and took on a lesser role. The younger Polian couldn't be fired without the other. The father undoubtedly wouldn't have tolerated that. A new general manager would want to choose his own head coach, which meant Jim Caldwell ultimately had to go, too.

Irsay stood at the media center lectern of the Indiana Farm Bureau Football Center and basically said he had to trust his gut instinct. The Polians were out. Caldwell was dismissed 15 days later.

"It's a new era," Irsay said, "and we're moving into exciting times by my estimation."

The use of the word "exciting" might have seemed an unexpected choice of adjectives, but Irsay had a sense for what was about to transpire and the uncertainty sparked a stimulating emotion. He didn't yet know his new general manager or head coach, but the owner realized quarterback Peyton Manning would have to be released to make way for rookie quarterback Andrew Luck. Manning was released March 7, 2012. Luck was selected with the No. 1 overall pick on April 26, 2012.

The Colts were on the verge of some serious salary cap problems, which meant they couldn't afford to keep both quarterbacks. And there was the lingering neck problem, for which Manning had endured four surgeries in 19 months. Before Manning departed in a tearful farewell and Luck was greeted as the face of new hope for a rebuilding team, Irsay plucked Philadelphia Eagles director of player personnel Ryan Grigson to be general manager, then they hired Baltimore Ravens defensive coordinator Chuck Pagano as head coach.

Bill Polian took a job with ESPN as an NFL analyst. Former Buffalo Bills coach Marv Levy, who went to four Super Bowls with teams Polian built, speaks highly of his former boss.

"Bill can be rather combative with the media from time to time, but he was fantastic to work with," Levy said. "He's intense, but usually when he gets angry, it's in defense of people who are working for him. He had opinions, but he would listen to other opinions. He had a knack for finding talent."

Bill Polian would say his biggest mistake was not having a quality backup quarterback behind Manning, who missed the 2011 season with those neck problems. After Polian's firing, the former Colts' boss had one more chance to show his disagreeable nature when he refused an interview request from *The Indianapolis Star* and spoke instead to the Associated Press.

"The family part of it is the hardest part, whether it's Chris or any of the people that are close to me," Polian said. "Saying

Best, Worst of Bill Polian

The front-office decisions that stood out the most in president/vice chairman Bill Polian's 14 seasons running the Indianapolis Colts.

Best

1. Picking Peyton—He took Peyton Manning instead of Ryan Leaf with the No. 1 overall pick in 1998. It might be the single most important decision in franchise history.
2. Along came Edge—Some draft experts thought the Colts should take running back Ricky Williams, but Polian selected Edgerrin James with the fourth overall pick in 1999. James became the team's all-time leading rusher.
3. "Free" instead—Coach Tony Dungy liked defensive tackle Albert Haynesworth, but Polian used his first-round pick in 2002 on defensive end Dwight Freeney, who would become the team's all-time sack leader.
4. Quite a find—The top picks everybody remembers, but Polian struck gold with the fifth-round selection of defensive end Robert Mathis in 2003.
5. Undrafted but useful—Every year, the Colts signed an undrafted player who made a name for himself. Middle linebacker Gary Brackett became a defensive captain. Running back Dominic Rhodes, cornerback Nick Harper, and safety Melvin Bullitt also became starters.

Worst

1. Passing on perfection—Polian considered a 2009 quest for a perfect season meaningless and along with coach Jim Caldwell had

goodbye to people is the hardest part. When you've been here 14 years, you've built up a lot of relationships. I've told the players for years and years to prepare for life after football because this is a terminal profession for all of us and that's true."

Irsay said he appreciated what Bill Polian did for the Colts. "I've always said there is a great loyalty in this business because when I walk into the locker room with my team on opening Sunday, I'm expected to make sure the circle that I've built is as strong as it can be for us to the starters of a 14–0 team benched to avoid possible injuries with the Colts leading the New York Jets in the third quarter of what would be a memorable home loss at Lucas Oil Stadium.

2. No go on Ugoh—It's referred to as the biggest draft miss of his career, when the Colts traded up in the second round in 2007 to take offensive tackle Tony Ugoh. It cost the team a 2008 first-round pick and a fourth-round 2007 selection. Ugoh never became the left tackle replacement for Pro Bowler Tarik Glenn and was released in the opening week of 2010 after just 37 games played.

3. Simon miss—The Colts thought they had a solid run stopper when they signed free-agent defensive tackle Corey Simon in 2005, but he was overweight and never returned to 2003 Pro Bowl form. He developed a complication from a knee injury and was placed on the non-football illness/injury list. He did not attend Super Bowl XLI with the other inactive players and said he never received a ring for the Colts' win. He retired in 2007.

4. Loud talk radio—The 2001 season was spiraling out of control when Polian agreed to appear on local talk radio with Mark Patrick and phone-in guest Jay Mohr. The debate about Edgerrin James' knee injury turned into a sparring match as Polian lost his temper. Polian was in the right, but the way he handled this couldn't have been more wrong.

5. Not a rush—The Colts thought they were looking to the future when they selected defensive end Jerry Hughes in the first round of the 2010 draft. But in three seasons, which included several healthy scratches early on, the pass rusher was a backup with five sacks and 62 tackles. He was dealt to Buffalo in the 2013 off-season.

win," Irsay said in announcing the Polian firings. "Sentiment and those things can't come between that, and that's the way I've always looked at it in seeing this business for over 40 years. So it was difficult, it was time, and it was the right decision to make. Fourteen years is a long time in this league, a lot of great memories, [I have] been through a lot with Bill, and I treasure all those memories, but it was time.

"In terms of how do you make a decision like this as an owner, it's an intuitive decision and a lot goes into it. From some of [the media] perspective, you only see a little bit of what goes on and all of the elements that go into making some of these big decisions. But I'm always well aware of everything that goes on in my organization. [I] keep a pulse on that, and [I] have always believed it's about timing, it's about energy, and it's about what the time calls for. Bill [Polian] is a Hall of Fame general manager. I hope to be there in Canton [Ohio] when he gets inducted. He is certainly a Ring of Honor individual in our stadium and our town, but it was time."

73 Tailgate with Blue Crew

Eric Van Wagner remembers his triumphant walk around the spiral corridors of Kansas City's Arrowhead Stadium after the Indianapolis Colts had defeated the Chiefs 10–7 in an AFC Divisional playoff game on January 7, 1996.

"A lady patted me on the back and said, 'Good job, Blue Crew. It's not easy to come in here and win,'" he recalled.

Thank you, Kansas City. That name would stick.

A year later, Randy Collins started walking around the RCA Dome's South Lot asking for signatures to form a group for tailgaters. The Blue Crew Fan Club was eventually born in 1998.

"The first few years were kind of tough," said club president Collins, 55. "Everybody thought we were trying to sell something. We said, 'No, we were just trying to start a fan club.' There was a fan club, the Thundering Herd, and it was doing okay. But we wanted a fan club for tailgaters."

Indianapolis had yet to embrace the idea of having parties in the parking lot before NFL games. They didn't know the fun they were missing from breaking out their grills and chairs, tossing bean bags at cornhole boards, painting their vehicles, and turning the experience into a full day of fun.

"That was when the worst of athletes could chuck a ball and not worry about hitting a car," fan club member Eric Griffin said. "Everybody was happy to see anybody else."

Van Wagner says he and Tim Millikan, who helped Collins create the Blue Crew, were in that parking lot long before that. "You could have 100 people out there and not hit one with a football," Van Wagner said.

Millikan mentions how fans teamed up before the club's inception to support sick children and others in need. When a family of seven lost a house to a fire, fans donated a box truck of items including beds and furniture.

"All the boys cared about was throwing the football and talking about Colts players," Millikan said.

That old South Lot is where Lucas Oil Stadium was built. Today, the Blue Crew has an active membership between 700 and 1,500 members, depending upon the year.

"It's the only fan club in the National Football League that was created by and for tailgating," said Blue Crew board member Dan Cole.

"Just being in the middle of Colts Central, you're with family," Griffin said. "Nobody is a stranger. If you're wearing a Colts jersey or a Colts hat, as soon as you hit the pavement, you're family. It's a great way to warm up for the game."

Nathan Tilse says if fans don't tailgate or check out the Blue Crew, they're missing out. "We put a lot into it," he said. "I know it sounds selfish, and I'm sure some people will say it is, but I love partying with other Colts fans and they're all the same ones. They're like family. You meet them and grow to know them."

He and his wife, Angie, "love to see the emotion in people."

So does Cole. In the beginning, Cole concedes, "We didn't know what we were doing." They do now.

Aside from elaborate party planning, such as deciding a menu as soon as the Colts schedule is released in April, the U.S. Army veteran organizes events to support the Indiana National Guard's units deployed overseas. A silent auction has raised about $1,200 each of the last three years to help pay for Internet services for those units. Other events raise money, including a cornhole tournament. Cole and friends walk around with 55-gallon trash bags to accept donations for care packages sent overseas.

"We collect everything," he said. "Soap, DVDs, key rings, Colts beads, money. You cannot send pork. They frown on that one."

He takes the money to the Dollar Store and buys more items.

Collins mentions the annual chili cook-off and all-nighter events. The Blue Crew raised $4,000 for the Leukemia & Lymphoma Society from the sale of "ChuckStrong" T-shirts after head coach Chuck Pagano was diagnosed with leukemia last season.

Tailgating starts at 9:00 AM for 1:00 PM games and typically ends at 5:00 PM.

"It's Hoosier hospitality," Cole said. "You'll get food and drink. We'll take care of you."

His food "faves" are tasty little snackburgers and zesty chili. "Snackburgers are undefeated if prepared properly. The two times I left something out, we lost," Cole said. One time he forgot mushrooms. Another time, during the memorable playoff loss to Pittsburgh in January 2006, he didn't have bacon. "That one is on me," he said.

A new generation of fans are selling out games these days. "Kids are growing up to be Colts fans now," Collins said. "I think we'll always have a great fan base now. It will be up and down with wins and losses, but the core is here. We'll be fine. I'm very proud of the Blue Crew. And the Colts appreciate the Blue Crew. [Chief operating officer] Pete Ward has always been awesome, and owner Jim Irsay has done a lot for us in the past, helping out, mentioning us in his tweets, and sending stuff over."

74 A Lot of Losses in Those Early Indy Years

The new Indianapolis Colts sold out all of their home games at the Hoosier Dome in the inaugural 1984 season. They just didn't win much. That took time.

A debut 23–14 home loss to the New York Jets would be an omen. While the Colts managed a 35–21 victory at Houston, then their first triumph at home 31–17 over Buffalo in Week 5, the wins would be few and far between in a 4–12 season that saw head coach Frank Kush quit with one regular season game remaining.

Mike Pagel, Art Schlichter, and Mark Herrmann took snaps at quarterback and were sacked 58 times. The Colts averaged just 14.9 points while allowing 25.9 per game. The 3-4 defense was led by right-side linebacker Barry Krauss.

"The '84 and '85 seasons were my best years as a pro player," said Krauss, who was voted MVP the first year for a 170-tackle season and received a Rolex watch. The next year, Ray Donaldson won the honor and received a mink fur coat. Krauss would have preferred the mink over the watch.

It wasn't the easiest transition to the NFL for Krauss who earned college acclaim on Alabama's national championship team. He made the *Sports Illustrated* cover with an infamous goal-line stop on fourth down against Penn State running back Mike Guman in the title game. Krauss hit Guman so hard he didn't remember much after that. He said he suffered from a reoccurring concussion as a pro and a pinched nerve in his neck that would sometimes leave him paralyzed from NFL hits. It all started with that hit on Guman.

"But it was worth it," insisted Krauss, a Sugar Bowl MVP who caught the eye of Colts owner Robert Irsay and became the sixth overall pick in 1979. "That one play, how it's changed my life, it's been incredible."

Krauss fought through the pain and injuries because of what he learned from legendary Alabama coach Paul "Bear" Bryant, who taught, "You're going to have to suck it up or you'll quit. And if you quit that, you'll quit anything." Krauss was no quitter.

He fought with some of his teammates in those early years in Baltimore. Opponents would ask him why he continued to play so hard in games that were already lost. That fired him up even more.

"The worst part is we had players on the team that didn't care," Krauss said. "I was appalled. I got into fights with other players. Losing was devastating to me."

When Krauss got to Indianapolis, fans loved his fighting spirit. Today, he suffers from cervical degeneration with arthritis in his neck. That pinched nerve always acted up.

"I used to paralyze myself two or three times a game," he said. "My left arm would just go dead. We'd rub some ice on it until the numbness would go away."

Suck it up, as Bryant said. Krauss kept reminding himself of those words, even when he would wake up with numb arms.

"Embrace pain or it will defeat you," Krauss said.

The fans' faithful support of a losing team inspired him. He did what he could to connect with them.

"These people in Indianapolis had grown up with all of these other team allegiances," Krauss said. "I knew it would take time to build this fan base."

He would arrive at the Hoosier Dome five hours before games and was typically one of the last to leave after icing down his pains.

After games, he chose kids to take to the locker room to meet players and get autographs.

"That AstroTurf was horrendous at the Hoosier Dome. It would burn you up," Krauss said. "I was always the last guy out."

The tailgate lots weren't packed. In those first few years when the Colts were continually losing, only the true die-hards stuck around until the time Krauss hobbled out of the locker room. He could always count on a group he referred to as the "Green Van Fan Club." They became his fan club.

"They would cook for me, and we'd have a couple of beers," he said. "I think about all of those fans now. I appreciate the fans who hung in there."

Kush's moody nature made for some anxious moments. And it went beyond just the players. Former strength and conditioning coach Tom Zupancic, who was hired by Kush in 1984, recalled a workout with Jim Irsay. The *Rocky* theme song was blasting on the boom box. Kush walked in and tried to turn it off. He couldn't figure out the buttons to silence the noise.

"He stepped back and just booted it against the wall," said Zupancic, who then advised the box belonged to the general manager and son of the owner.

The next two versions of the Colts probably had a few fans kicking the proverbial dog. Rod Dowhower went 5–11 in '85 and was fired after an 0–13 start the next season when Ron Meyer came in and won the last three games.

"You're killing me," Krauss said when reminded of the records.

There would be so many better days ahead for the franchise, most after Krauss ended his 11-year career in 1989. He's still connected to the team as a postgame radio show analyst.

"It's a classy organization," he said. "Obviously it was tough in the beginning. But to see where it is now, to win a Super Bowl [in 2007] and be associated with that, that I played for the horseshoe, it's an honor."

75 Hit the Road

Blue Crew Fan Club members tend to agree on two road trips that are bucket-list musts for a die-hard Colts fan—Kansas City's Arrowhead Stadium and Green Bay's Lambeau Field.

"Here I am," Nathan Tilse said of making a road-trip statement. "I'm here for you."

Kansas City and Green Bay have two of the finest NFL tailgate lots with passionate fans who are friendly to visitors.

"Those are just the Meccas," Tim Millikan said.

"They're like Xanadu for football fans," Eric Van Wagner said. "Green Bay is fantastic. You get treated like gold there. And Kansas City is my favorite. You're welcome there."

He will never forget visiting a Piggly Wiggly supermarket to pick up charcoal for tailgating before a January 1996 playoff game at Kansas City. A loudspeaker surprised him with, "Attention, shoppers. We'd like to welcome the Colts fans in aisle five."

Van Wagner has told his 22-year-old twin sons that they need to go to a game in Kansas City and Green Bay. "That's what we wanted to get started here," Millikan said.

And they did. Millikan and Eric Van Wagner joined Randy Collins' movement to create the Blue Crew, which started in 1998.

Dan Cole also considers Green Bay and Kansas City among his favorite stops along with New Orleans. His bottom three are Cincinnati, Cleveland, and Pittsburgh, although he advises, "I've never been to New England."

Eric Griffin has made that trip, and it wasn't pleasant. "They were throwing batteries at us one year in New England," Griffin said. "They had some toy giveaway, and fans were taking the batteries out and throwing them at us."

Van Wagner thought he was in a cordial suite environment for the Colts' AFC Championship Game at Pittsburgh's Three Rivers Stadium on January 14, 1996. A Steelers fan in his seventies sat behind him. When the Colts' final-play Hail Mary hit the AstroTurf for an incomplete pass and the Steelers started celebrating a 20–16 victory, Van Wagner turned to congratulate the fan and wish him luck in the Super Bowl.

"But the guy smacked my hand away and said, 'Get out of here,'" Van Wagner said. "They should go to Kansas City or Green Bay and see how it's done."

Griffin didn't care for a trip to Philadelphia, either, where an Eagles fan shouted at him to take off his Colts jersey. "I came into this stadium wearing a Colts jersey," Griffin responded, "and I'm leaving this stadium wearing a Colts jersey."

When the Colts became perennial playoff contenders with nine consecutive winning seasons from 2002 to 2010, more fans showed up on the road.

"You've got to travel to see your team," Cole said. "That's part of being a fan. We make a weekend of it. We usually run into a few Colts fans because we've become a better travel team. We go once a year somewhere."

Perhaps the best part is when the Colts win on the road. The stadium is silent when the outcome is inevitable. Home fans leave early. When the Colts won at Jacksonville in a Thursday night game last season, the visitors' lopsided early lead prompted many Jaguars fans to depart at halftime. By late in the third quarter, the stadium was about a third full. Boisterous Colts fans could be heard.

"There's nothing like watching guys throw their hands in the air or cry," Griffin said. "Watching the fans give up and head to the exits, that is fun. I don't taunt them. I just smile. It's a nice, quiet victory for me."

76 Where to Watch the Colts in Town

If you can't get a seat at Lucas Oil Stadium or if the Colts are playing on the road, two Indianapolis establishments pride themselves in creating an inspired atmosphere to watch the game.

The Blue Crew Sports Grill is near Fishers at 7035 East 96th Street. If you're downtown, the Indianapolis Colts Grille is at 110 West Washington Street.

The first place, which opened October 15, 2006, is an extension of the team's Blue Crew Fan Club and is run by club president Randy Collins. It's typically packed for away games with as many as 200 fans. When the Colts score, the roar is so loud you can't hear a siren sound off. You can't miss the white horseshoe bar, the large blue light overhead, and blue walls covered with everything Colts, including 83 Peyton Manning pieces. There's a Blue Crew Wall of Fame with pictures of fans and famous patrons.

One of the more amusing sights is behind the bar. On that far wall is the likeness of a goal post. Look to the extreme right and spot a football embedded into the wall next to a jersey of Mike Vanderjagt, the kicker who missed a last-second field goal way right in a 2007 AFC Divisional playoff loss to Pittsburgh.

"The place is kind of a landmark. It's 100 percent Colts in here," Collins said. "Everybody in Indianapolis knows about it. It's a place they call home. It's definitely a game-day experience. I wanted a place where you could see it and hear it. It's cranked up in here. That's what I'm proud of. That comes from being an owner who really gets into it, too. I'm from right here. I love my Colts."

The menu features popular tailgate items with a few twists. There's the Best of Luck burrito, named for Colts quarterback

Andrew Luck. It's $7.95 with chicken, peppers, onions, cheese, queso, and pico de gallo. Add $1 for steak.

"We don't have enough Andrew Luck in here yet," Collins said of the decor.

An ordained minister, Collins has performed six marriages for Colts fans at his place. Each time, he has to mention the Colts in the vows.

Collins makes his living in construction. The Blue Crew Sports Grill doesn't turn a profit, but he keeps it going.

"This is my passion," he said. "I love the place. I love Colts fans."

Indianapolis Colts Grille manager Michael Duganier, 33, grew up in Buffalo, New York, but also takes pride in the atmosphere he and his staff have created and expounded upon since an August 28, 2011, grand opening. There's Colts memorabilia everywhere, a Super Bowl XLI mural the length of the wall next to the bar, 40 beers on tap with a majority of them local brews, and 66 flat-screen TVs. If you go to the men's bathroom, there's a two-way mirror that enables fans to see the bar TV screens while at the urinals.

The menu includes normal bar food and appetizers, but the Grille prides itself in being a "unique, food-favored, sports-themed restaurant." That means gourmet items such as Moroccan BBQ chicken or the Skirt steak chimichurri, which is aged Argentinean-style skirt steak with caramelized plantains, salsa, spring mix, and a fresh lime squeeze.

Colts players have autograph signings on Mondays during the season. A $500,000 audio/visual system sets the game-day mood and keeps fans jacked up.

"What we do is create an experience," Duganier said. "We do a lot of interaction songs and activities with the guests. You get goose bumps."

Fans are alerted that kickoff is approaching by The Black Eyed Peas' "Let's Get It Started" and Michael Buffer's booming voice, "Let's get ready to rum-m-m-b-l-l-l-e!" When players line up for that kick, expect to hear The Rolling Stones' "Start Me Up." Spinning lights slow down and dim, then speed up and get brighter.

Before a field goal, here comes "Under Pressure" by Queen and David Bowie. A Colts touchdown means a celebration song. Patrons often hear stadium sound bites from fans as if they were at the game. During commercial breaks, it's more high-energy music. The popular "Everybody Clap Your Hands!" by Joshua's Troop gets the expected loud reaction.

Rooms are named after Peyton Manning, Raymond Berry, Reggie Wayne, and Tony Dungy. A popular secluded spot is Mr. Irsay's VIP private owner box, which has Skype on one of three TVs and Sony PlayStation3 hooked up to another. A picture of Irsay hoisting the Vince Lombardi Trophy is on the wall.

"During the season, players are texting and calling all the time, asking if they can get the VIP box," Duganier said.

Wayne always asks. After a Tennessee home victory last season, the wide receiver brought Luck, safety Antoine Bethea, and punter Pat McAfee to the place.

"I wanted to show the guys my spot," Duganier recalled Wayne saying.

77 Visit Baltimore's Sports Legends Museum

If you want to appreciate genuine Colts history, take a trip to Baltimore.

Step through a time portal in the shape of a large blue horseshoe to enter the Baltimore Colts exhibit at the Sports Legends Museum at Camden Yards. It's a journey back in time that John Ziemann is only too happy to share.

The museum's deputy director was born and raised in Baltimore. Nobody is more proud of his city's history. Ziemann, 65, can tell you how the museum building was first built in 1856. He can take you to the room where President Abraham Lincoln was brought to lie in state for 90 minutes as part of the 1865 funeral train. The museum opened on May 14, 2005, as part of the Babe Ruth Birthplace Foundation. "The Sultan of Swat" was born in Baltimore in 1895.

Ziemann has more of a connection than being the museum's deputy director. For 51 years he has been involved with the Baltimore Colts Marching Band, which kept playing after the Colts left Baltimore in 1984. They were the subject of the 2009 ESPN 30 for 30 documentary, *The Band That Wouldn't Die*, directed by Baltimore native Barry Levinson. "I kept it together when we didn't have a team for 11 years," said Ziemann, band president.

When walking into the museum, the first turn to the right showcases how band uniforms changed over the years. Ask Ziemann about how he once pawned his wife's wedding ring to buy band equipment. There's a pair of black high-top cleats worn by Hall of Fame quarterback Johnny Unitas. Check out the jerseys worn by Unitas, Buddy Young, Raymond Berry, Gino Marchetti, Jim Parker, Art Donovan, and Lenny Moore. There's head coach Weeb Ewbank's hat and playbook. Helmets, footballs, a Super Bowl ring, the Vince Lombardi Trophy for Super Bowl V, this place has it all.

"The people from Indianapolis come to this museum," Ziemann said. "We tease them, and they tease us. Once they come through and see the Colts exhibit and see the Colts videos from 1947 to 1983, one person who came from Indianapolis said to me, 'Now I know why you hate us.' I said, 'We don't hate you, we hate the situation.'"

There's a Mayflower exhibit, a display encapsulated in what looks like the back of a moving van, complete with rear brake lights. The Mayflower vans were used to relocate the Colts to Indianapolis in 1984. There's a front-page story on the day the Colts left town. "For some reason, Mayflower didn't want to sponsor it," Ziemann said with a smile.

Ziemann recalled going to games at Memorial Stadium as a kid, beginning in 1955. A friend's father was a police officer. Whenever the cop had stadium duty, the son would ask Ziemann if he wanted the extra ticket. They would hop a bus and head to 900 East 33rd Street.

"There will be generations after me that will look at this as ancient history," he said of the exhibit.

But it's a history Ziemann and many others are dedicated to preserving.

"The Indianapolis Colts should be separate in the Hall of Fame, and the Baltimore Colts should be separate in the Hall of Fame," Ziemann said. "I had the pleasure of being good friends with Johnny Unitas. John always said it should be separated. He said, 'I never played a down for the Indianapolis Colts.' He was adamant. All the Colts alumni are adamant about that.

"Don't hurt us. Don't take our history. That's why our museum has been established, to set the record straight."

78 Want More Money? You're Traded.

The second overall pick in the 1994 NFL Draft provided the Colts with a Hall of Fame running back. Problem is, Marshall Faulk played just five years in Indianapolis before the team's concern about Faulk's possible holdout for a new contract prompted president Bill Polian to trade the star to St. Louis for second- and fifth-round draft picks.

The seven-time Pro Bowl selection had his best years with the Rams, most notably in 2000 when he was NFL MVP. He ran for 1,359 yards and a career-high 18 TDs, and he also caught 81 passes for 830 yards and eight more TDs. Faulk earned his only Super Bowl ring that postseason.

In his time with the Colts, there wasn't any question as to whom the offense counted on. At 5'10" and 211 pounds, Faulk used his speed and elusiveness to thrive as a runner and receiver. He led the team in rushing each year and was the reception leader in 1995 when the Colts advanced to the AFC Championship Game. He had tied for the team lead in catches the year before as a rookie.

In 1998, his swan song with a 3–13 team, Faulk was instrumental in providing rookie quarterback Peyton Manning with his first comeback victory. The Colts trailed the New York Jets 23–17 at the RCA Dome and were facing fourth-and-15 at their 33. Manning dumped a short pass to Faulk, who did the rest to gain 18 yards. The Colts drove 80 yards in 15 plays, the last a Manning 14-yard TD pass to tight end Marcus Pollard with 24 seconds remaining for a 24–23 triumph.

Those are a few of the positives. Unfortunately, there were negatives, too, that explain why Faulk didn't stay with the Colts.

His reputation took a hit in 1996 when a dislocated toe injury caused him to miss three games. Fans would be excited to see him warm up before games but were then disappointed after learning Faulk wouldn't play. After one missed game, he was spotted playing golf during the week. Already somewhat distant with people, that public scrutiny didn't go over well.

"Great player, but he was temperamental," said Mike Chappell, longtime Colts beat writer for *The Indianapolis Star*. "He wasn't

Marvin Harrison by any means, but he was very guarded. He did not let you get very close to him."

Retired offensive lineman Joe Staysniak doesn't hide the fact he didn't care for Faulk, and that he wasn't the only one. When quarterback Jim Harbaugh made the Pro Bowl, he bought Rolex watches for not just every offensive lineman but the strength coaches, too. When Faulk made the Pro Bowl as a rookie, the guys blocking for him didn't get anything except one party tray of subs per week during the season.

"Not 15 party trays so everybody could enjoy it, just one," Staysniak said.

In a game at Jacksonville, the Jaguars jumped into a 4-6 defensive scheme. The Colts called a trap play to exploit the alignment. Staysniak pulled and kicked out his man on the edge, but somebody else missed a block and Faulk was dropped for a two-yard loss. The running back jumped up and started screaming at Staysniak.

"I guess you're going to have to watch the game film, superstar," Staysniak recalled telling him.

Head coach Ted Marchibroda got wind of "this big rift" between the O-line and Faulk. He called Staysniak, Will Wolford, and Kirk Lowdermilk into his office. The coach eventually relented in his demand that Staysniak apologize to Faulk, which wasn't going to happen.

Staysniak remembered when Faulk showed up one hour late without an apology for a TV show taping. And then there was the time he arrived to do a radio show with Staysniak and parked in the most convenient place.

"A Mercedes parking in the handicap spot," Staysniak said. "He was just that kind of guy."

Faulk had two more years on his contract that was to pay him $2.9 million in 1999. But he was dissatisfied and made it known that he wouldn't report to off-season minicamps without a new contract. That demand convinced Polian his leading rusher would hold out come training camp, hence a trade that earned the team boss some criticism from fans and media.

"If we gave Marshall his [new contract] money, we would be capitulating to a holdout," Polian said after the trade. "I don't want to make this personal, but you assume that any player had one good year, that we should tear up his contract and renegotiate. We paid a hefty signing bonus [$5.1 million] to get that contract, and I didn't see Marshall's agent knocking on the door when Marshall was injured and giving us back any money. If we should have given him money, why didn't they give us something back when he was hurt?"

At the time, Faulk said he was upset about the trade. Years later, he tried to downplay his exit from Indianapolis.

"I don't think it was as much personal as people perceived it to be," he said on a conference call. "When you look at it, it was one of the smart decisions that they could have made."

Faulk played his last game in 2005 and finished with 12,279 yards rushing, 100 rushing TDs, 767 receptions for 6,875 yards, and 36 TDs. When he retired, his receiving yards were the most for a running back, his reception total and receiving TDs were second all-time for the position, his 19,154 total yards ranked third, and his rushing total was 10th in league history.

The Rams retired Faulk's No. 28 jersey in 2007. The Colts did not do the same, nor have they added him to their Ring of Honor. In his first year of eligibility in 2011, he was enshrined into the Pro Football Hall of Fame.

79 Another Trade Backfires

After pulling off one big trade that paid immediate dividends with running back Eric Dickerson in 1987, Colts general manager Jim Irsay tried another. But 1990's maneuvering to use the No. 1 overall selection on quarterback Jeff George didn't produce the same results as the Dickerson deal.

The Colts dealt Pro Bowl offensive tackle Chris Hinton and promising wide receiver Andre Rison as well as a fifth-round pick in '90 and a first-round choice in '91 to Atlanta for the No. 1 overall selection and a fourth-round pick.

"They basically blew up the team to get Jeff," said Robin Miller, a longtime columnist who covered the Colts from 1984 to 2001 for *The Indianapolis Star.*

The chance to get what they thought would be a franchise quarterback was too much to pass up. The hometown product out of Warren Central High School had a great arm and tremendous potential. The Colts gave him the richest rookie contract in NFL history, a reported six-year $15 million pact, including a $3.5 million signing bonus.

"Obviously, we feel that this trade will prove to be very significant for this organization," Irsay said. "Our position is, let's let time decide."

It was significant, but for the wrong reasons. In kindest terms, George didn't pan out. While that passing arm would keep him in the NFL eight years after he was no longer a Colt, the bottom line is he lost 35-of-49 starts in Indianapolis through 1993 with 46 interceptions and 41 touchdown passes. He fought with everyone: fans, media, teammates, coaches, and management. He held out for 36 days at one point and demanded a trade.

Jeff George, quarterback from the University of Illinois, was selected as the first overall draft choice by the Indianapolis Colts. He was announced and introduced by NFL Commissioner Paul Tagliabue at the 1990 NFL Draft on April 22, 1990, in New York, New York. (AP Photo/NFL Photos/Ben Liebenberg)

"The main problem with Jeff George, aside from being immature or whatever you want to call it, the team did a terrible job surrounding him with players," said Mike Chappell, longtime Colts beat writer for *The Star.* "They just didn't have anybody around him. And he wasn't a leader."

Career statistics show George had talent: 80.4 passer rating, 27,602 passing yards, and 154 TDs with 113 interceptions. Compare those numbers to a famous quarterback who finished with a 77.1 passer rating, 25,092 passing yards, 192 TDs, and 172 interceptions. That would be Miami's Bob Griese, and Griese is in the Pro Football Hall of Fame.

"Jeff George wasn't the train wreck everybody said he was, but then you try to defend him and you can't," Chappell said.

That's because George had a 46–78 career win-loss record.

Former strength and conditioning coach Tom Zupancic liked what he saw from George in the weight room.

"The local media really plastered him," said Zupancic, 57. "It was all about the attitude. But the thing that always impressed me about Jeff is he had a tremendous work ethic. He took pride in working hard. He just probably could have used a public relations guy walking around with him to help him out."

George took a physical pounding from 146 sacks in four seasons, including 56 in 1991 behind an offensive line that was initially blamed. Robin Miller defended George during the passer's rookie year before offensive lineman Ray Donaldson took the scribe aside to enlighten him that it wasn't all on the O-line. Miller and former defensive coordinator Rick Venturi watched film, and the journalist came away with a different take on how George didn't mesh with his line and was responsible for many of the sacks.

"Jeff, for all his God-given talent, just didn't understand the locker room," said Miller, 63. "Guys told me he would change plays in the huddle just to show off his arm with a 30-yard out."

At the end of his NFL career, after being released by Washington, George still didn't embrace the idea of being a team leader when he said, "That leadership stuff is all overrated."

Chappell mentions a comparison of George to Colts quarterback Peyton Manning, the NFL's only four-time MVP who was drafted No. 1 overall in '98. "As far as throwing the football, holy cow, George was awesome," Chappell said. "But whatever the 'it' Peyton Manning had, Jeff didn't have."

In the 15th game of the 1992 season, George led the Colts to a 16–13 victory over Phoenix at the Hoosier Dome. George pointed to the press box in the final moments, a gesture aimed at Miller. The columnist had hosted the high school Mr. Football banquet and cracked a joke that Jeff and his mother, Judy, had called to see if the quarterback received any first-place votes in the balloting.

If there was any doubt about George's animosity toward Miller, the quarterback made it clear in the locker room after that game. Miller was talking to defensive tackle Tony Siragusa when George entered and started shouting profanities at the columnist, then threatened him. When Miller basically ignored the verbal tirade, George became more enraged and had to be restrained by defensive end Sam Clancy.

"He went nuts," Miller said. "He called me a scrawny mother [expletive], which I am."

"That was Jeff," Chappell said. "He just wasn't wired to be quarterback sometimes."

When Marchibroda benched George for backup Jack Trudeau, who threw a game-winning touchdown pass, it didn't sit well with the starter. George said the next day that it was a decision Marchibroda "would have to live with."

George didn't show up for 1993 training camp until 16 days before the season opener. That just made his situation worse. The Colts had finally seen enough after a 4–12 season. New vice president of football operations Bill Tobin took the job after the Colts gave him the okay to trade George. The quarterback, ironically, was dealt back to Atlanta, the team that could have selected him in '90, in a swap for three draft picks—first- and third-rounders in '94 and a '96 pick that became a first-rounder.

At least the Colts salvaged something out of the George debacle. That latter pick was used to take wide receiver Marvin Harrison, who would rewrite the franchise record books and end up in the Ring of Honor.

George has said in later years that he wished he would have handled certain situations differently. He has been approachable, appeared on radio, and didn't have the same persona fans and media remembered from his playing days. He continued to work out and stay in shape, that strong throwing arm always ready to whistle another pass, but the NFL didn't call again.

"You're talking about two different people and two different attitudes about him," Zupancic said of George, who retired in his hometown. "He is a very generous guy. He's given a ton to his church and helped out Warren Central. And he's done it under the radar. He really is a good guy."

Even Miller acknowledges George has grown up a lot. "People have seen in the last five to 10 years, he's not a bad guy," said the man who was George's harshest critic. "He's got a heart."

80 Mayor Hudnut Saves the Day

Counterfeit tickets were a problem when the Colts started out in Indianapolis as ticket manager Larry Hall turned away fans who had purchased bogus seats on the street.

One time, a larger group got scammed by scalpers.

"It's probably 10 minutes after kickoff, and I'm in the lobby between the ticket office and the stadium," he said of the Hoosier Dome. "There's a police room across the hall. I always made sure there were a few police officers with me when I had to inform people, 'I'm sorry, folks, but these tickets you purchased from someone on the street are actually either lost, stolen, or counterfeit tickets.'

"I'm having this conversation with a decent-sized group of maybe 15 people. Some are more excited than others about it. 'This is ridiculous. I've got this ticket. I paid a lot of money for this ticket.' Yeah, but you didn't buy it from me. The analogy I would give is if you bought a watch on the street and the watch broke, would you take it to the jeweler on the corner or would you try to find the guy on the street? You'd try to find the guy on the street because that's who you bought it from."

As the upset fans persisted, Indianapolis Mayor Bill Hudnut passed by.

"Oftentimes the mayor, because he had so many other things he was doing, would come to the game a little late," Hall said. "He always cut by the ticket office. That was kind of his path in. There was an elevator right by the ticket office. I knew the mayor a little bit. We had talked, and he knew who I was.

"As I'm having this conversation with this group of people, I hear somebody go, 'Larry, Larry' as the voices are getting louder. Sure enough, it's the mayor. I say, 'Excuse me, folks, one second. The mayor needs me.'"

Hudnut inquired about the problem.

"These people unfortunately bought counterfeit tickets," Hall said. "I really can't let them in."

The mayor was sympathetic to the fans.

Hall recalled Hudnut saying, "You know what? I had a small group cancel in my suite. I'm going to let them come up to my suite."

A surprised Hall said, "'Mayor, I just want to make sure you understand what you're doing here.'

"He said, 'Absolutely. They look like nice people.'"

"They are nice people. If you want to do it, that's fine, I just want to make sure you understand what you're doing."

"You know what? I do."

Hall was glad to deliver the good news.

"Okay folks, you've gone from not having a ticket to buying a ticket on the street to being told it's lost, stolen, or counterfeit and being asked to leave because the rightful owners are already in the seats. Now the mayor of our fine city would like to have you up to watch the game and eat his food in his suite.

"They all roared."

Score one for Hudnut, who Hall commended as "good-hearted."

"I've always had a sympathetic ear for fans, period," Hall said. "While it's not my fault, it is my problem. We want to take care of Colts fans."

The 45th mayor of Indianapolis, from 1976 to 1992, is now 80 years old and living in Maryland. When told how Hall remembered his good deed that game day, Hudnut said, "That's a nice story. I just wish I could remember it. Frankly, it sounds like something I would have done."

81 Bert Jones Plays His Pants Off

The 1973 off-season trade of quarterback Johnny Unitas to San Diego meant the Baltimore Colts were in the market for his replacement. LSU's Bert Jones was selected with the second overall pick.

Jones possessed one of the strongest throwing arms in league history—it was suggested he could throw a football 100 yards. And he didn't mind showing ball boys during practice.

"Sometimes he would throw it as far as he could even if the receiver was wide open," said linebacker Barry Krauss, who joined the team in 1979. "He would give the ball boys a workout. The ball boys would look at him and be like, 'Damn, Bert.'"

Jones became a trusted field general who called his own plays. He earned the respect of teammates with his talent, but his entertaining sense of humor also helped teams bond.

Krauss recalled a grueling training camp practice when the players would go about three hours in the morning and then another three hours in the afternoon. Film study would add to the drudgery of preseason.

"Tick, tick, tick, that film reel would roll," Krauss said. "And it was in a dark room, guys were exhausted and just trying to stay awake."

So Jones thought of something during practice to get his teammates' attention in film study.

"Bert would pull his pants down, and you would see his white ass," Krauss said. "The guys watching the film would start cracking up. And then he would go ahead and run the play with his pants down!"

Jones was NFL MVP in his fourth season. He passed for 3,104 yards and a career-high 24 touchdowns in 1976. He could take a pounding and keep playing hurt. He endured with so many injuries, including cracked ribs, shoulder problems, and even a neck fracture. He missed 25 games over the course of the '78 and '79 seasons with shoulder injuries. After missing 13 games in '78 with a separated shoulder, he got crunched in a 14–0 season-opening loss at Kansas City to start '79. Jones tried to play through the pain, as he had so many times before, but he couldn't keep going. Over the course of those two seasons, the Colts were 5–2 with him as a starter and 5–20 without him.

Former Colts coach Ted Marchibroda was convinced Jones had the talent to be a greater player than what many will remember.

"Had Bert been healthy, he'd be in the Hall of Fame," said Marchibroda, who had Jones from '75 until the coach was fired after the '79 season. "He's as fine a football player as I've ever been around. He was a leader and a little more gutsy and also flamboyant. Bert had it all. He was like [Green Bay quarterback] Aaron Rodgers, and he was probably a little bit quicker."

Jones passed for a career-high 3,134 yards despite missing one game in '80, but the Colts weren't the same team anymore and finished 7–9. In one game, Jones set the wrong kind of NFL record as he took 12 sacks. He played in 15 games again in '81 and had 3,094 yards passing, but the Colts ended up 2–14.

In the off-season, Jones vented his frustration about being unable to come to an agreement on a new contract. He blamed owner Robert Irsay. It started before the '81 season when Jones said Irsay reneged on a verbal agreement to give Jones a four-year, $3 million deal that would have made the quarterback the game's highest-paid player. As the losses mounted, Jones thought he was made the scapegoat. After the season, he said he couldn't play for the Colts anymore and asked to be traded.

History had repeated itself with a beloved Baltimore quarterback. Unitas had also demanded to be traded at the end of his career after being benched in 1972. Irsay pulled the trigger and sent Jones to the Los Angeles Rams for first- and second-round draft choices. Just like Unitas, Jones was at the end of his career. He suffered a neck injury in '82 and played in just four games for the Rams, then he retired.

Elway Says, "No Way."

The Colts' final go-around in Baltimore began with a humbling turn of events in the '83 off-season. Quarterback John Elway had no interest in joining the team, but the Colts chose the Stanford star anyway with the No. 1 overall pick.

Elway didn't like the idea of playing for Colts owner Robert Irsay or head coach Frank Kush. The quarterback was also a touted baseball prospect who had been drafted by Kansas City out of high school and then again in 1981 in the second round by the New York Yankees. In '82, he played 42 games of Class A ball for the

Oneonta Yankees and hit .318 with four homers, a team-high 25 RBIs, and 13 stolen bases. Elway suggested he might pursue a full-time baseball career if the Colts didn't trade him.

Irsay had dealt Bert Jones a year earlier after the franchise quarterback demanded to be traded. He pulled the trigger again. On May 2, 1983, the Colts traded Elway to the Denver Broncos in exchange for quarterback Mark Herrmann, the rights to offensive tackle Chris Hinton, and a 1984 first-round choice that became offensive guard Ron Solt.

Herrmann was born and raised in Carmel, Indiana, and played his college ball at Purdue. The Broncos had selected him in the fourth round in 1981. He played in just two games for Denver before the Elway deal. After two seasons with the Colts, he was traded to San Diego. He eventually returned to Indianapolis for the final three years of his career through 1992. Herrmann was just 3–9 in 12 career starts, completing 59.5 percent of his passes for 4,015 yards with 16 touchdown passes opposite 36 interceptions.

Hinton became one of the Indianapolis Colts' first great players, named to seven Pro Bowls, six for the Colts and the last for Atlanta. Hinton was involved in the 1990 deal that sent him and wide receiver Andre Rison as well as two other picks to the Falcons for the No. 1 overall selection used to take quarterback Jeff George in addition to other pick considerations. Hinton was the second player to be inducted into the Colts' Ring of Honor.

Solt played five seasons for the Colts, was selected to one Pro Bowl in 1987 then joined Philadelphia for four years before returning to Indianapolis for his final year in 1992.

As everyone knows, Elway became a Hall of Fame legend in the Mile High City. He's still working his magic in Denver as the team's executive vice president of football operations. In an Elway move that once again pained Colts fans, he persuaded free-agent quarterback Peyton Manning to come to Denver in 2012 after Indianapolis released the NFL's only four-time MVP.

83 Know Autograph Do's and Don't's

Everywhere Colts players go, a fan is waiting for an autograph. The best opportunity is at training camp. Players know fan interaction is expected. They don't all sign every day, but you'll see a decent share of them walk over to the ropes at Anderson University after each workout.

Some fans are resourceful and find out the hotels where the Colts are staying the nights before home and road games. There's nothing wrong with hoping to run into a player at the right time, but most hotels are mindful of this. Before home games when the Colts are staying at The Westin in downtown Indianapolis, there's a path players take to the elevators. Respect the rope as well as hotel staff, but fans often stand there near the front lobby and are typically rewarded as players begin their trek to Lucas Oil Stadium.

Public events are a great chance to get something signed. Colts wide receiver Reggie Wayne obliged autograph seekers in-season after his Tuesday radio show in Carmel, Indiana. Players have Monday autograph signings at Indianapolis Colts Grille, 101 West Washington Street, Indianapolis. If you hear of an open-to-the-public event involving players, it's usually a golden opportunity. But it must be open to the public. A player showing up at a school function might not have time to give an autograph to hundreds of kids, let alone you.

Don't be shy. But don't be rude, either. It never hurts to say, "Please." If the player asks your name to personalize the autograph, that's a bonus. Don't command, "Make it out to Johnny," and try to strengthen the request by saying the signature is for your son. It still comes off like you're telling them what to do. Some players won't take offense. But some will.

Don't come unprepared. These guys don't walk around toting Sharpie pens in the highly likely event they will meet their biggest fans. You need to have your own Sharpie. In fact, carry two in case one fails. The dark ink works best. What's the point of getting a signature if it doesn't show up well?

Unless it's a special circumstance, don't bring a half dozen things to sign. Sure, it would be great to get an autograph on that jersey, hat, T-shirt, picture, program, and football, but if you're part of a group, the general rule is one autograph per fan. Players might make an exception or two, if it's a special item, but there's typically only so much time to sign and they have the mind-set of trying to please as many fans as possible in a short amount of time.

One other thing—which should go without saying but you would be surprised how often it happens—if Wayne signs that No. 87 Colts jersey to make you the happiest fan in the world, frame the prized possession so it never ends up in the laundry. You could be one rinse cycle away from that keepsake being just a jersey again if it somehow ends up with your dirty clothes.

84 One Lucky Fan

Jay Williamson didn't consider himself a lucky person. His wife, Caryn, used to say he shouldn't carry money around because it burns a hole in his pocket.

So imagine the wife's reaction when the printing salesman from Franklin, Indiana, spent $100 on raffle tickets for the Colts' "Quest For The Ring" contest in 2007. A business meeting had been canceled at the last minute. On a whim, he walked across the street to the RCA Dome and took a chance on Colts owner Jim Irsay's quest, which offered Super Bowl XLI rings valued at $23,000 apiece to five lucky fans.

"I had all this money in the parking meter and $100 in my pocket," Williamson said. "When I told my wife I bought 20 of these raffle tickets, she flipped."

More than 45,000 fans paid $5 for raffle tickets with about $1 million being donated to charity. One of Williamson's numbers was selected for the next round of the quest, a two-day scavenger hunt around town. Each contestant selected a four-person team. Williamson's team included his wife. His team finished third out of 10 finalists. That earned him a trip to the Jacksonville game on December 2, 2007. Ten boxes were brought onto the field at half-time. Fans chose in the order of their scavenger hunt finish.

"Everybody kept telling me to take the number three, that it was the best statistical number. I wanted to pick seven," he said. "I kept going back and forth, three or seven?"

As he took the field, he looked up at the scoreboard, which read: "Colts 7, Jaguars 0." "Something was telling me seven," he said. "It's a good thing because there was a ring in seven and there wasn't one in three."

Chris Carr, Bryan Snyder, and Jeff Haggard of Indianapolis as well as Ed Ressler of Avon also won Super Bowl XLI rings.

The moment Williamson's box was opened and he won, his wife came "charging out there." The ring fit perfectly. He wore it all the time and informed admirers it was white gold, had 52 diamonds, and weighed 63 grams. Last year he had it polished then placed in a safety deposit box.

"Jim Irsay said when we started this that it was going to be a life memory. And it was. I'll never forget it," said Williamson, 52. "I still don't let my wife live it down. The best part is she doesn't give me a hard time about carrying around money anymore."

85 "Team Nobody Really Wanted"

Before they were Colts, they were Texans.

Strange as it sounds today considering the Lone Star State's affinity for football, not enough NFL fans cared for a struggling excuse of a franchise in Dallas in 1952. Just 17,499 people filed into the 75,000-seat Cotton Bowl to see the Dallas Texans open with a 24–6 loss to the New York Giants. The results were increasingly embarrassing as the season sputtered on.

The lack of sponsor support led to the Texans being returned to the league with five games remaining. Franchise operations were moved to Hershey, Pennsylvania. The last home game was played at the Rubber Bowl in Akron, Ohio.

"That was a disorganized operation," defensive end Gino Marchetti said, 61 years later, of where he played his rookie year.

The Texans finished 1–11 and folded. A group led by Carroll Rosenbloom was awarded the remaining assets, and the Baltimore Colts were born in 1953. There was a previous Baltimore Colts venture that disbanded after 1950, but it would not be linked to the 1953 version, except for the nickname derived from the city's horse racing tradition. The Colts kept the Texans' blue and white colors.

Rosenbloom asked fans to give him five years to build a winner.

"Carroll Rosenbloom was a great owner," said Marchetti, who became a Hall of Famer. "He would do anything for you."

Joining Marchetti for the move was defensive tackle Art Donovan, who would also be enshrined in the Hall of Fame. Marchetti went to 11 Pro Bowls, Donovan five. The Colts roster also included halfback/quarterback George Taliaferro, a three-time

Indiana University All-American who earned Pro Bowl selections in 1951, 1952, and 1953. "Whenever the ball was snapped, it came to me," said Taliaferro, who lives in Bloomington, Indiana.

The Colts started their inaugural season with a stunning 13–9 win over the Chicago Bears at Baltimore's Memorial Stadium. This team would be far more competitive than the Texans, although that's not saying much. Two games later, they beat the Bears again, 16–14 at Wrigley Field, to improve to 2–1. After a 27–17 home win over Washington bumped the Colts to 3–2, the team lost its last seven games.

"We really didn't have the personnel to sustain the record," said Taliaferro, who also played for the Colts in 1954.

Taliaferro was a workhorse in more ways than one. He played quarterback, running back, wide receiver, cornerback, punter, and returned kickoffs and punts. "I am the only football player in the history of the National Football League to play seven positions," he said.

He caught Rosenbloom's attention on a kickoff return late in a 37–14 loss at Green Bay on October 18, 1953. Boxed in near the Colts' sideline with a tackler speeding in, Taliaferro didn't take the easy way out. "I put my head down and drilled his ass like you wouldn't believe," he said.

Rosenbloom asked Taliaferro why he took on the tackler instead of running out of bounds, especially in a game already decided. "You can't score if you run out of bounds," Taliaferro said.

That resonated with Rosenbloom, who informed Taliaferro what the owner had told *The Baltimore Sun*, "I decided then that if these guys will play like that, I will bring a championship team to Baltimore."

"Here's a city, Baltimore, that had a very bad inferiority complex," said John Ziemann, deputy director of Baltimore's Sports Legends Museum, which has a Colts exhibit. "We were a whistle stop between Washington, D.C., and New York. We were made fun of all the time, gritty little Baltimore. All of a sudden, here's a team nobody really wanted. Here's a city everybody made fun of.

"We more or less got together, loved each other, formed a bond, and knocked this block off our shoulder, the fans, the team. It's 1953. And by 1958, we're world champions in the most historic game ever played. Baltimore got its first pride in sports from the Baltimore Colts. That '58 championship game made NFL football, this team that nobody wanted in a city that everybody made fun of. It was a love affair. It was our Baltimore Colts."

Unitas led the Colts to a 23–17 overtime win over the Giants at New York's Yankee Stadium in the 1958 NFL Championship finale dubbed, "The Greatest Game Ever Played."

Rosenbloom more than made good on his build-a-winner timetable.

86 Line Up for Colts Tickets

Indianapolis Colts ticket manager Larry Hall hasn't missed a home game since he was hired in May 1984. That's 29 seasons and 299 consecutive home games, counting preseason and postseason. The most anxiety he has ever experienced was before his first preseason game.

As the Colts were trying to get organized at Fall Creek Elementary School, it was apparent the team needed to take over ticket processing for the Hoosier Dome's part-time staffers. Applications had flooded in—30,000 requests for 143,000 seats—before Hall was hired. The team held back a few thousand tickets for players, coaches, staff, city officials, and sponsors.

"As we grew closer to the season and the summer going on, we were really behind our normal process for NFL ticketing," Hall said. "The company that was going to produce the tickets, we asked them if there was any way we could pay to get the tickets earlier. They said, 'No, sorry, we can't do it. You guys are at the end of the line.'"

These were the days before computer emails. The team tried to keep people informed through media releases. But fans were understandably antsy.

"The tickets came in maybe eight to 10 days before the first game," Hall said. "People are used to having event tickets much earlier than that."

The few thousand set aside had to be processed by hand without the benefit of computers—a tedious process to say the least. Many long days turned into nights with basically two staffers performing the work—Hall and Sue Kelly.

"The one day, I think I worked like 7:30 in the morning until 2:00 in the morning and then got back and started working at 8:00 in the morning and went until 4:00 the next morning," Hall said. "All of a sudden, we go, 'What about the players?' It's like the Thursday before the first game."

Hall and Kelly headed to Anderson University where the Colts practiced during training camp. The tickets came in complete sheets, which presented more last-minute work.

"I'm tearing the tickets apart as we're driving up to Anderson," Kelly said. "I had to tear off Game 1 as he is driving."

When they arrived, they stared at a group of exhausted players. Head coach Frank Kush had put the Colts through multiple daily practices in full pads.

"We get to the dining hall at maybe 6:00 or 6:30, and the players are pretty hot and bothered," Hall said. "They've been through weeks of training camp. It's been a long, hot day, it's been a long, hot week, and it's been a few long, hot several weeks leading up to our first game at home.

"We show up and the players come at us maybe 12 to 15 wide. There's no line. There's no structure. The first guy says, 'I need two of these and four of those.' So they're all coming at us at once. At the time, I'm 24 and most of the players are older than me. But I realize this situation is getting out of hand."

Although sleep deprived, Hall took charge, albeit with some trepidation.

"In the heat of the moment and in my fatigue, I stood on a chair and then stood on a table and yelled at the whole team, 'If you guys will make one line, this will go a whole lot faster or we can just go back to Indy!'" he said. "As I'm saying that, there's a little voice in my head thinking, *Somebody is going to turn this table over while I'm standing on it, and I'm going to end up on my back side.*"

Initial player reaction was predictable.

"Some of them said some not-so-nice things," he said. "Some said, 'Just go back to Indy.' And then some said, 'Hey, guys, I really need these tickets. Let's make a line.' So you know what happened? They made a line."

Distribution took a little more than one hour.

"At that point, we were just happy to have it over," Hall said. "We were very exhausted."

87 Bob Lamey at the Mic

Indiana University broadcaster Don Fischer cracks up about what initially comes to mind about longtime Colts radio voice Bob Lamey.

"The first thing that pops into my head is that I played the last round of golf with him that he ever played," Fischer said with a hearty laugh.

They were at Golf Club of Indiana in southern Boone County near Zionsville, Indiana. The foursome was Lamey, Fischer, well-known Indianapolis radio voice Jerry Baker, and professional hockey coach Jacques Demers. They reached the sixth hole, a challenging par-five test with two water hazards that stretches from 501 yards to 564 yards depending upon the tee box.

Fischer looked around for Lamey and didn't see him. It took a moment.

"I look toward the parking lot, and he's already halfway to the clubhouse," Fischer said. "He got frustrated obviously. We joke about it every year."

That was years ago, but Lamey remembers.

"I don't think I've been on a golf course since," he said. "I got to the point where I was throwing the club farther than what I was hitting the ball. It wasn't any fun anymore."

When behind a microphone at Lucas Oil Stadium, Lamey doesn't leave any proverbial clubs in his bag. He takes his best shot. And listeners can immediately detect the momentum shifts from his distinctive tone of voice.

"I enjoy listening to him on the radio now," said retired Colts tight end Ken Dilger. "Boy, he is dramatic. He's up when the Colts are up, and he's down when the Colts are down."

Fischer, who has been calling Hoosiers games for four decades, loves Lamey's play-by-play style. The Colts' voice has been a constant for 26 seasons, every year in Indianapolis except from 1992 to 1994 when another station carried the games.

"Nobody works at it harder than Bob Lamey does," said Fischer, 66, who handles Colts TV broadcasts in the preseason. "The first guy I walk up to is Bob Lamey because I know he's got it all.

"I can be pretty excitable myself when I'm on the air. I've always liked that kind of broadcasting. That's how I fell in love with play-by-play. I listened to [baseball broadcaster] Harry Caray.

Colts quarterback Andrew Luck, who was the first pick of the NFL draft, is interviewed by Colts announcer Bob Lamey (left) at a draft party in Lucas Oil Stadium after he was introduced by the team in Indianapolis on Friday, April 27, 2012. (AP Photo/Michael Conroy)

He wore his emotions on his lips. Part of our job is to entertain. We're not perfect. We all make mistakes. It's all ad-lib when it comes to play-by-play. To me, that's the best part about it."

Colts chief operating officer Pete Ward says Lamey, 74, combines reactionary emotion with statistical preparedness.

"He's a lock for the Ring of Honor, I think," Ward said. "He's a homer, and we love it about him. Some people may not appreciate it, but we sure do, and we think the majority of our fan base does. He's a legend."

When Lamey was told of Ward's Ring of Honor prediction, he said, "I am not sure that is going to happen, but if it does it would be a great honor."

What he does know is he loves his job and the Colts. "I've been a Colts fan forever," he said. "The first time I really knew I was going to follow the Colts was 'The Greatest Game Ever Played' [in 1958]. I watched it in Texas. Johnny Unitas and Raymond Berry. Raymond played at SMU. I went to TCU. I knew all about him and then followed him to the Colts. It was kind of a natural progression. But I never thought I would see a Colts game, let alone broadcast them."

Landing the Colts job in 1984 was a case of being in the right place at the right time after the franchise relocation, he said.

"I try to do a broadcast as if I was talking to the people in the building and the people who can't afford to get there," he said. "I've had two or three people over the course of my career tell me this, and it means a tremendous amount: 'Listening to you puts me in the game.' And the last thing they say is, 'You know I'm blind.' If a blind person can see what you're trying to describe, to me that's the ultimate compliment."

When running back Dominic Rhodes headed for the goal line in the AFC Championship Game against New England in 2007, the ball popped out and Lamey reacted with a disappointed call, "He fumbled the frickin' football." When bodies were uncovered, Colts center Jeff Saturday had recovered the fumble for a touchdown. Lamey's tone went from his lowest decibel to his highest.

"Jeff Saturday got on my fanny the next day," Lamey said. "It was one of those things. I was very, very hard on myself at the time because, you know, 'You came really close, you dumbass, to saying something you shouldn't.' And then [former coach/color analyst] Ted Marchibroda shouted over the top of me, 'Friday recovered it!' He called Saturday 'Friday.'

"As the years have gone by, it gets funnier. Guys have said worse."

Lamey studies year round. A game development can trigger the recollection of a former player, perhaps one he never saw play but is aware of due to research. Even when the Colts lost early on, he liked most players.

"You knew down deep that somewhere along the line it was going to turn for the better," he said. "I'm luckier than heck that I was there. Ted Marchibroda had a tremendous amount to do with it, the players, Peyton Manning, all the guys."

He's looking forward to next season.

"For me, personally, it's been the greatest 26 years of my broadcast career, more fun than I could ever imagine," Lamey said. "I hate to lose, some of the losses are tough, but even the 1–15 year when you win one game, you remember that game and you try to forget the losses. It's not that easy, but the whole thing is fun."

More fun than golf, anyway. He laughs.

"Yeah, just by a little bit." Then he adds, "Maybe I should say by a lo-o-o-ng drive."

88 Give to Books For Youth

Stacy Lozer refused to let the Books For Youth program fizzle. For two years, the Department of Child Services' program director worked out of her garage to keep alive this annual mission of placing 25 age-appropriate books in the hands of every foster child in Marion County.

"I wouldn't give it up. That's me," said Lozer, 46, a married and extremely active Indianapolis mother to three sons. "I had librarians in my family room sorting books sometimes. We kept it alive."

The program had been around since 1998 but desperately needed a boost. Lozer decided to pick up the phone and call Nicole Duncan, the Colts' director of community relations. They agreed to do a game-day collection and another book drive.

Books For Youth soared from there.

The program was relaunched in 2005 when former Marion County Judge James Payne became director of the Indiana Department of Child Services. The Colts came on board that next year, and the goals became more aggressive—place a backpack with 25 books in the hands of every foster child in the state. That's about 10,000 children each year, but Books For Youth has met that challenge and collected more than 750,000 books.

"We would be nowhere without that relationship with the Colts," Lozer said.

Stephanie Pemberton, then an intern and now the senior director of marketing, has overseen the Colts' involvement.

"I have had the opportunity to see the Books For Youth initiative evolve from a vision to a living, breathing program that touches the lives of hundreds of foster children each year," Pemberton said. "There is something so special about the moment when a foster child receives his or her very own backpack filled with books from a caring adult. It is those life-changing moments that we've focused on creating for the past several years. These backpacks and books are about so much more than just reading—they're about empowerment and about hope."

A 2006 book drive put Washington Township Schools to the test to see which elementary school could come up with the most books. The schools came up with 60,000 books.

"We decided to use that as the rollout to the relationship with the Colts," Lozer said. "We had box trucks being unloaded by [players] Antoine Bethea and Marlin Jackson."

The Indianapolis Public Library has been instrumental in helping the program realize the books needed to be age appropriate.

The Marion County Public Library signed on from the get-go and continues to be a drop site for book donations. New or gently used books can be donated to any Marion County Public Library or county Department of Child Services office throughout the state.

"We collect any book anybody will donate," Lozer said. "Then we sort them. Each book goes through somebody's hands who has been trained. I'm not giving you something you can't read or that doesn't have a value. We will not pass along books with a child's name in it. They open those pages, they're theirs."

Last year, with the help of presenting sponsor Cargo Services Inc., blue or pink backpacks with a picture of Blue the Colts mascot were offered for $22. The "Buy One Give One" offer, launched in 2010, meant the Colts would match each backpack purchase with another for the program. About 7,000 backpacks have been distributed.

A foster family was a special guest for the Colts' regular season finale on December 30, 2012, at Lucas Oil Stadium. Lozer and the family were preparing to take the field for a promotional appearance during a timeout when the Colts' Deji Karim returned a kickoff 101 yards for a touchdown in a 28–16 win over Houston.

"We come through the Northeast corner tunnel," Lozer said. "The place is going nuts. People are screaming."

Except for a 12-year-old foster child, Mackaleigh.

"There's this little girl sitting on the floor of the tunnel, pulling out the books and stacking them because we gave them their backpacks," Lozer said. "She could have cared less about the game in that moment.

"I got a great picture of Stephanie bending over in the tunnel and saying to her, 'Aren't these great?' And she's trying to stuff the books back in the backpack."

89 Enroll in Women's 101, 201 Clinics

A game program advertisement for the Indianapolis Colts' Women's 101 and 201 Clinics caught April Nading's eye about a decade ago, so she checked out the informative class that educates female fans on the NFL's basics and intricacies.

She's been going ever since.

"I just thought it was incredible," said Nading, 50, of Newburgh, Indiana. "There's so much camaraderie, and it's so much fun."

The last three years she's been joined by about 15 women on a bus that drives the group three hours from the Evansville area to the Indiana Farm Bureau Football Center in Indianapolis. The 101 clinic explains the basics of player positions, vocabulary, and strategy in a classroom setting. The 201 clinic provides an opportunity to participate on the team's indoor practice field in various activities including passing, catching, kicking, and defensive drills.

"I understand so much more now," Nading said. "I used to have such a hard time in the beginning understanding downs and everything. I recommend every female signs up for this camp. You can go every year and get something different out of it."

Colts players and alumni, NFL officials, and team personnel take part in the three-hour sessions. Punter Pat McAfee has been a popular instructor and was joined last year by offensive guards Mike McGlynn and Joe Reitz and center A.Q. Shipley.

"They're getting the knowledge from the players themselves, so it means that much more," said Colts marketing coordinator Ashley Powell, 28. "When I go to them, I still find myself learning things from hearing the players talk. That's not something people get to hear on a daily basis."

Women don't have to take 101 to get to 201.

"They lighten up in 201 when they run around and we let them tackle things," said retired safety Mike Prior, an instructor since 2005. "It's a blast."

The sessions draw between 100 to 150 women. Last year's clinics cost $70 each, but check Colts.com by clicking the FanZone tab for 2013 fees.

"They ask really good questions. The women really come prepared," Powell said. "I think sometimes they even surprise the players. The fact that these women can show they know the game and they know as much as their husbands or boyfriends, it's empowering to them."

The 101 class has been around since 1996, the 201 class since 2002.

"Even if you know football, it's a great opportunity to see inside the Colts complex and get on the practice field," said Dee Johnson, 46, Indianapolis. "It's fun to be there. You feel special."

Linda White, 44, from Indianapolis, has attended four sessions. Two sisters were curious and joined her. Last year, a niece took part. "I'm still learning," she said, "but I'll be watching a game and it will be like, 'Hey, I've done that play.'"

She impressed former Colts wide receiver Blair White one year by showing up in his No. 15 jersey. Linda White liked the idea of sharing that last name on her jersey. After the on-field exercises concluded, she was walking off the field with McAfee when Blair White said, "Hey, wait. What about me?" The free-spirited, fun-loving White has a way of attracting his share of fans.

"I absolutely love him," she said. "He is a hoot."

90 Implosion of 2011

The first sign of serious trouble came during preseason on August 24, 2011, when the Indianapolis Colts signed 38-year-old quarterback Kerry Collins.

He had retired a month earlier. The fact he was back in the fold for the Colts, as insurance for quarterback Peyton Manning, heightened concern about the franchise quarterback's neck problem.

As everyone soon learned, there would be no such thing as an insurance policy for Manning. When the NFL's only four-time MVP needed another surgery in September, speculation swirled that his career was in jeopardy. The Colts floundered with Collins. A 34–7 opening loss at Houston was written off by some as the passer being rusty because he had not practiced much with his new team. But the losses mounted. Collins didn't finish the third game, a heartbreaking 23–20 home loss to Pittsburgh in which the Steelers prevailed on a last-second field goal.

At 0–3, it was Curtis Painter's turn to start at quarterback. He wasn't the answer. The low point of what quickly became a forgettable season came in Week 7 at New Orleans when the Saints rolled 62–7 in prime time.

"Man, they scored so much, their fans got tired of cheering," said defensive end Robert Mathis.

Advised it was the most points the Colts had allowed in their 59-year history, Mathis said, "It sums up this season so far."

Collins was placed on injured reserve with what the team said was a concussion. Fans and media began to focus more on what the winless team would do if it ended up with the No. 1 overall selection in the NFL Draft. Stanford quarterback Andrew Luck had already distinguished himself as a popular choice. Fans took to Twitter to debate what became known as "Suck For Luck." Some suggested the Colts would be better off if they lost and came away with that top pick. Conspiracy theorists questioned if the Colts were losing on purpose to land the pick.

The Colts kept losing. It became obvious from Manning's monthly briefings that his recovery from a neck fusion surgery was going to take time. Manning held out hope that he could return at some point, and the team evidently thought it was possible because he wasn't placed on injured reserve and kept on the active roster. When the Colts fell to 0–13, they were the first team in NFL history to do so after reaching the playoffs in nine previous seasons. Manning started throwing in mid-December, raising expectations that he might play, which didn't make much sense considering the team's fate. But he never suited up.

Dan Orlovsky, cut in training camp but later re-signed, started for Painter in the 13th loss, 24–10 at Baltimore. The winless skid finally ended in Orlovsky's second start as the Colts defeated Tennessee 27–13 at Lucas Oil Stadium. When wide receiver Reggie Wayne caught a one-yard touchdown pass with 19 seconds remaining for a 19–16 home upset of AFC South champion Houston the next week, fans celebrated but the No. 1 pick was now in doubt.

A 19–13 loss at Jacksonville in the season finale locked up the top selection as the Colts finished 2–14. Colts owner Jim Irsay said more than a year later he knew change was inevitable as he exited EverBank Field. Vice chairman Bill Polian, general manager son Chris Polian, head coach Jim Caldwell, and Manning would soon be gone.

"I knew when I walked out of that locker room, I knew that it had ended," Irsay said in an exclusive interview with *The Indianapolis Star* columnist Bob Kravitz on February 28, 2013. "I saw players in that locker room who I'd known for years and knew they wouldn't be back. On my way to the airport, there were tears rolling down my face."

But it also meant, among other things, that the Colts would end up with a new franchise quarterback in Andrew Luck.

91 Last of Colts Playoff Days in Baltimore

After one-and-done playoff exits the previous two years, the 1977 Colts thought they were poised to go farther. They instead played their last playoff game in Baltimore and enjoyed their final winning season in the city before the 1984 move to Indianapolis.

Head coach Ted Marchibroda's team gave every indication the year would be different. The Colts started 9–1 as an offense led by quarterback Bert Jones and running back Lydell Mitchell put up 223 points in those victories and a defense that would generate 47 sacks brought constant pressure on opposing passers.

A three-game losing streak put the playoffs in jeopardy, and then the Colts trailed New England 21–3 at home in the season finale. A furious four-touchdown comeback with the deciding score at the end of a 99-yard drive propelled the Colts to a 30–24 triumph to finish 10–4 and take first place in the AFC East. Jones passed for 2,686 yards, second in the NFL. Mitchell ran for 1,159 yards and caught a league-high 71 passes.

The defending Super Bowl champion Oakland Raiders (11–3) visited Memorial Stadium for an AFC Divisional playoff game on December 24, 1977. The Raiders had piled up a league-high 351 points.

A double-overtime endurance test of nearly four hours with eight lead changes is still considered among the all-time playoff classics.

Oakland Raider John Matuszak tugs on the jersey of Colts quarterback Bert Jones as officials step between them during AFC playoff action on Saturday, December 24, 1977, at Memorial Stadium in Baltimore, Maryland. (AP Photo)

The Raiders scored first on a Clarence Davis 30-yard touchdown run. Baltimore responded with 10 second-quarter points, the highlight a Bruce Laird 61-yard interception return for a score. Tight end Dave Casper caught an eight-yard TD pass, but the Colts' Marshall Johnson returned the ensuing kickoff 87 yards for a go-ahead score. Ted Hendricks blocked a punt to set up another Ken "The Snake" Stabler scoring pass to Casper, this one covering 10 yards. The Raiders led 21–17.

Back and forth the teams went. Ron Lee scored on a one-yard, fourth-down run as the Colts reclaimed the lead. Pete Banaszak answered with his own one-yard TD run to put the Raiders back on top. But Lee scored again on a 13-yard run to give the Colts a 31–28 lead late.

The Raiders went for the clincher. Stabler lofted a long pass to Casper, nicknamed "The Ghost" after the cartoon character Casper the Friendly Ghost. The third-and-long throw seemed overthrown.

"When I looked up over my shoulder, I took one look and said, 'The ball isn't going where I'm going,'" Casper said, in a quote posted on the Raiders.com website in a 2012 story honoring the 35th anniversary of "one of the greatest games played in the history of any sport."

Casper adjusted to the ball in flight and hauled it in for a remarkable over-the-shoulder reception that gained 42 yards. "The Ghost to the Post" play enabled the Raiders' Errol Mann to kick a game-tying, 22-yard field goal with 26 seconds remaining in regulation to force overtime.

Neither team scored in the first overtime. Finally, 43 seconds into the second overtime, the game ended with Casper finishing off the Colts with a 10-yard TD pass from Stabler for a 37–31 triumph. It was then the third-longest game in NFL history. Casper, an All-American tight end from Notre Dame, would be inducted into the Pro Football Hall of Fame in 2002.

"Playing checkers with your daughter is fun. Not this," Casper said after the game in a quote posted on the Pro Football Hall of Fame website. "This was the hardest football game I ever played."

92 Visit Pro Football Hall of Fame

If you're a Colts fan, it should be understood there are a few modern-era players from your team destined to be enshrined in the Pro Football Hall of Fame in Canton, Ohio.

So it's probably worth a trip at some point. If you live in Indianapolis, it's about a five-hour drive. Check it out so maybe some day you will know where you're going if you want to see quarterback Peyton Manning have his bronze bust unveiled.

Tony Dungy, the first black head coach to win a Super Bowl, is eligible next year, as is wide receiver Marvin Harrison.

Former Colts president/vice chairman Bill Polian, a six-time NFL Executive of the Year, will also probably get the call at some point.

Kicker Adam Vinatieri, who has two game-winning field goals in Super Bowls, should also receive strong consideration. But he spent most of his career with New England, so expect him to go in as a Patriot. The voting committee might take a while on this one, though, considering there is only one true kicker in the HOF, Kansas City's Jan Stenerud.

Arguments could also be made in those closed-door meetings for running back Edgerrin James, defensive end Dwight Freeney, wide receiver Reggie Wayne, and center Jeff Saturday. They might not all make it, but consider the possibilities if most of them do.

The HOF website makes planning a trip easy. Just click on the "Plan Your Visit" link on the home page. The Hall's hours and admission rates are on that page. There's a travel link which estimates how long it will take to drive there depending upon where you live. If using an iPhone map, punch in "Pro Football Hall of Fame, 2121 George Halas Drive NW, Canton, Ohio, 44708."

The site has links for preferred hotels, places to eat, fan packages and special offers, group rates and other packages. There's even a link for anyone interested in being a HOF volunteer.

Tickets are sold for more than just museum admission. There are autograph signings, the annual HOF Game, and the enshrinement ceremony. So if you never could score a Manning autograph when he was a Colt, here's an autograph signing to count on down the road.

Interactive exhibits are known to change, but there's so much to look at, you won't be disappointed. The museum recommends allowing at least two hours to see everything. Don't be surprised if you stick around longer than that.

93 Jim Nantz's Special Ties

Craig Kelley and Jim Nantz were third-grade classmates who were even in the same Cub Scout pack in Metairie, a New Orleans suburb.

Kelley became the Colts' vice president of public relations. Nantz is known for having one of the most distinctive voices in sports broadcasting. You remember his calls for CBS, specifically at The Masters' golf tournament: "A tradition unlike any other, The Masters."

Nantz called the Colts' 38–34 AFC Championship Game victory over New England on January 21, 2007, at the RCA Dome.

"We've been friends for a long time, and he is very gifted in commemorating special moments," Kelley said. "Over dinner during the week, he told me if we won the game, he would give me the tie he wore during the broadcast. He is very thoughtful. It was a nice blue tie. Sure enough, Jim gave it to me after the game. How he found me on the field after the game in the scrum, I'll never know."

Kelley wore that nice blue tie at Super Bowl XLI, when the Colts defeated Chicago 29–17 in a steady rain at Dolphin Stadium in Miami.

"It got soaked," Kelley said. "I figured, 'Gosh, we had this great comeback against the Patriots, I'd better wear this tie.' I did and we won and it got drenched. I brought it home and just laid it out. I can still wear it to this day. It didn't get stained. I don't know how, maybe some divine intervention, but the tie is okay."

When the Colts returned to that same conference title game three years later, Nantz was on the mic for CBS at Lucas Oil Stadium.

"Same thing," Kelley said. "'If you guys win, I'll give you my tie.'"

The Colts won again, 30–17 over the New York Jets on January 24, 2010.

"I didn't see him after the game, but we had a family area on the field and Jim saw Katie, my wife. We've had dinner with him more than once," Kelley said. "He immediately took his tie off, winked, hugged her, and said, 'That's for Craig.'"

That had Kelley in a quandary for Super Bowl XLIV, once again in Miami.

"So now what do you wear?" he said. "The one that won the Super Bowl, or the other one? I had to go with the same pattern. I wore the new tie, but we got beat."

The Colts lost 31–17 to the New Orleans Saints.

"The symmetry guy I guess trumped the superstition guy on that one," Kelley said. "Both ties made the trip. I should have packed the other one in my briefcase. I might have switched at halftime rather than listening to The Who."

94 Give Carepack Tip, Join Community Event

The Indianapolis Colts strive to reach out to as many fans as possible.

Take Jackson Hartman, for example. The Colts couldn't have had better timing with the 12-year-old fan from Virginia Beach, Virginia, on January 22, 2013. He had just completed his sixth and final round of chemotherapy for Hodgkin's lymphoma at Children's Hospital of The King's Daughters in Norfolk, Virginia. Hartman endured days of throat sores yet never complained about the pain.

On the drive home, his mother's cell phone rang. His father, Steve, told Lisa Hartman there was a package at home from the Colts. She told Jackson, who immediately asked his mother to phone the hospital to share the good news with a favorite nurse, Teresa Black, a devout Colts fan.

"After feeling so bad that day," Jackson recalled, "as soon as I got home from the hospital I saw where the package had come from and it made my day."

Jackson put on his ChuckStrong bracelet, placed the Colts hat on his shaved head, then sat down and read the team yearbook from cover to cover.

"It came the best day it could have possibly come," said Lisa, 40.

The boy's envious nurse, who has been in the profession for more than three decades after completing nursing school in Indianapolis, phoned later to find out the details about the special delivery.

"Jackson is an incredible young man, and we have had a great time together talking about the Colts," Black said. "We hit it off immediately. He had a Colts T-shirt and hat on when I first met him. Jackson always came into the clinic for his treatment on Wednesdays, so we always talked about upcoming games and the following week about the games that were played. Jackson was always quick to say the Colts would win.

"I have told Jackson that he needs to write to coach Chuck Pagano since Jackson was so inspired by the coach going through his [leukemia] treatment. Jackson always had a great attitude from

9/11 Drive

Instead of playing football after the 9/11 terrorist attacks, the Indianapolis Colts took part in a Big Blue Drive Through on September 16, 2001, at the RCA Dome.

The event began at noon, what was the kickoff time for their postponed game. It started with one lane but eventually grew to four lanes because so many people stopped by to make donations to the Red Cross.

Players were not told they needed to take part, but they did anyway. Marcus Pollard, Adam Meadows, Ken Dilger, Peyton Manning, head coach Jim Mora, and others visited. What was supposed to end at 3:00 PM continued until 7:00 PM, after more than $100,000 had been raised.

day one. These kids are always so inspiring. I love getting to know my patients and families. I know that being a Colts fan and being able to talk about [Andrew] Luck, Reggie [Wayne], and all of the team helped Jackson get through his long chemo days."

Jackson is now 13, his cancer is in remission, and he has check-ups every three months. The seventh grader has returned to class at Princess Anne Middle School.

"He doesn't wear a hat to cover up his shaved head," Lisa said. "If he's cold, he wears his Colts beanie. He's doing great."

It's stories like Jackson's that make Stephanie Pemberton smile. The Colts senior director of marketing shares these feel-good reactions with her staff as a reminder of why their work is so important.

"We send hundreds and hundreds of these carepacks out every year, and it includes a letter from the team that we personalize and a plethora of Colts items," said Pemberton, 30. "I'm getting chills just talking about this. That's what this is about. It's about spreading that to as many people as we can.

"Whenever I get a new group of interns, I know some days when you're packing these carepacks and writing these letters that it seems long, I tell them, 'Never underestimate what that does.'

When they hear back or get letters, it really hits home. It can make their whole week, their whole month."

Pemberton grew up a Colts fan in Columbus, Indiana, went to Purdue University, and started out as a Colts intern in 2004. She's ecstatic to be part of the team's outreach program. It starts at the top with owner Jim Irsay.

"We've all had the experience in our lives when we've been down and out," Irsay said. "When a hand reached down, we grabbed hold of it and got pulled up. We all know how that felt and how much it meant."

95 Donate at Bleed Blue Blood Drive/Health Fair

Colts fans who say they bleed blue have an opportunity at one game each year to prove it. The Bleed Blue Blood Drive and Health Fair, the largest single-day blood drive in Indiana, has been a constant for 13 years.

Last season, a record number of about 2,300 donors came to Lucas Oil Stadium before a game to "Raise Their Sleeve," as the Indiana Blood Center slogan asks. The drive was moved to the Colts' stadium when the venue opened at 500 South Capitol Avenue in 2008.

"They say one pint of blood can save up to three lives," said Stephanie Pemberton, Colts senior director of marketing.

When Colts head coach Chuck Pagano was hired in January 2012, he agreed to be an Indiana Blood Center spokesman for the blood drive that year. When Pagano was diagnosed with leukemia on September 26, his personal fight inspired fans to action—the drive had drawn about 2,000 donors in the past.

"October comes and his commitment takes on a whole new meaning," Pemberton said. "Suddenly the mission that we had been asking our coaches and players to share was more personal than ever. This year was the largest Bleed Blue Blood Drive to date. It was just unbelievable. Our exhibit halls were filled. Hundreds were there in line to donate blood, and 75 percent of them were wearing their Colts jerseys or ChuckStrong T-shirts."

Donors received a football with Pagano's laser signature. But the benefit went beyond a keepsake. That blood is like a mini-physical in that it will be screened for anemia, body temperature, pulse, and blood pressure. Donors at the Indiana Blood Center receive a free cholesterol screening.

The center's website, indianablood.org, states that hospital patients use about 40,000 units of blood throughout the country each day. The average donor gives less than two times per year. If donors gave twice per year, blood shortages would be rare. Each pint can help up to three people through four components: red cells, plasma, cryoprecipitate, and platelets. The site lists daily blood drives and Indiana center locations including Indianapolis, Avon, Carmel, Columbus, Fishers, Greenwood, Lafayette, Muncie, and Terre Haute.

"Yes, you get a football," Pemberton said, "but fans make the trek to come down, and we open it up and go on the field to do fun activities with their kids."

Mr. T. Needs a Ticket

It had to be one of the more unexpected, last-minute Indianapolis Colts ticket requests. Ticket manager Larry Hall doesn't remember the year, just that it happened in one of the team's earliest seasons at the Hoosier Dome.

"We had a very, very sold out game," Hall said. "We really didn't have any tickets. Our players maxed out. It was a high-profile team in the early years, I don't remember which team it was."

His phone rang. Laura Dougher, who ran the suites, was on the line.

"Larry, Mr. T. is at the back door," he remembers her saying.

"What?" said Hall, taken aback.

"Mr. T is at the loading dock with a bunch of his friends," she said.

"Laura, you're making no sense," Hall said. "What are you talking about?"

"Mr. T. from *The A-Team*..."

"I know who he is," Hall interrupted, "but what are you talking about?"

"He's at the back of the building. They'd like to come in. Do we have any tickets?"

"Honestly, I have sold everything we have to sell," Hall said. "I might have a single or two, but I don't have much else."

"Okay, let me call you back," she said.

Back then, Mr. T. was known for his roles in movies and television. The former bodyguard is perhaps best remembered as Clubber Lang in *Rocky III* as well as being a regular in *The A-Team* series. His popular preface to a definitive statement was, "I pity the fool..." In this instance, it might have been, "I pity the fool who can't get me a ticket."

Hall prides himself in being accommodating. But who just shows up expecting to get in? Well, evidently Mr. T.

"Anybody over 35 I hope would remember Mr. T.," Hall said. "He was driving in a limo with some of his friends from somewhere down South, back home to Chicago, cutting through Indy. They turn on the local radio and hear the Colts are at home. He shows up at the back dock of the Hoosier Dome and decides they want to come in."

Dougher arranged to squeeze Mr. T. and his five friends into a suite. She called Hall back.

"'Will you go with me? I'm not sure if it's an imposter,'" Hall recalled her saying. "To be candid, I wasn't a big fan of the show but everybody knew who Mr. T. was, right? He was in a *Rocky* movie. He was big at the time."

Hall headed down to the back loading dock.

"I go back with her and sure enough, it is unmistakably Mr. T.," Hall said. "Gold chains everywhere. The Mohawk. He said, 'Brother Larry' about 22 times. 'Brother Larry, thanks for getting us in.'"

They took Mr. T. and his entourage up to the suite. Brother Larry wasn't a fool to be pitied.

97 Danny Webber's Last Wish

Danny Webber knew he was dying and wanted more than anything to spend one of his last Sundays watching a Colts game at Lucas Oil Stadium.

Heritage House, the senior community in Greensburg, Indiana, where the 74-year-old Webber resided, granted that wish on September 23, 2012. A Heritage House friend donated the tickets.

In the days leading up to the game, Webber spoke of his excitement about his first trip to the Colts' spacious NFL home. He had seen Colts games before, but this would be his first at Lucas Oil Stadium.

"This one will be very special…" Webber said in a phone interview the Thursday before the game. His voice cracked with emotion as he tried to finish the sentence. "...because this will be the last one I ever see."

Webber had cheered the Colts since the 1950s. A visit to his room was testament to that fact. Colts items were everywhere.

"He's one of the first dreams we're helping to fulfill," activity director Myranda Hartwell said that Thursday. She and her husband, Doug, joined Webber for the special day. "You can see how much better it makes him feel."

Six years ago, Webber's cancer was in his prostate gland. Last December, it had reached the lungs. In the week prior to the game, he learned the disease had spread to his spleen.

But you wouldn't know it from how Webber endeared himself to others, be it the Heritage House staff or fellow residents. When he rolled up in his wheelchair, you could count on a handshake and/or a hug. He enjoyed cooking his homemade macaroni and cheese for the staff and sweetened up everyone by offering candy.

One of his favorite phrases was repeated often: "I love you all like a hog loves slop."

On game day, Hartwell painted Webber's face blue. A bright blue, spongy wig was placed on his head. His blue T-shirt read: "The Luckiest Man." He would also hold a sign that read: "Today is my Lucky day!" He hoped to meet Colts quarterback Andrew Luck and get his autograph.

When the Colts learned of Webber's story the Friday before the game, they were quick to provide an upgrade. Instead of being seated high above in section 531, Webber and the Hartwells enjoyed pregame sideline access as well as VIP admittance to the club lounge. When the game started, they had one of the best views from section 135, seats 5–7, in the handicap accessible area.

Webber was understandably excited just to see the stadium. When it came into view on the drive, he fixed his eyes on Lucas Oil Stadium and just stared. "He was just in shock," Hartwell said on Showtime's *Inside the NFL*, which fixed a camera on Webber for the game. "He wouldn't take his eyes off it."

Before the game, his wheelchair parked just beyond the Southwest corner end zone, Colts players came up to say hello. Head coach Chuck Pagano, who would be diagnosed with leukemia five days later, stopped by, too.

"Thank you for coming," Pagano said, in a moment caught on film. "We're so glad to have you. You're an inspiration to all of us."

After Webber was wheeled to the tunnel, Colts chief operating officer Pete Ward advised him there was one more person who wished to say hello.

It was Luck.

"How you doing, sir?" the quarterback said as he reached to shake Webber's hand. "Andrew Luck, very nice to meet you."

"I know who you are," Webber said.

The fan shared his crystal-ball optimism.

"You're the greatest football player the Colts will ever have," Webber said.

"Hopefully so," Luck said. "I appreciate you coming out."

Luck handed Webber an autographed football.

Webber spent a few moments wiping away tears. It didn't really matter that the Colts lost the game.

"Just meeting Mr. Luck was an experience of a lifetime," Webber told *Inside the NFL*.

Three days after the Colts ended their season with a 24–9 AFC wild-card playoff loss at Baltimore, Webber died on January 9, 2013. The former U.S. Navy Seabee was survived by his wife of 39 years, Ramona, and five children. He was buried in Glen Cove Cemetery in Knightstown, Indiana.

There wasn't any doubt he cherished his last game. Webber knew he would before he even made the trip.

"Oh boy," he had said the Thursday before. "It's a highlight of my life."

98 Head to Hawaii, Golf with Rohn Stark

When Colts punter Rohn Stark traveled to Hawaii for the Pro Bowl in 1985, he spent the week before in Maui, made some friends, and played some golf.

These days, he's still soaking up the sun and golfing with buddies in Maui.

"I'm playing with the same guys today," said Stark, now 54 and owner of his own real estate company. "I work in the morning, finish at night, and play golf in the afternoon.

"I'm kind of known as the ambassador of golf in Maui. A lot of people look me up. If you come, you've got to bring your wallet. We've got to play for something."

Be advised, Stark can hit the sticks. The Kapalua resident plays as a pro in the Aloha Section PGA and has a listed handicap of plus 1.5. So the offer to play 18 with him is good-natured and probably not to be taken too seriously.

"That's the point," he said. "That's why they need to bring their wallets."

And he will probably be too busy to fit you in for a tee time, anyway.

That said, if you can make it to Hawaii for any reason, does it matter if there's any availability for Stark to take your money?

He's got at least one taker in a former teammate, kicker Dean Biasucci. "That would be a good thing on the bucket list," Biasucci said, although he's already been there and done that. "I went out there, and we spent 10 days together. It was a blast. I'd love to go out there again."

Stark and Biasucci were Colts from 1984 to 1994. Biasucci retired in 1995. Stark punted three more years for three other teams before calling it a career after 1997. Then it was Aloha time for the married father of two.

"It's like you're on a different planet," Stark said of Maui. "The travel is extensive, but it's not some place you want to come out for just a week or a weekend. It takes you that long to settle down. You need to spend at least a couple of weeks out here. It's a whole different culture and lifestyle."

As his longevity suggests, Stark was an excellent punter. And the four-time Pro Bowl selection was called upon often on mostly losing teams. He still holds several franchise records, including career punts (985), career yardage (43,162), punt yards in a season (4,383), games averaging at least 40 yards per punt (143), 50-yard average games (15), and punts downed inside the 20 (224).

"The Colts are still my team and my son is a huge fan, which keeps me into it," he said. "I enjoyed Indianapolis a lot. We had some rough years, but we started getting better in the '90s. You pull together, and you make a lot of good friends."

He laughs when talking about his first Colts head coach, Frank Kush. While some players didn't care for Kush's demanding ways, Stark liked him.

"I guarantee we could have taken on any team in a marathon," he said. "We did a lot of running."

Stark was the last of the old Baltimore Colts to retire, excluding quarterback John Elway who refused to play for the Colts when drafted in 1983 and was traded six days later.

"A lot of good memories," Stark said. "But I'm happy where I'm at now."

Who wouldn't be?

99 Colts Complex Walls

A guided tour around the Indiana Farm Bureau Football Center in Indianapolis is worth sharing since it's not open to the public. There's so much to see and appreciate. And that's just on the walls—in the hallways and offices, a splash of history is seemingly everywhere.

A considerable amount of space is devoted to framed jerseys. Many were worn by the Colts' Pro Bowl players, including everybody from Jerry Logan to Johnny Unitas, John Mackey to Ted Hendricks, Ray Donaldson to Will Wolford, to the more current stars, such as Bob Sanders, Tarik Glenn, Robert Mathis, Jeff Saturday, Reggie Wayne, Edgerrin James, Dwight Freeney, Marvin Harrison, and Peyton Manning. They're all up there somewhere. Yes, rookie quarterback Andrew Luck's No. 12 from 2012 has already joined the club.

Equipment manager Jon Scott explains that another long hall contains a framed jersey representing each year of the franchise's existence since 1983. The Colts put up two jerseys each for 1983, the last season in Baltimore, and two more for 1984, the inaugural run in Indianapolis. Randy McMillan's No. 32 and Mike Pagel's No. 18 are for '83. It seems odd to see an 18 jersey and not the name "Manning." The '84 jerseys are a Barry Krauss No. 55 and Ron Solt No. 66.

Barring a couple exceptions, the jerseys alternate between royal blue and white. Ray Donaldson's No. 53 is blue for 1985, Jon Hand's No. 78 is white for 1986. And on it goes. Albert Bentley's No. 20, Mike Prior's No. 39, Chris Hinton's No. 75, Jeff Herrod's No. 54, Brian Baldinger's No. 62, Bill Brooks' No. 80, Jason Belser's No. 29, and Will Wolford's No. 67.

Tony "Goose" Siragusa's No. 98 is for 1995. Scott pauses and chuckles. "Goose's jersey we had to make a little bigger," he said. "He kind of filled it out there."

Jim Harbaugh's No. 4 is from 1996. Lamont Warren's No. 21, Glenn's No. 78, Cornelius Bennett's No. 97, Terrence Wilkins' No. 80, Dominic Rhodes' No. 33, Mike Vanderjagt's No. 13, Dallas Clark's No. 44, Brandon Stokley's, No. 83, Saturday's No. 63, Antoine Bethea's No. 41, and Sanders' No. 21 brings the chronological journey up to 2007.

Most jerseys are framed with the back showing, the exceptions for uniforms worn with patches. Gary Brackett's No. 58 in 2008 has a lot of patches: a special one-game addition commemorating the opening of Lucas Oil Stadium, a Gene Upshaw No. 63 patch worn league-wide in honor of the Hall of Famer's passing, and a captain's "C."

The last jerseys are of Ryan Diem's No. 71 in 2009, Joseph Addai's No. 29 in 2010, and Robert Mathis' No. 98 from 2011. The next jersey added for 2012 will be Freeney's No. 93. Just like on the field, the Colts' all-time sack leader will be displayed across from Mathis.

"That's kind of nice that Freeney's is going in after Robert's," Scott said of the Pro Bowl tandem. "I guess they're still bookends."

At the rear of the facility is a picture of Harrison's touchdown to set the NFL record with Manning for 112 touchdowns by a quarterback-receiver tandem. There's also a shot of Harrison screaming, in a rare display of emotion, after scoring a touchdown on the road at New England.

Then there's another long wall where the players pass by on their way to and from practice. This is worth a lengthy stop to study this massive mural with its collage of images through the years. What stands out to Scott about this collection of photographs overlapped on top of a large Lucas Oil Stadium shot?

"That it could have been bigger," Scott said.

PHILLIP B. WILSON

There's Manning and owner Jim Irsay with the Vince Lombardi Trophy from Super Bowl XLI. Harrison is stretching to make a one-handed catch. Safety Melvin Bullitt making a fourth-and-2 stop when New England coach Bill Belichick went for a first down at his own 28 and paid the price in a Colts 35–34 home win in 2009. Kelvin Hayden is running in the rain with a TD interception return at Super Bowl XLI. Sanders forcing the Bears' Cedric Benson to fumble in that same memorable game. A football fluttering in the air after Brackett hit Pittsburgh's Jerome "The Bus" Bettis in the AFC divisional playoff game from January 2006. A favorite picture, according to the men included, shows the offensive line on the bench "getting ready" before an AFC divisional playoff win at Baltimore in January 2007—Glenn, Ryan Lilja, Saturday, Jake Scott, and Diem.

Older images include Krauss, Herrod, Eugene Daniel, Belser, Harbaugh, Eric Dickerson, Marcus Pollard, and Brooks, to name a few. The lower left corner of the collage has a picture of the RCA Dome.

If there's another treat to the behind-the-scenes visuals, it's in Scott's equipment office area. They have a poster for the movie *Scarface* with a letter from none other than the actor who played him: "To my little friends in the equipment room. Tony Montana. Al Pacino."

Scott is shown with Harbaugh on the field at Pittsburgh's Three Rivers Stadium before the AFC Championship Game in 1996. The inscription reads, "A man I truly respect. I'll never forget the memories we all shared. God bless you and yours. As always your friend, Jim Harbaugh."

Manning signed his picture: "Jon, The best equipment man a QB could ask for! Thank you for all of your help, support, and friendship! Love, Peyton Manning 18"

Super Bowl XLI–winning coach Tony Dungy, who is talking to CBS broadcaster Jim Nantz after the game in his photo: "To Jon, Best wishes. Thanks for helping make this moment! Tony Dungy"

Irsay's image is of him holding up the Vince Lombardi Trophy after Super Bowl XLI: "Down the long and winding roads…. The dancing in the windy halls of friendship, you and me, my friend, world championship forever…Friends for 41 eternities…Love you bunches, you red-headed, detailed mother of a dude. Jim Irsay"

Next to Irsay's autograph is a smiley face.

100 Room to Remember

Welcome to the Colts' National Treasure.

That's what longtime equipment manager Jon Scott calls a culmination of collecting more than a half century of memorabilia then displaying these historical keepsakes in one room.

The room to remember at the Indianapolis Colts' complex was completed in November 2012. And it's beyond overwhelming, from photograph images and wall murals to the familiar jerseys and helmets worn by the stars, and trophies including a Vince Lombardi replica, footballs, and lockers. Some unexpected items show up, too, like a baseball autographed by Babe Ruth and a red guitar signed by Bob Dylan (owner Jim Irsay collects some neat stuff, too).

Scott decreases the dimmer light switch. The contrast of light and darkness with shadows gives a distinctive hallowed effect, reminiscent of how displays are showcased with such awe-inspiring reverence at the Pro Football Hall of Fame.

"To prepare this, I took a trip to the Pro Football Hall of Fame," Scott said of the Canton, Ohio, facility. "I took the real tour, the tour downstairs, when you have to use the white gloves."

Left of the door is the Super Bowl XLI section. The cleats that offensive left tackle Tarik Glenn wore in that 2007 championship victory still have orange confetti stuck to the studs. In front of a picture of Tony Dungy is a mannequin resembling the head coach dressed with the clothes he wore that night in Miami, and the orange cooler overhead that is dumping artificial water is the same container from the actual sideline celebration at Dolphin Stadium.

There's a large snapshot of running back Joseph Addai seeing the gaping hole on his game-winning touchdown run in the AFC Championship Game victory over New England in January 2007. The ball he carried is on display. So is the No. 63 jersey of center Jeff Saturday, who is in the picture, delivering a pancake block on the Patriots' Vince Wilfork. A smaller cut-out picture of cornerback Marlin Jackson celebrating his game-clinching interception extends from the wall, and his No. 28 Colts helmet rests on a plastic shelf. Another image is of Irsay holding up the Lamar Hunt Trophy, and that same shiny hardware given to the AFC champion is on a shelf in front of the picture.

Above that showcase and across the wall are the words:

"We had heard about a time
A time that might be ours
Then on a rain drenched windy night
Hiding deep inside a magical Florida winter
We finally walk softly into OUR TIME"

"That was just put up," Scott said. "I love that."

Asked to point out his favorite display, Colts chief operating officer Pete Ward said, "I love the pieces that are associated with the Super Bowl victory."

Another wall has lockers with helmets and jerseys. Jersey and helmet numbers are synonymous with greatness: 18, 88, 87, 93, 7, 19, 32, 78, 4, 75. More jerseys are hanging from the rafters around

Colts team history is on display in its Room to Remember.
(Photo courtesy of the author)

the room, including red Pro Bowl attire. There's a case with Pro Bowl items, a Marshall Faulk jersey, a football, and a red Hawaiian lei around Peyton Manning's red No. 18 uniform.

Three wall murals separate the franchise's stadium history. The first on the right is of Lucas Oil Stadium with a ground-breaking shovel resting in dirt below. The next is of the RCA Dome from when an AFC Championship Game banner hung over the entrance, and memorabilia from that era displayed in front. The last is of Baltimore's Memorial Stadium. The artifacts out front include lockers for the legendary Johnny Unitas and quarterback Bert Jones. You can't miss a picture of linebacker Mike Curtis about to throw a field-rushing fan to the ground on December 11, 1971. A scout's 1954 player evaluation card on some Louisville quarterback named Unitas reads, "This lad is great. Can play pro ball, had to throw on the run, can hit receivers." A Memorial

Jim Irsay's Legacy

Colts owner Jim Irsay was once asked how he would like to be remembered:

"I did everything I possibly could to give ourselves a chance to win and achieve greatness. That commitment came from me as a sportsman, a steward, a caretaker always looking for greatness and that type of success, but also someone who understood the work that we do in the community.

"I always like to say I can taste my peasant roots because of my grandmother. She was a poor, inner-city maid raising five kids alone because my grandfather died in 1927. When the horseshoe goes out and tries to affect people's lives, it's not done for brand and promotion. It's not done so we can make our brand look shinier so people spend more money on it. That is not the intention. It's about when you're blessed and you can affect the world and make the community a better place. When we played in the Super Bowl in Florida, we won it, and at the same time, the Colts sent a lot of financial aid to a different part of the state to help the hurricane victims. That's what the horseshoe does.

"I remember playing the 49ers and taking my kids to a homeless community shelter and bringing a large check along. We met the people in need and began to understand the terrible homeless problem in San Francisco. The horseshoe is that way. It's used for good. I did everything I could to make the world a better place and to make the community better, and at the same time, my fierceness in terms of competing and the desire to win was unparalleled. I guarantee you the fire that burns in me when it comes to winning to taking that field and trying for greatness out there, that is something which is absolutely a part that drives me.

Stadium seat, marked No. 19, is signed by Hall of Famers John Mackey, Raymond Berry, and Lenny Moore, among others.

"The horseshoe has been in the NFL for so long," Ward said. "To finally have a collection of memorabilia that symbolizes key aspects of the franchise, great games and great players, means a lot to everybody associated with the Colts.

"To make tough decisions, being very emotional and very loyal, is a challenge because I know it needs to happen even though it will put me in the difficult position of needing to bear the weight of the great emotion that goes behind our fans. I understand that emotion of a fan because when I was eight years old, I would get on an 'L'-train and wait 45 minutes in line to get Ernie Banks' autograph. I understand the love and the loyalty of the players. But at the same time, as I told Jeff Saturday when he retired as a Colt, when we all put our hands in the middle and we're going out to take the field to win, you have the fiercest competing owner you can find.

"That's the reason why years ago, when we were $15 million cash over cap, playing in the smallest stadium in the league, losing tens of millions of dollars, we signed defensive tackle Corey Simon because my people came to me and said, 'This guy could be a difference maker.' Although that deal didn't work out, it represents my commitment to winning. Like I've said, when it comes to competing, when it comes to winning, there's no fire that burns more strongly in my heart.

"When we hear about a difficulty somewhere in the state, it's let's go, let's get money down there, let's get Colts hats down there, let's go raise spirits, let's send our caravan, let's go. I think the community views us that way, a franchise that's there to do what we can to make Indiana a better place and to really bring joy and inspiration. There's a special thing about inspiration that comes from the greatness and what these great athletes do on the field and the pressure they face. With that inspiration, a small little dose can be so powerful with its ripple effect that touches communities and people in general. You can't underestimate its effect. Hopefully, people will always see the horseshoe as something driven to inspire."

"Jon and his staff took the bull by the horns and put a lot of time into it, and that's time they really didn't have because they have busy jobs. They did a spectacular job. This is the result of years and years of acquiring and saving key pieces of team history."

Scott has creative ideas for adding interactive elements. When entering the room, he would like to have NFL theme music playing, then the sound would shift to the voice of Colts radio voice Bob Lamey. Scott visualizes how a visitor would walk in and a video screen would drop down from the ceiling with Unitas throwing a pass. After a few more steps, another screen would drop down, the video of a ball spiraling through the air with the blue sky background. A third screen would show wide receiver Marvin Harrison catching a pass.

What a way to bring together Colts eras.

Scott picks up a Manning helmet and shares another idea. Wouldn't it be something to put on that helmet and hear Manning interacting with offensive coordinator Tom Moore, then as the quarterback surveys the field and makes his pre-snap adjustments, a video screen shows what is being heard. Then Manning runs the play, giving the visitor the sound and visual from the experience.

"I'm sure Tom Moore would agree to recreate this," Scott said.

The Colts would love to be able to share this museum with the public. That's the long-term goal according to Ward, to find a place where fans can immerse themselves in history.

Just like at the Pro Football Hall of Fame, there isn't enough room for everything that has been saved. For so many years, the memorabilia just sat in brown cardboard boxes.

"It went from closet to closet," Scott said. "It was all in boxes, then we'd move them to another room. We've still got so much more stuff in storage."

Room to Remember expansion is obviously limited. Scott points to a brown box on the floor.

"That's Andrew Luck's stuff over there," he said of the 2012 rookie quarterback.

Scott takes out footballs. The first is the one Luck threw for his first NFL touchdown pass to Donnie Avery in Chicago. He also has the No. 12 Luck jersey from his first win.

"We kept his pants, too," Scott said.

The next keepsake is an NFL Draft football from when the quarterback was selected with the No. 1 overall pick. There's two blue T-shirts, "ChuckStrong" and "Build The Monster." Scott also has the white road jersey Luck wore when he set the NFL rookie passing record at Kansas City. Scott also hung onto the jersey, pants, and socks from Luck's first NFL playoff game.

"I keep everything," Scott said, stuffing it back into that box.

Hopefully, some day, fans can see it all again.

"It's a special room," Ward said, "because the Colts are one of the NFL's classic franchises."

Sources

Books

Chappell, Mike, with Phil Richards. *Tales From The Indianapolis Colts Sideline: A Collection Of The Greatest Colts Stories Ever Told.* New York: Sports Publishing, 2004, 2012.

Gifford, Frank, with Peter Richmond. *The Glory Game: How the 1958 NFL Championship Changed Football Forever.* New York: HarperCollins, 2008.

Hutchens, Terry. *Let 'Er Rip, The Colts in Indianapolis: A Look Back, A Look Ahead.* Indianapolis: Masters Press, 1996.

Smith, Hunter, with Darrin Gray. *The Jersey Effect: Beyond The World Championship.* Bloomington, Indiana: WestBow Press, 2011.

Indianapolis Colts. *Colts Media Guide*, 2012.

Magazines

Sports Illustrated

Stadium Journey by Paul Swaney.

Newspapers

Chicago Tribune

Newsday

The Baltimore Sun

The Indianapolis Star (archives)

The New York Times

The New York Daily News

USA Today

News Outlets

Associated Press

Gannett News Service, Mike Lopresti

Websites

Anderson.edu, Anderson University (Indiana)
Colts.com
duketumatoe.com
ESPN.com
howardschnellenberger.com
indianablood.org, Indiana Blood Center
IndyStar.com
johnnyunitas.com
naplesnews.com, Yahoo!Sports The PostGame
NBC.com, *Saturday Night Live*
NFL.com
profootballhof.com, Pro Football Hall of Fame
Raiders.com
wikipedia.org, Wikipedia
youtube.com, YouTube

Movies

The Band That Wouldn't Die, ESPN 30/30 documentary, 2009
48 Hours, Paramount Pictures, 1982

Television

ESPN
Fox News' *On The Record with Greta van Susteren*
Showtime's *Inside the NFL*

Radio

The Bob & Tom Show, Indianapolis, WFBQ 94.7-FM

TV Commercial References

DirecTV
MasterCard
NFL Sprint Mobile